INTERPERSONAL COMMUNICATION
The Real World Approach
PRELIMINARY EDITION

D1712403

DEBRA
HARPER-LEBLANC, PhD

Kendall Hunt
publishing company

Kendall Hunt

p u b l i s h i n g   c o m p a n y

www.kendallhunt.com
Send all inquiries to:
4050 Westmark Drive
Dubuque, IA 52004-1840

DEDICATION

This workbook is dedicated to my family on both sides. One should only know how important communication is within family. If you were in my family, you would know. We are there for each other, believe in each other and are able to communicate and understand each other. Due to my family being so large, I will omit the names though they all mean a lot to me. I do want to mention four family members in particular; Ms. Mae H. Sanders-Mitchell (mother), Ms. Savannah LeBlanc (mother-in-law), Mr. Rodgers Haynes, Sr. (father, deceased), and Mr. Wilton LeBlanc (father-in-law, deceased). My parents place a premium on family, striving to complete their education, and being the best as you can in your chosen career. I would be remiss if I did not mention Miles J. LeBlanc my husband and Niaya A. Harper my daughter. The two of them will always be near and dear to me. A quote that I heard at the graduation of my nephews sums it up about family and that is: *"Even though you graduate from high school or college, you never graduate from family"* *(Curtis Warren)* Family you are the best. May God bless all of you.

CONTENTS

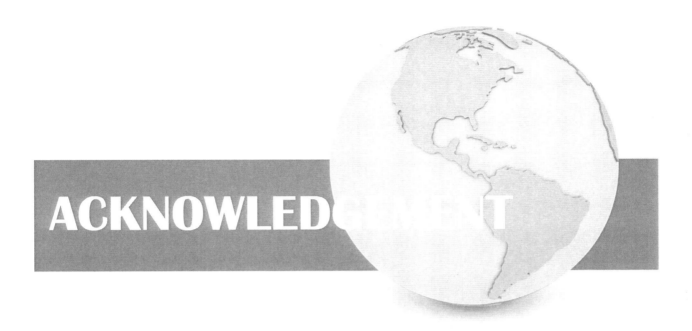

ACKNOWLEDGMENT

It has been a great honor and pleasure to work with Stephanie Ramirez and the Kendall Hunt team on this project. Thank you for being very patient with me. I would also like to specially thank two wonderful people who provided me with their artwork for this workbook. Thank you, Niaya A. Harper for the perception pictures used for one of the activities and for helping me with the design of the book cover. Your love for photography and design is unbelievable and astounding. The detail and life you show in your photos are breathtaking. What can I say about thirteen year old Michael "Mickey" Tillman, Jr. you are a young creative genius to be able to captivate your craft the way you do. You have a great life ahead of you and I am sure you will be the next Jim Davis, Matt Groening, or Seth MacFarlane to name a few. Thank you all for lending me your talents.

PART ONE

Exploring the Fundamental Principles of Interpersonal Communication

CHAPTER 1

Your Thoughts Regarding Interpersonal Communication

STUDENT LEARNING OUTCOMES

Critical Thinking			Communication			Team Work		Social Responsibility	Personal Responsibility	Activity Measured
Creative Thinking/ Innovative	Analysis & Evaluation	Synthesis of Information	Writing	Visual	Oral	Differing Viewpoints	Work with Others	Intercultural Competence	Ethical Decision Making	Activity
X		X			X	X	X			1.1
X	X		X	X			X			1.1 and 1.2
			X					X		1.3
X	X	X	X	X	X	X	X			1.4
X	X		X		X				X	1.5
X	X	X	X							1.6
X	X	X	X		X	X	X	X		1.7
X	X	X	X	X	X					1.8
X	X	X	X			X				1.9
X		X	X		X	X	X	X		1.11 and 1.13
X		X	X			X			X	1.10, 1.12,1.13

YOUR THOUGHTS REGARDING INTERPERSONAL COMMUNICATION

Daily we communicate verbally (orally) and nonverbally (not orally and written). For example when we wake up in the morning we say "good morning" and at night before we go to sleep we say "good night". This form of communication is verbal communication. On the other hand, nonverbal communication to this example is when you give a "hug". This type of communication, you are showing a behavior that does not include speaking orally or writing but its meaning could mean the same. These examples define communication which is a process of acting on information. This section of the workbook relates to your thoughts regarding interpersonal communication that includes 1) the definition of interpersonal communication, 2) the process of communication, 3) life and interpersonal communication, and 4) communicating electronically: social media and theory. The activities in this section will focus on student learning outcomes (SLO) and how they are measured. The Student Learning Outcomes Chart on page 3 will match each activity to the SLO and show the activity that measures that SLO.

DEFINITION OF INTERPERSONAL COMMUNICATION

ACTIVITY 1.1

PURPOSE

This exercise is designed to discuss and develop critical ideas by communicating them clearly and in terms of others being able to communicate openly with each other. Each discussion question will be addressed by gathering and assessing the communicator's thoughts that are relevant to the question.

DIRECTIONS

Reflect on your understanding of interpersonal communication, mass communication, public communication, and/or small group communication (forms of communication). This exercise may be completed either individually or in teams (based on the number of students in class). When the individuals (or teams) have completed the exercise, each question will be discussed and the results compared with others in the class.

1. Mass communication, public communication, and small group communication are forms of communication. Discuss each of the forms and give an example of each of the forms. Then explain how interpersonal communication is compared with the forms of communication discussed.

2. Compose a problem that occurred at home, school, or at work. In the problem provide a list of interpersonal communication characteristics or factors. Describe any lessons you personally learned from the problem and any lessons you would change. Why or Why not.

3. Interpersonal communication is expressed through tone of voice, facial expressions, gestures, and body language. Click the link *"How I Met Your Mother: Superman Scene"* http://www.youtube.com/watch?v=iegjX-DS85M or another video of our choice and view the video. After viewing the video, on a piece of paper, draw lines and label headings called "tone of voice", "facial expressions", "gestures", and "body language". Under each labeled heading, write the scene in the video that relates to the labeled heading. Discuss in class what you wrote and your thoughts on how the scene relates to interpersonal communication. This exercise may be completed either individually or in teams (based on the number of students in class).

4. Think of an example of a TV commercial in which mass communication did not display a positive image. What would you have done to improve the commercial? Allow another person to read your revised example and see how they interpret the example (positive or negative). Why or Why not.

5. Every day we are engaged in interpersonal communication. How we communicate determines how effective our interpersonal skills are. Some interpersonal communication skills can be used to 1) influence the attitudes and behaviors of

others, 2) give and receive emotional support, 3) regulate power, and give and collect information. Choose two of the interpersonal communication skills and compare them with your personal skills. Which one do you need to develop or improve? Explain.

6. Employers today are interested in effective communication skills. Many of the job descriptions may state that one must have good verbal and written interpersonal and communication skills. Interview someone in human resources and ask why they feel that should be a skill that employers should have. Discuss the results of the interview in class.

ACTIVITY 1.2

PURPOSE

This activity is to analyze and interpret how interpersonal communication is translated in the video clip from *"Pursuit of Happiness: The Basketball Scene"* or another video or your choice.

DIRECTIONS

Click the video link http://www.youtube.com/watch?v=UZb2NOHPA2A and view the scene from *"Pursuit of Happiness: The Basketball Scene"*. After looking at the video, discuss the questions below. This exercise may be completed either individually or in teams (based on the number of students in class).

1. Describe and discuss the nonverbal and verbal messages in the video and interpret how the nonverbal and verbal messages relate to interpersonal communication.
2. Based on the nonverbal and verbal messages you discussed, how do they relate to an incident that occurred in your life or the life of someone you know?
3. How would you respond if someone speaks to you like Will did to his son (the message that was said in the video)?
4. Write two paragraphs or a one page dialogue about an incident that involves you or someone (others) being told something that made you believe in yourself or think about your life. Explain how you felt and how would you respond to the dialogue written?

ACTIVITY 1.3

PURPOSE
This activity is to research, write and understand how interpersonal communication is viewed in other countries with others.

DIRECTIONS
The way we communicate differs from one part of the country to another. The way we dress, speak, and interact with others all includes how we interpret or express interpersonal communication.

1. Research a country (not your country) and write about how that country communicates in business setting and leisure setting.
2. Include gestures for hello, goodbye, etc., basic information about the country (history, language, dress, culture, etc.).
3. Include what is important about that country that we should know.
4. In the paper, doubled space, include 12 point fonts, cite in the document and the reference page.
5. The paper should be two no more than four pages in length and include page numbers.
6. Lastly, include a title page with your name, professor name, the course name, the date, and the country name.

THE PROCESS OF COMMUNICATION

ACTIVITY 1.4

PURPOSE
This exercise is designed to discuss and develop critical ideas by communicating them clearly and in terms of others being able to communicate openly with each other. Each discussion question will be addressed by gathering and assessing the communicator's thoughts that are relevant to the question.

DIRECTIONS
Reflect on your understanding of the process of communication. The communication process is a process where there is a sender (speaker) who encodes (creates message to understand) the message and a receiver (listener) who decodes (interpret the message) the message that is conveyed to one or more people or in a group. The information may be communicated in several ways. Those ways may consist of e-mail, telephone, and other types of mediums (this way is called channels). If information is not clear or distorted due to noise (interferences), one may not be able to interpret the message correctly. Below is a diagram of the communication process to help better understand effective communication when completing the exercises. These exercises may be completed either individually or in teams (based on the number of students in class). When the individual(s) (or teams) have completed the exercise, each question will be discussed and the results compared with others in the class.

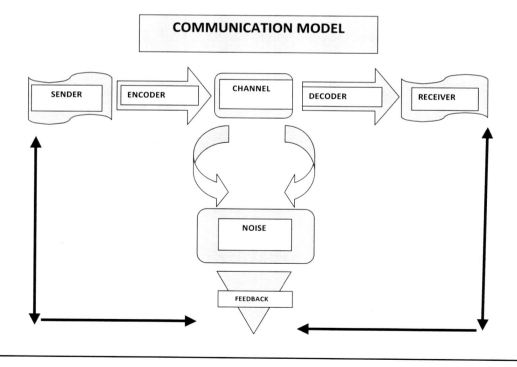

1. When communicating at home or in the workplace, how is the communication processed? State the environment (home or workplace). Which communication process is more effectively, verbally, nonverbally, by telephone, e-mail, etc. Based on the way the communication is processed stare why or why not the way is effective or not.

2. Observe someone communicating (talking) and answer the questions below.
   a. Who did you observe communicating?
   b. Where did the communication take place?
   c. If the process was not effective, state how it could have been improved based on the communication model in this exercise.
   d. If the process was effective, state how it was effective by incorporating the communication model process.

3. By using the communication model process, create an effective communication process dialogue to use at work when talking to your supervisor at why you feel there should be a change in the current communication process in the department. Include all the part, label each, and explain what they are and why they were used based on the dialogue.

4. Identify and define some noises that interfered in a conversation that you had that was not effective. State why the conversation was not effective and what noises caused the conversation not to be effective.

5. Explain and list as many factors as you can in how a message can be distorted? Write a time when you were in a conversation and told someone something but when you heard the conversation again it was distorted. Explain at least three factors or more as to what was said to make the original conversation distorted.

6. Draw and label an effective communication model that can be used to fire someone who has missed too many days of work. Write out a scenario explaining the model. Discuss in class why your communication model is the best model for the scenario. This exercise may be completed either individually or in teams (based on the number of students in class).

ACTIVITY 1.5

PURPOSE
This activity is to interpret and express how to connect actions and consequences to ethical decision-making for teachers.

DIRECTIONS
In November 1999 the National Communication Association Legislative Council adopted a code of professional ethics for communication teachers. The National Communication Association believes that in the area of academic integrity, as teachers, a high standard of academic integrity should be maintained by:

- Teaching those courses for which a teacher has academic credentials that are, preparation in the subject matter area and knowledge of current thinking and research related to the course material.
- Helping students to develop their academic potential; encouraging them to become engaged in learning, to think critically about readings and lectures, to reflect on what they learn and, when appropriate, to disagree with what is presented; and to participate with faculty and other students in research projects and activities.
- Acknowledge scholarly debates where they exist and helping students understand the nature of scholarly controversy, rather than presenting controversial material as "truth."
- Engaging in classroom practices only to the extent that one is qualified to do so. For example, communication teachers should not assign exercises requiring self-disclosure by students, unless they have provided ways for students to avoid making significant disclosures without penalty. Nor should communication teachers attempt to lead exercises designed to reduce communication apprehension without being trained to do

Discuss or write why you as a student agree or disagree on the academic integrity standards that teachers should uphold. Why or why not. Explain.

ACTIVITY 1.6

PURPOSE
This activity is to demonstrate and identify the communication channel in a conversation. The students will be able to list and give examples on what communication channels are used when communicating and why.

DIRECTIONS
How much time in a day do you spend communicating with others? Keep a log of how you communicate to others (e.g. verbally, nonverbally, telephone, e-mail, etc.). In the log label the headings as date, hours, communication channel. Include 20 – 30 hours of tracking in the log. Explain why you chose that method to communicate and also state two different types of methods to deliver the same message.

ACTIVITY 1.7

PURPOSE
This activity is to demonstrate and identify different types of noises that may interpret a message differently. The students will be able to list and give examples of noise and explain how the noise you listed is used when communicating.

DIRECTIONS
During the communication process there may be noise where the message may be interpreted differently. Sometimes noise could refer to jargon, slang, or specialized professional terms. In this exercise, draw three columns, at each column heading write jargon as one, slang as another, and specialized professional terms as the last column heading. Under each heading, give five examples of each and state your interpretation of the noise you listed. This exercise may be completed either individually or in teams (based on the number of students in class).

LIFE AND INTERPERSONAL COMMUNICATION

Interpersonal communication is experienced every day in our lives. This may include communicating with those we live with such as learning how to understand interpersonal communication skills and principles with family members. By doing this, more constructive solutions to family conflicts and how to interact with others may create harmonious relationships. With friends, overtime, developing friendships may develop into one falling in love. In the work place, you may not be able to choose who you can work with but you can understand how to avoid stress or conflict and how to get along with your peers and supervisor. Having positive interpersonal relationships with others can cause good health and happiness.

ACTIVITY 1.8

PURPOSE

The activities listed are to demonstrate and identify interpersonal communication among family, friends, colleagues, and loved ones. The students will be able to think critically, list and give examples on various types of real world and interpersonal communication relationships.

DIRECTIONS

In our professional and our personal lives, strong interpersonal communication skills are needed. Many employers search for applicants who can work well in a team, have good decision-making skills, problem solving skills, and listening skills. Applicants should also communicate effectively with colleagues and clients, and be assertive. This may also mean being proactive and having the initiative in the workplace or at home. Some examples are organizing a group, leading a project, designing policies and procedures, and working together collaboratively.

1. Think of two examples in which interpersonal communication was used in a project that you lead with your colleagues or a family member. State the name of the project, how the decision was made to come up with the project, what were the positive and negative project results, how it was positive or negative and what could have been improved about the project and why?

2. Select three people from your family or identify friends that you have known for a year or more. Use magazines or books to find pictures and sayings that demonstrate the qualities of your relationship with the three people based on the number of years you stated. Cut out and paste the pictures or sayings to create a collage and bring to class. In class, stand and discuss the meaning of the collage that you created and state how the experiences influenced you positively or negatively. Discuss for 3 – 5 minutes (or the timeframe based on your instructor).

3. Locate a job description that includes four of the seven interpersonal skills (1) verbal communication, (2) non-verbal communication, (3) listening skills, (4) problem solving, (5) decision making, (6) assertiveness, and (7) negotiation. Explain in one typed page (no more than two) as to why the position should include the four skills that were listed in the job description and define the four interpersonal skills that were listed.

COMMUNICATING ELECTRONICALLY: SOCIAL MEDIA AND THEORY

Communicating electronically is when no face-to-face communication is involved but communicates is sent by using computers, facsimile machines (fax), telephones or other ways to transmit information to each other that is not face-to-face whether the person is miles away or close by. Social media is part of electronic communication and is when a conversation is supported by online tools. Social media transform passive audiences into active participants in the communication process by allowing them to share content, revise content, respond to content or contribute new content. Some examples of social media are Facebook (conversation), YouTube (videos), Twitter (conversations), LinkedIn (professional business network), Flickr (photos), Wikspaces (collaboration), and slideshare (presentations). Cunningham and Antill (1981) stated three theories that electronically mediated communication (EMC) identifies the richness of the communication medium based on (1) cues-filtered-out theory, (2) media richness theory, and (3) social information-processing theory. Cues-filtered-processing theory restricts the use of emotions when communication is used electronically in e-mails and text messages because you are unable to see the non-verbal cues such as facial expressions, gestures, and tone of voice. Media richness theory identifies (1) the amount of feedback that is received by the communicator, (2) the number of cues the receiver can interpret through flyers, notes, memos, videos, or more, (3) the different languages that are used by the communicator, and (4) the potential for expressing your feelings and emotions. Social information processing theory messages from people will take longer to express without nonverbal cues on the Internet when messages are communicated relational and emotional.

PURPOSE
The activities below are to help understand, demonstrate, and identify interpersonal communication through social media and theories. The students will be able to think critically, define and list examples on various types of social media through research, demonstration, ethical laws, policies, and rules, and show how they apply to them.

DIRECTIONS
Media is a means of communication with the intent to influence a large audience (Random House Webster's College Dictionary, 11th edition). According to a 2011 Pew Research Internet Project, stated that 79% of American adults used the internet and 47% or 59% of the internet adult users used the social networking sites (SNS) at least once which doubled the 2008 adults over 35 who used SNS. Fifty-six percent are females. Facebook had over 92% of users; My Space had 29%, 13% Twitter users, and 18% were LinkedIn users. On an average day, F14% of Facebook users updated their own status, 22% commented on various post, 10% sent private messages, and 20% commented on another user's photo. With social media come more problems, rules, policies, and laws. Some of the problems consist of cyber bullying, harassment, identity thief, scam artists, and stalkers. Today, once information is posted in the networked world, it is accessible to the world immediately. This section consists of activities to better help users to understand communicating electronically. The activities can be completed individually or in groups.

ACTIVITY 1.9

Think of different types of Electronically Mediated Communication (EMC) media that you (or someone you know) have used. Describe and name five – ten types of electronically mediated communication media and compare and contrast how each are used when you want to express your facial or emotional feelings.

ACTIVITY 1.10

People are constantly receiving e-mails that are requesting some personal information. Explain what could happen if you were to disclose or not disclose the personal information and why? Name three – five ways you can avoid this type of action in taking place and why?

ACTIVITY 1.11

In a group of four (or based on your instructor), use some type of communication medium where you can chat with each other. Each person in the group chat for 3 – 5 minutes about why you think it is important to communicate effectively in your daily lives. State why or why not and give one-two examples why you stated the examples. When chatting in the chat rooms, use complete sentences instead of emoticons (i.e. LOL, BTW, happy face, sad face, etc.). After chatting in your groups, answer the questions without being in the groups (individually). (1) How long did it take you to come up with what to say correctly in the chat room? (2) How did you feel because you were unable to use the different emoticon? (3) State which communication medium did you use if your instructor did not state one and how comfortable were you in using the communication medium? (4) State how different would the chat be if you had someone from another country, ten plus year older than you, and from a different environment from you? (5) Turn in your chat log and the questions you answered after the chat.

ACTIVITY 1.12

List five – ten social networks. State the name of the network, its purpose, what you will use it for, and how old one should be in order to use the social network that you stated.

ACTIVITY 1.13

When communicating on the different types of social networks, you should keep in mind certain rules, policies and laws in protecting yourself and others. Choose two types of social networks and research the rules, policies, and laws you are to abide by in order to protect yourself and others. Type in paragraph form your results. What type of communication is appropriate for the social network medium that you stated (i.e. chatting, video conferencing, email, presentations, etc.)? How should you accept who should be your friends or be part of your community? Why or why not? How would you design your message to those who are from other countries? Give three examples of what you should say to those who are in your community for each of the two types of social networks that you listed?

CHAPTER 2

Who Are You: Self

STUDENT LEARNING OUTCOMES

Critical Thinking			Communication			Team Work		Social Responsibility	Personal Responsibility	Activity Measured
Creative Thinking/ Innovative	Analysis & Evaluation	Synthesis of Information	Writing	Visual	Oral	Differing Viewpoints	Work with Others	Intercultural Competence	Ethical Decision Making	Activity
X	X		X	X	X	X	X			2.0
X	X		X	X	X	X	X			2.1
X	X		X	X	X	X	X	X		2.2
X	X		X							2.3
X	X		X							2.4
X			X		X			X		2.5
X										2.6

WHO ARE YOU: SELF

Sensitive, Energetic, Loving, and Friendly are words one can think of when describing self or who you are. These words as well as others help you to understand who you are and how others think of you. As human beings, we try to identify ourselves based on how others perceive us, our behavior, our circumstances, or how we view life. To understand who we are, we will begin with defining self. Your Dictionary (2013) defines self as knowing who you are and what your purpose in life is. The American Heritage Dictionary (4th edition) defines self as the identity, character, abilities and attitudes in relations to a person or thing outside oneself or itself. The average person looks in the mirror at least five times a day which is 1,825 times a year. If we look in the mirror we tend to see the reflection of ourselves which some may see as being the opposite of how people may see us. This can be interpreted as the "looking glass self" which is a concept where we learn who we are based on interactions with others who reflect ourselves back to us. Understanding who you are helps you interact with those who are around you and those who work with you. The URL is to a Utube video on teens expressing their body image based on how they see themselves (http://www. youtube.com/watch?v=PpFBKeuKf7M&feature=youtu.be). After looking at the video, discuss if you or someone you know think of themselves as some of the teens in the video. State why or why not. A quote by Albert Einstein on inspiring greatness within you was written by Ilya Pozin in Forbes stated that **"Strive not to be a success, but rather to be of value."** In other words, bring value to your company or your environment as being the best way to move up the corporate ladder or to bring value to your organization or to those who are around you. Don't play politics whether it is in an office environment or not.

This section of the workbook relates to who you are: self that includes 1) self-concept, 2) self-esteem, and 3) current self and future self. The activities in this section will focus on student learning outcomes (SLO) and how they are measured. The Student Learning Outcomes Chart on page 17 will match each activity to the SLO and show the activity that measures that SLO.

PURPOSE
The purpose of the assignments will help students and others in the class understand who they are. The assignments will involve ways where students can identify, compare, understand, and show ways how to understand who they are.

ACTIVITY 2.0

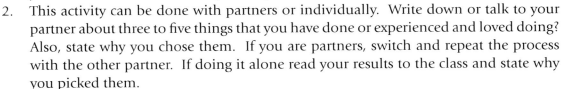

1. What advertisements in the magazines, TV, or other type of media have contributed to your identity as to who you are? Write in a journal and discuss. State why or why not.

2. This activity can be done with partners or individually. Write down or talk to your partner about three to five things that you have done or experienced and loved doing? Also, state why you chose them. If you are partners, switch and repeat the process with the other partner. If doing it alone read your results to the class and state why you picked them.

3. Bring to class an item that represents you. This can be food, clothing, picture, object, etc. Stand in front of the class and talk about the item without showing it to the class. Have the class to guess what the object is for 2 minutes. If someone in the class guesses the object before or by two minutes, show the class the object. If the class is unable to guess the object in two minutes, show the object to the class. The person who guesses the object will be the person to come up to describe how their object represents them.

4. Personality Test: **Objective**: To explore interpersonal communication by keeping a journal related to who you are (self) and creating a PowerPoint about you and your results.

    Description of Activity: Go to the URL of Carl Jung (http://similarminds.com/jung.html). You can use a personality test of your choice if you are unable to locate Carl Jung's Personality Test. Complete the personality test (Carl Jung) of 48 questions. After answering the questions, click the Submit Results Button. Read, print, or write your results in a journal and compare to how you are in compared to the results. You can also see the meaning of the results by clicking the URL (http://www.123test.com/carl-jung/) to review and include in your results.

    Create a PowerPoint of your results from the Personality Test and state how the results relate to your personality.

    Your assignment should have (1) the results of the online personality test [include your letters], (2) how you relate to or do not relate to the personality test results [explain and give examples of the results from the test], (3) create a PowerPoint discussing and showing your results, (4) include a title slide [your name, title of the project, date, course, professor's name], (5) be creative and specific, and (6) give a brief overview about the Personality Test.

SELF-CONCEPT AND SELF-ESTEEM

When we look at self-esteem, we tend to view ourselves as having low or high self-esteem. Having high self-esteem will allow you to go a long way. Low self-esteem may cause a person not to believe in themselves and others will not believe in you as well. Therefore, if you know who you are and understand who you are you may also be able to build your self-concept and self-esteem. This may also prevent you from being a bullying target. If you have high self-esteem and you know who you are, you tend to look at yourself with positive goals and commitments and you are more likely to control your goals and commitments for the present self and the future self. A UTube video on self-concept and self-esteem shows positive words and images on how you can look at yourself and how you can build your self-esteem. The URL is (http://www.youtube.com/watch?v=oNC9cc5ZsyU). View the video and discuss how some of the information in the video applies to you or not. State why or why not.

In 1955, Joseph Luft and Harry Ingram developed the Johari Window Model which is useful for helping people understand their awareness and personal growth as well as how others see them. The Johari Window Model has four quadrants. Quadrant 1 – Open Area is information about our behavior that is known by ourselves and others (i.e. our height, weight, hair color, etc.), Quadrant 2 – Hidden Area is information about ourselves which we would not share with others (i.e. hide things that we are a shame of), Quadrant 3 - Blind Area are things we do not know but others do know (i.e. mannerisms we are not aware of but others are), and Quadrant 4 - Unknown Area is the area we are not aware of and others are not aware of (i.e. things we forgotten or is buried in our subconscious mind). The concept of the Johari Window Model is to make the Open Area the largest of the four quadrants which can be done through self disclosure, feedback, and shared knowledge.

ACTIVITY 2.1

PURPOSE

The purpose of this activity is to understand who you are by comprehending your knowledge of the Johari Window Model through drawing, naming, associating, and illustrating.

DESCRIPTION

Johari Window Model: View the three minute video of the Johari Window Model and answer the questions below. (http://www.youtube.com/watch?v=Zd597GMHNYA&feature=results_main&playnext=1&list=PL56AC4459DCD11E46)

1. In the video, Wilbur identifies himself by using the Johari Window Model. He uses the four quadrants of self (i.e. open, closed, blind, and unknown self).
   a. Take a piece of paper and fold it into four squares.
   b. At the top of each square, write the name of one of the four quadrants and underneath each quadrant topic, write four things about you that relates to the quadrant topic.
   c. Partner up with someone in the class and discuss your answers that you wrote based on your instructor's timeframe.
   d. After discussing the answers, first state to the class, the name of your partner, choice one of your partner's quadrant and draw it on the board and have the class to guess what it is for three minutes and vice versa (not your own).
   e. The instructor can give a small prize to the person who guesses the most of the right answers.
2. Choose someone in the class and state something about that person that relates to open self (quadrant). The instructor will have some of the students in the class to state who they chose from the class and state what they said about that person that relates to open self (quadrant).
3. Keep a one week Johari Window Journal on someone you know by observing that person. Based on the Johari Window Model list and state what you observed about that person based on the Open and Blind quadrants.

ACTIVITY 2.2

PURPOSE

The purpose of this activity is to understand and identify self-disclosure through knowledge, synthesis, and application.

DESCRIPTION

Self-disclosure is open communication of private information about yourself to others. View the video by clicking the link https://www.youtube.com/watch?v=H8p2dYpeO6U state the time when you self-disclosed something to someone and what was their nonverbal or verbal reaction?

1. In a group create a 1 minute or less video explaining self-disclosure. Be creative and be sure the video is clear and loud enough to hear. After creating the video, the instructor will have the class present and explain the video.

2. In a group or individually, choose a video or movie that displays self-disclosure. Write down your results, explain how the clip(s) of the video displays self-disclosure and present your findings to the class or in writing.

3. On a job interview, an interviewer should not ask certain self-disclosure questions because they may be illegal. Research and write as many of the self-disclosure questions that an interviewer should not ask and state why the question should not be asked.

CURRENT AND FUTURE SELF

Current and future self may be viewed as self-fulfilling prophecy. For example, a parent constantly told a child that he/she will never amount to anything. The child's behavior was always negative and as the child later was not successful. Since the parent constantly told the child that he/she was not going to amount to anything, the child believed that and it was displayed in the behavior of the child (current self) and later because of constant negative behavior from the child the child was not successful because the parent constantly told the child that he/she was not going to be anything (future self). Another example, your professor expects you to be a good student academically. Your professor spends a lot of time with you to prepare you for a major exam and because of the extra time you spent with your professor, you make an "A" on the major exam. Your current self was pushed in studying hard to be prepared for the major exam. After the hard work and your professor pushing you to study, your future self made the "A" on the major exam because you wanted to show your professor that you could pass the exam. The two examples show current and future self and how they are viewed as self fulfilling prophecy. The activities in this section will help students understand self fulfilling prophecy and current and future self along with examples.

Purpose: The purpose of the activities is to understand and identify self fulfilling prophecy as it is viewed through current and future self. Also, recognizing self fulfilling prophecy as it relates to other countries.

ACTIVITY 2.3

Think about a time when you were told something (negative or positive) that related to self fulfilling prophecy and in turn, you believed what that was and it reflected in your behavior. State what that something was, how you reacted towards that something, how you were conditioned to react that way (based on your behavior), and what was your outcome.

ACTIVITY 2.4

Look at the 1 minute 7 seconds clip of the TV show called Criminal Minds. (Click the link: http://www.youtube.com/watch?v=OXIEo_DyS0I) Based on the short clip, state how it relates to self fulfilling prophecy and why? Analyze the segment stating your thoughts based on the current and future self of self fulfilling prophecy. This should be a 12 point font, doubled spaced one page no more than two page paper.

ACTIVITY 2.5

People sometimes say because of your environment or culture, you react a certain way. Discuss two countries and explain how self fulfilling prophecy is related to the countries. Also, draw and label a design on how current and future self applies to the culture or environment that you discussed.

ACTIVITY 2.6

Improving yourself can be difficult at times. If you could improve or change something about yourself, what would you improve or change about yourself and why? In your response, state what needs to be changed or improve. Be specific and detailed. Type at least one page, doubled-spaced.

CHAPTER 3

Perception

STUDENT LEARNING OUTCOMES

Critical Thinking			Communication			Team Work		Social Responsibility	Personal Responsibility	Activity Measured
Creative Thinking/ Innovative	Analysis & Evaluation	Synthesis of Information	Writing	Visual	Oral	Differing Viewpoints	Work with Others	Intercultural Competence	Ethical Decision Making	Activity
X	X	X	X	X	X	X	X	X	X	3.0 and 3.2
X	X	X	X	X	X	X	X			3.1
	X	X	X	X	X	X	X	X		3.3

DEFINITION OF PERCEPTION

Perception is viewed as the ability to view things or people uniquely based on their experiences, environments, or cultures. Although, people perceive things differently, it does not mean that one person is right or wrong; it means that communication between individuals may have different perspectives, requires more understanding and persuasion of those differences.

This comes to how we tend to judge people and/or things based on our perception. When we meet people or see things for the first time, we begin to formulate our opinion regardless if that opinion is true or false. For example, when we see a person for the first time and that person is dressed as though he or she is homeless, we begin to formulate our bias opinions without knowing the real story. That person may not have been homeless but instead wanted to be comfortable in his/her environment and lead a comfortable, affluent life. As we formulate our opinions of others, we tend to rely on our own ideas and guesses. This section will help one understand, identify, and explain perception.

This section of the workbook relates to perception: 1) the definition of perception, 2) the stages of perception, 3) perception theories, and 4) perception barriers and how to improve them. The activities in this section will focus on student learning outcomes (SLO) and how they are measured. The Student Learning Outcomes Chart on page 25 will match each activity to the SLO and show the activity that measures that SLO.

PURPOSE
The purpose of the assignments will help students and others in the class understand perception. The assignments will involve ways where students can identify, compare, understand, and show how perception can be understood or not.

ACTIVITY 3.0

1. Many times we perceive and assume things by formulating an opinion about the person, place or thing. Below are three photos. Review the photos and state your opinion about what is going on with the person or animal in the picture. Write three – four doubled-spaced paragraph about 1) What is going on in the pictures? 2) What do you see? and 3) Write a brief story about the picture and what you perceive is going on. State why or why not.

Picture 1   Picture 2   Picture 3

Source: Niaya A. Harper   Source: Niaya A. Harper   Source: Niaya A. Harper

2. Click the link (http://www.youtube.com/watch?v=nxKcpfFvuf8) to view the video on perception by Psych Files. The show how the Gestalt Principles are applied to perception. The video is 4 minutes and 13 seconds. After looking at the video, write down your answer to see if you see the image or not. If you see the image, state what the image is and if it is what is stated in the video. 1) Image one: the face of the Virgin Mary in the lemon. 2) Image two: the symbol of the Swastika on the Navy Base. 3) Image three: faces and patterns; what are they. 4) Image four: the image of a face on Mars. 5) Image five: the image of a happy face on Mars.

3. In pairs, list 5 – 10 characteristics that others may not know about you. Each person should try to name 3 - 5 characteristics about their partner and vice versa. The partner who names the most correct characteristics will be the person who states two of the corrected characteristics about their partner aloud in class. The partner who could not name the correct characteristics would say one of the incorrect characteristics that were stated aloud in class. After all the groups have stated their characteristics aloud in class, ask the members in the class how many thought of some of the same characteristics about a particular person in class (do not spend a lot of time on this). It will be interesting to see what your classmates perceive you as being.

4. Have the students to locate a scene from a video that relates to perception. (they can look online or they may have a video) Have them to save the link (if online) and show the class the video along with discussing why and how the scene relates to perception.

5. Bring to class and show pictures of people working from other countries (the pictures can come from magazines, newspapers, books, or online) and have the students to guess which country and name some things that they perceive about the person in the picture and why.

6. Discuss in class things that happened at work where the supervisor or colleague perceived you as doing although you were not. Briefly describe the incident and state the outcome.

7. Many times we tend to meet people and formulate perceptions as to how they are. Describe a situation in the workplace of your first impression of someone you met who turned out to be different than your original impression. State why you formulated that opinion of that person and what made you change your perception of that person?

PERCEPTION STAGES

Let's examine the stages of perception closer by using the works of Dr. Floyd. According to Kory Floyd, he viewed the following stages. 1) Selection as a process of attending a stimulus. In other words, your mind and body help you select certain stimuli to attend. For example, when we notice something negative or positive about a person but they may have done something else that may not catch our eye and we may not have been aware of. 2) Organization as a process of categorizing information that has been selected for attention. When we want to make sense out of the different stimulus that has been received and we want to understand the stimulus. By fully gathering information about a person or thing, we may begin to make or have a perception about that person or thing. 3) Interpretation is the process of assigning meaning to information that has been selected for attention and organization. Our interpretation is based on the full stimulus that is selected and organized. This type of stimulation should be placed last in our conversation so we can fully evaluate the given situation. Although three stages were listed by Dr. Floyd, some say that there are five stages. The last two perception stages are 4) Memory which is the ability to store and recall information and 5) Recall is when past information is retrieved.

PURPOSE
The purpose of the assignments will help students and others in the class understand the stages of perception. The assignments will involve ways where students can identify, compare, understand, and show ways on how they understand and perceive things.

ACTIVITY 3.1

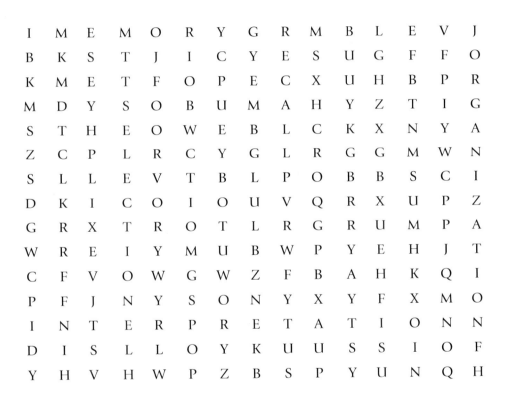

1. List one of the five stages of perception and write or type a one page doubled-spaced story on how one can relate the stage to the workplace. Be specific in the story.
2. Define the five stages of perception and give an example for each stage.
3. In the word puzzle below, find the five stages of perception and circle them. This can be played in class in groups or individually. The class can play against each other.

Perception Stages

```
I   M   E   M   O   R   Y   G   R   M   B   L   E   V   J
B   K   S   T   J   I   C   Y   E   S   U   G   F   F   O
K   M   E   T   F   O   P   E   C   X   U   H   B   P   R
M   D   Y   S   O   B   U   M   A   H   Y   Z   T   I   G
S   T   H   E   O   W   E   B   L   C   K   X   N   Y   A
Z   C   P   L   R   C   Y   G   L   R   G   G   M   W   N
S   L   L   E   V   T   B   L   P   O   B   B   S   C   I
D   K   I   C   O   I   O   U   V   Q   R   X   U   P   Z
G   R   X   T   R   O   T   L   R   G   R   U   M   P   A
W   R   E   I   Y   M   U   B   W   P   Y   E   H   J   T
C   F   V   O   W   G   W   Z   F   B   A   H   K   Q   I
P   F   J   N   Y   S   O   N   Y   X   Y   F   X   M   O
I   N   T   E   R   P   R   E   T   A   T   I   O   N   N
D   I   S   L   L   O   Y   K   U   U   S   S   I   O   F
Y   H   V   H   W   P   Z   B   S   P   Y   U   N   Q   H
```

- interpretation
- memory
- organization
- recall
- selection

4. Below are the five perception stages that are scrambled. Unscramble the five stages on the line to the right of each scrambled word. This can be played in class in groups. The winning team who can unscramble the word first, can receive an inexpensive token or points.

Perception Stages

YROMEM   _____

RLECLA   _____

CEOISTENL   _____

GAOIANTRIONZ   _____

NRNPTEEIRTAITO   _____

PERCEPTION THEORIES

When interpreting perception, not only do we look at the stages of perception, we also interpret the different perception theories. This section of perception will focus on eight perception theories. Those theories are 1) Impression formation theory, 2) implicit personality theory, 3) uncertainty reduction theory, 4) predicted outcome value theory, 5) attribution theory, 6) causal attribution theory, 7) standpoint theory, and 8) intercultural communication theory are also ways we organize and interpret interpersonal perception.

Impression formation theory was founded by Solomon Asch (1946). The purpose of the theory was to understand how a person's impressions were established based on adjective traits. This included bits of information and selected cues to form general impressions. For example, meeting someone for the first time and thinking they are a certain way because of the way they look or based on their environment. *Implicit personality theory* is assumptions and expectations that we attribute to people in order to understand them and help us organize information we have about their personality. For example, we may assume that quite people or shy and timid. Berger and Calabrese (1975) developed the *Uncertainty reduction theory.* The uncertainty reduction theory is how knowledge is gained of others as well as being able to reduce the uncertainty about others. For example, when networking in the community and dressed professionally, one would think that the professional dressed person has an important position and job. *Predicted outcome value theory* (POV) is when future predictions are made about a relationship based on initial interactions with the person you meet. The future predictions can be negative or positive predictions. For example, when you meet someone for the first time, you use your early knowledge to decide if you want to continue or diminish the relationship. *Attribution theory* is when someone interprets events and how their thinking impacts their behavior whether it is a success or failure. The Weiner's model noted that certain emotional responses were associated with causal dimensions (Weiner 1985, 2006). For example, when a person normally does poorly on a test and then pass a test, he or she would say it was because of luck. *Causal attribution theory* identifies three probable causes for a person's action: circumstance (the person acted a certain way because he/she had no choice), a stimulus (the person acted that way because of an incentive), or the person herself or himself (the person acted that way because of a quality about that person). For example, you were at a restaurant and overheard a person complaining about the service. After hearing this person for a while, you concluded that this person is never satisfied about anything. *Standpoint theory* states that a person's power, social position, or culture influences how they perceive the behavior of others. For example, when one see a person who is wearing a professional suit and driving an expensive car, they automatically feel that that person has a high status job and make a lot of money. *Intercultural communication theory* is a form of communication that shares information across different cultures and social groups that may be made up of individuals from different religious, social, ethnic, and educational backgrounds. For example, if a communication specialist in New York asks a marketing specialist in Asia that he/she needed the design "soon", the two parties may have different interpretation of the word "soon". Sometimes language is a reflection of culture and different cultures have different ways of word meanings.

PURPOSE
The purpose of the assignments will help students and others in the class understand the theories of perception. The assignments will point out those assumptions that may be fact or fiction through showing how students are able to identify, compare, understand, and explain how to understand the perception theories.

ACTIVITY 3.2

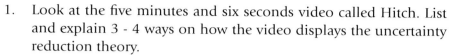

1. Look at the five minutes and six seconds video called Hitch. List and explain 3 - 4 ways on how the video displays the uncertainty reduction theory.
   Hitch video: http://www.youtube.com/watch?v=x-CBqcb0Kcc

2. Discuss a time when you experienced an event or task and based on the outcome of the event or task, you did not take the responsibility for it. State why or why not.

3. Compare and contrast the following: attribution theory, causal attribution theory. What are the key concepts of each theory? What are the primary influences or behaviors of each theory? According to each theory, how do the actions of other people influence an individual's behavior? In your opinion, what are the major strengths and weaknesses of each theory?

4. Cindy has just turned in her presentation outline which was very well done. What should her instructor say to make the best of the probability that Cindy will continue to work equally hard on upcoming assignments in the future?
   a. "Great job. I knew you could do it."
   b. "Great job. I can see that hard work pays off."
   c. "Great job; but I think with more studying, you can do better."
   d. "You can do better than this if you put your mind into it."
   e. "You're the best student we have in this class."

5. Jerry grew up in a bad neighborhood in the inner-city where he and most of his friends had to wear clothes handed down from older brothers, cousins, or second-handed. Jerry can't understand why Cindy, who grew up in an affluent family doesn't take better care of the nice clothes that she has. Jerry's difficulty in understanding Cindy's behavior is best explained by which of the eight personality theories?

6. Look at the three minutes and 49 seconds video called Crash and how they viewed their perception according to the StandPoint Theory. Look at the three scenes and state how you would react towards the three scenes and why? Write 1 -2 doubled-spaced paragraphs for each of the scenes.

7. The movie Mr. Baseball is one that demonstrates intercultural communication. Look at the video (2 minutes 10 seconds) http://www.youtube.com/watch?v= bdeFdFEbuqk&list=PLVexp9xeeoEVgYwhm1hUPQGPAYgM9JetN and discuss the two culture's etiquette differences. How would you respond if you were in Japan and during a meal you noticed the Japanese way of eating a meal such as that? Would you try to fit in or not? State why or why not in your answer. This should be a have page to a page long doubled-spaced activity.

PERCEPTION BARRIERS AND HOW TO IMPROVE THEM

How many people feel that when they travel to another country or go to a different environment that everyone should adapt to their culture, values, or beliefs? This is true to some people but we need to be able to adapt to the culture or environment that we are in as well as accept their behaviors and values. This also holds true if someone from another country or environment was to come to your country. Therefore, how can we improve perception barriers? Some ways to improve the perception barriers is to be aware of the perception barriers, try to understand or research as much as possible about that country or environment, keep an open mind by putting your preconceived ideas aside, and show respect to others culture. To seek information through passive perception in order to confirm or refute our interpretation is indirect perception checking and being upfront in asking if your interpretation of a perception is correct is direct perception checking. One scenario that occurred one day when I was out of the country is that a person that I met in that country assumed that everyone in the United States was against the people of that country. When I asked why she thought that, she stated because in her country, they show a lot of negative things as to how the United States view her country based on television. That scenario showed me how people perceive or assume things because of media and we should be sure that we have our facts correct before assuming things.

Purpose: The purpose of the assignments in this section will help students and others in the class understand intercultural communication. The assignments will point out those cultural assumptions that may be fact or fiction through showing how students are able to research, interprete, understands, and explain how to understand the intercultural communication theory.

ACTIVITY 3.3

1. The video called "The Big Bang Theory" (21 seconds) consist of a scene that displays an example of intercultural communication theory. http://www.youtube.com/watch?v=PcOBJnnz1kE and state what you would do or responded if someone told you what was stated in the video? Explain why?

2. Look at the video that involves intercultural communication stereotypes. Video Link: http://www.youtube.com/watch?v=LQQtoyStMe4 (7 minutes 30 seconds). The video consist of how people view different cultures and stereotypes. Look at the video and give your view point of how you feel about intercultural communication and research a country and include a brief history of the country, how they communicate (gestures and language), their dress, money, and how they are different from your country. This should be a 1 – 2 page doubled-spaced paper.

3. Create a 2 – 3 minute professional video on intercultural communication and how you view culture elements such as belief systems, language, and behaviors (social and personal). This activity can be done individually and in a group of 3 – 4 people. Edit the video and be sure that the sound is clear and loud as well as the picture is clear.

4. You were hired at a global company and became friends with someone from another country. After meeting this person, you realized that many of the false judgments that you heard about your friend's values, beliefs, and country were not true. As a friend, what would you do to become better informed about your friend's country, values, and beliefs? Explain and state why?

CHAPTER 4

Diversity

STUDENT LEARNING OUTCOMES

Critical Thinking			Communication			Team Work		Social Responsibility	Personal Responsibility	Activity Measured
Creative Thinking/ Innovative	Analysis & Evaluation	Synthesis of Information	Writing	Visual	Oral	Differing Viewpoints	Work with Others	Intercultural Competence	Ethical Decision Making	Activity
X	X	X	X	X	X	X	X	X	X	4.0
X	X		X	X		X		X		4.1
X	X		X	X	X	X		X		4.3
X	X	X	X	X		X		X		4.4
X	X		X			X				4.5
X	X	X	X	X		X				4.6
X	X	X	X	X		X		X		4.7
X	X	X	X	X	X			X		4.8

UNDERSTANDING DIVERSITY

When we talk about diversity, we are not only talking about race, we are including a large scope such as gender, age, sex, sexual orientation, and social class. When looking at gender, we look at the psychological and emotional characteristics where people assume different roles such as masculine, feminine, or androgynous. Sex on the other hands refers to the biological aspects of a person such as male or female characteristics. As the world continues to change when looking at sexual orientation, those who are gay or lesbian are still negatively judged but are getting better.

Today we are seeing more states to agree on same sex marriages and who are now beginning to treat gay and lesbian equal as those who are not. When we look at race and ethnicity, traditionally they relate to biological and sociological factors. For example, race relates to a person's physical appearance, such as skin color, eye color, hair color etc. On the other hand, Ethnicity is cultural factors such as nationality, culture, ancestry, language and beliefs. According to University of College Cork chair of anatomy and physiology M. A. MacConaill, he viewed Caucasian race as people being light skin and eyes, narrow nose, and thin lips. Their hair may be straight or wavy. As far as ethnicities within the Caucasian race, they are Irish, Welsh, German, French, Slovak etc. Their language, cultural heritage and traditions, and beliefs are some things that differentiate their ethnic groups from each other. Age refers to the amount of time a person lives. Age could also relate to generational differences on misunderstandings among ages. For more information regarding the generation differences, look at the table below that consists of the generation differences based on age, work ethics and values, motivation and more.

The last reference to diversity is social class which is a broad group in society that relates to education, money, family, job, and the way of life.

This section of the workbook relates to diversity: 1) understanding diversity, 2) understanding culture, and 3) diversity barriers and how to improve them. The activities in this section will focus on student learning outcomes (SLO) and how they are measured. The Student Learning Outcomes Chart on page 35 will match each activity to the SLO and show the activity that measures that SLO.

PURPOSE
The purpose of the assignments will help students and others in the class understand diversity. The assignments will involve ways where students can identify, compare, understand, and show how diversity relates to various characteristics and cultures.

ACTIVITY 4.0

1. Look at the Generation Chart in the Diversity section. Look at when you were born to see what your generation is and when your mother was born. Explain the differences of the two generations based on the chart, your research, and how you see the relation between you and your mother. State where you see age differences and where you see age similarities in the workplace, home, and other ways among you, your mother, and others. This activity should be at least one page long and no more than two pages long. Doubled-spaced and typed.

2. Students will work in pairs and ask the questions below about each other. After discussing the questions in pairs, then a member from each pair will disclose one of the questions from each person in the pair to the class. Have three people from the class to ask one question related to diversity to three members of the class. The question should be one that has not been discussed by other members in the class.

    *   Are you living with your biological mother and father? Explain how you feel living with your biological parents, living with your single mom or dad, of step parents.

    *   If you are not the only child in your family, how are you ranked based on your other siblings (first child born, last child born, in the middle, etc). Explain how you get along with your siblings based on how you are ranked. Explain why you get along or why you do not get along so well with your siblings. Does being close or far in age makes a difference as to how you and your siblings get along? Explain why or why not.

    *   Being the race or ethnicity that you are, have you been able to bond with others outside of your race or ethnicity easily? Why or why not.

3. Research three ethnicities and state 2-3 races that are derived from the ethnicity that you researched. Include your references in APA or MLA format.

4. Ask each student to make a collage of the type of social class they would like to live in. They can use newspapers, magazines, books, etc. Have the student to bring their collage to class and show the class and state why they included the items as their social class. Allow 3 -5 minutes long as their presentation time in class.

5. Pam is a Black female whose biological parents consist of a White mother and a Black father. Pam's skin color is very light and her hair is wavy. Pam portrays herself as being white and not Black. Write your view point of how you see Pam based on her race and ethnicity. Do you feel that she is doing the right thing? Why or why not? What would you say to Pam if you were her parents? Explain. You can include examples where need. This should be at least a half page – 1 1/2 pages long, doubled-spaced and typed. Include references in APA or MLA format.

6. State your view points on same-sex marriages and if it should be legal in your state or country. Why or why not. This should be at least a half page – one page long, doubled-spaced and typed. Include references in APA or MLA format.

UNDERSTANDING CULTURE

To understand culture, you first have to define culture. Culture is a knowledge of learned characteristics such as language, behaviors, attitudes, beliefs, values, and religion that is shared by a group of people. Learning his/her culture through generation to generation is called enculturation. Enculturation may come from experiences, observations, and instructions. For example, in Japan, one would have to go through a process of enculturation. They would have to learn all of believed to be appropriate behaviors.

As we become a more global society and work with other people from other countries, one must understand Hofstede's Model on dimensions of culture. Hofstede's six dimensions of culture that are found in all cultures are 1) individualism; 2) high and low context; 3) masculine and feminine culture; 4) high and low tolerance for uncertainty; 5) centralized and decentralized culture of power; and 6) time as it relates to short-term and long-term. Let's begin with *individualism* which includes individualism and collectivism.

Individualism stands for self because they tend to take care of themselves and their immediate families. Some examples of individualism culture are United States, Great Britain, Canada, France, Italy, and Australia. When looking at individual audiences they respond better when emphasis is placed on personal reward. *Collectivism* stands for the group because they expect support from others and they place their values of "we" rather than "I". Some examples of collectivism culture are Costa Rica, Venezuela, Pakistan, Chile, and South Korea. When looking at collectivist audience, they will respond when emphasis is placed on community and a sense of duty. Next is high and low context. *High context* draws information from surrounding context such as interpreting messages nonverbally. Countries such as China, Japan, Saudi Arabia, Italy and Greece are considered high context countries. *Low context* prefer to communicate in words rather than nonverbally and low context feels that those who are high context are not trustworthy. Countries such as Switzerland, Germany, Sweden, United States, Finland, and Australia are considered low context countries. Masculine and Feminine cultures emphasize on male values and female perspectives. *Masculine cultures* place emphasis on material wealth and assertiveness. Countries such as Japan, Italy, Mexico, Ireland, and Jamaica are considered masculine cultures. *Feminine cultures* value caring, attention to quality of life and are more sensitive. Sweden, Norway, Chile, Portugal, Thailand, Denmark are some countries that focus on feminine cultures. Next high and low tolerance for uncertainty tolerate may be more ambiguity and uncertainty than others. Cultures who need to feel secure through stability and rules consist of countries such as Greece, Japan, Peru, Spain, Belgium, and France are *high-uncertainty cultures* whereas cultures who prefer new ideas, more adventurous and embrace change are countries such as Canada, United States, Great Britain, and the Philippines which are *low-uncertainty cultures.* When looking at cultures with more *centralized power* expect individuals to have more power than others. They have clear defined lines of authority and responsibility. Countries under a centralized/high power culture are Mexico, Arab countries, Malaysia, India, Guatemala, and Venezuela. *Decentralized/low power cultures* tend to minimize the difference in power between people and accept fewer people having authority and power. These countries are Denmark, United States, Germany, Costa Rica, Switzerland, Nigeria, and New Zealand. Hofstede's last dimension of culture is time as it relates to long-term and short-term culture. *Time* as it relates to long-term culture focuses on the future and value perseverance and thrift because will pay off over a period of time. Long-term culture also has a strong work ethic, structure, and status. Countries that fall under long-term cultures are China, Japan, Brazil, and other Asian countries. Short-term culture values spending rather than saving they want quick gratification and results. Countries that are short-term cultures are United States, Canada, Great Britain, Spain, Nigeria, Portugal, and Philippines.

PURPOSE
The purpose of the assignments will help students and others in the class understand culture. The assignments will involve ways where students can identify, compare, understand, and show how culture relates to Hofstede's Dimensions of Culture.

ACTIVITY 4.1

DIRECTIONS
This exercise will help you understand your culture and its beliefs and values.

Contact someone in your family and ask what are some of the beliefs and values of your culture. If there is no one in your family who can answer your questions regarding beliefs and values, research your culture and find out about the values and beliefs that you found during your research. Once you have your answers, write how you feel about your culture's belief and values. Also state if you have children do you plan to pass your findings down to your children? State why or why not?

ACTIVITY 4.2

DIRECTIONS
View the video on culture gestures. After viewing the video answer the questions that relate to the video. http://www.youtube.com/watch?v=2h0V1YkccEE&list=PL_LftoeVJpNQMXC6kxGKg4_Y8KyS5hYPT

QUESTIONS
1. If you were in Iran and you flashed the thumbs' up (which is a vulgar insult), how would you correct the gesture so they will know that you did not mean what you said?
2. If you were in Italy and you brought your finger together, what does that gesture mean in Italy? Write an example of the gesture for Italy and Egypt?
3. What do the thumb and the forefinger mean in China and Italy?
4. If you were in the UK, what gesture would you use for Good or alright?

ACTIVITY 4.3

DIRECTIONS

You work for a global advertising agency in Japan and were given the account to sell the HSBC (a bank) ads in the United States (U.S.). After looking at the video state which one of the ads you would choose to promote to a US advertising agency and why? Then write 1 – 2 paragraphs on how you will communicate to a United States advertising agency on how to purchase and show the ad(s) in the U.S. Video Link: http://www.youtube.com/watch?v=GOHvMz7dl2A

ACTIVITY 4.4

DIRECTIONS

You are a member of your school college band. Every year there is a band concert in Argentina and this year your college band will attend the concert. Before you leave for the concert, your band director asked all the members to view Argentina's culture and perceptions as to how they differ or are similar to your country. Also, list some of the gestures, greetings, clothing, and other cultures or co-cultures you may face in Argentina.

ACTIVITY 4.5

DIRECTIONS

Review and research Hofstede's Dimensions of Culture. Based on your findings compare and contrast Hofstede's culture dimensions of China and Australia.

ACTIVITY 4.6

DIRECTIONS
Click the link and look at the video on Hofstede's Dimensions of Culture Theory. After looking at the video, answer the questions that relate to Hofstede's Dimensions of Culture Theory. List the dimensions of culture theory and give one example of each. Hofstede's Dimension of Culture Theory video Link http://education-portal.com/academy/lesson/hofstedes-cultural-dimensions-theory.html#lesson

ACTIVITY 4.7

DIRECTIONS
Look at the Hofstede's Dimension of Culture Theory video again and relate Hofstede's Dimension with the scenarios below. Video Link: http://education-portal.com/academy/lesson/hofstedes-cultural-dimensions-theory.html#lesson

SCENARIO 1
Pamela Jones has been chosen to start a new accounting division in Tokyo, Japan. Most of the employees at the Japan office are Japanese and Pamela would like to transfer two employees from the US office to help train the Japanese staff who will be working in the new department. The two US employees will be offered a great salary and two months housing cost. When Pamela discussed this with the two US employees they turned down the position. They preferred to stay in the US with their current employers. After reviewing the Hofstede's Dimension Culture Theory, discuss and apply your answer as to why the two US employees turned down the position?

SCENARIO 2
Ablah has been working at a global communication company in Saudi Arabia and the headquarters is located in New York, New York. The New York office decided to close the Saudi Arabia office and wanted Ablah to transfer to the New York office. Since Ablah is Arabic, she did not want to move to the New York office. Based on the Hofstede's Dimension Culture Theory, state four reasons as to why you feel that Ablah may not have wanted to move to New York and why? If you feel that Ablah should move to New York, New York, state why?

DIVERSITY BARRIERS AND HOW TO IMPROVE THEM

As stated earlier about diversity we know that race, gender, age, sex, sexual orientation, and social class are areas that we tend to focus on. Not only do we focus on those areas of diversity, we face barriers that consist of stereotypes and prejudice. When looking at stereotypes it is fixed over generalized beliefs about a particular group or class of people (Cardwell, 1996). Stereotypes are seen as a barrier when the uniqueness of individuals, groups or events fail. Some negative, positive, racial, and gender stereotype examples are saying "all blond women are dumb" (negative) and all Asians know kung fu (positive), all Italians are good cooks (racial), and women are always moody and men likes hats (gender). Every race, culture, country, religion and a community has a stereotype. It is a way some establishes identity in people or things. Prejudice on the other hand is an opinion or judgment of someone that is formed before you know the facts or the background of a person. An example of prejudice is when an organization hires more men candidates and rejects women candidates (and vice versa) due to their gender. We tend to say that we are prejudice against people when we assume that they have certain characteristics. How can we improve these barriers? This can be done by becoming knowledgeable, motivated, and skilled.

To develop knowledge, one must seek information about others, ask questions and listen for the answers, and establish common ground by merging cultural traditions to develop understanding. To develop motivation, strategies to appreciate others who are different from you may help you appreciate diverse culture approaches to communication and relationships. One must be mindful. You want to be conscious of what you are doing, thinking, and sensing at any given moment. You want to avoid negative judgments. Lastly, to develop skill, you must adapt to others focuses on specific behaviors that can help overcome barriers and cultural differences. Put yourself in someone else's mental position and emotional mindset and be creative and flexible. Learning the mentioned skills will help you relate to others who are different than you.

PURPOSE
The purpose of the assignments will help students and others in the class understand how to improve diversity barriers.

ACTIVITY 4.8

DIRECTIONS
Look at the different videos and relate them to how one would handle diversity barriers, stereotypes, and prejudice.

1. Discuss how you would handle stereotypes and prejudice in the workplace. Defend your position on each and state why?

2. If you were the diversity director of a global company and you were asked to write procedures on how to improve diversity in your company, what would you write? List five procedures and state why.

3. Look at the 7 minute video on Diversity Challenges. Discuss how you will handle the situation with Felix and as the hiring manager, would you hire him? State why or why not? Diversity Challenges Link: http://www.youtube.com/watch?v=n6kUaDp5FVU

4. Look at the 6 minute and 19 seconds video on Culture Competence: Managing Your Prejudice. Discuss how you would handle culture competence as it relates to prejudice. Look at the four (4) pictures and give your viewpoint on your thoughts about each person in the picture. State why. Culture Competence: Managing Your Prejudice Link: http://www.youtube.com/watch?v=E1MI_h0HIcw

5. Look at the 5 minute video on Culture Diversity: Tips for Communicating with Culture Awareness. After looking at the video, state whether you agree or not on the tips that are mentioned. State why or why not. Would you apply the tips? Why or why not. Write an example that relates to two of the tips that were mentioned in the video. Culture Diversity: Tips for Communicating with Culture Awareness Link: http://www.youtube.com/watch?v=ZDvLk7e2Irc

6. View the 10 minute video on Culture Differences in the Business World. Research the countries that were visited in the video and discuss how you would have reacted in each of the situations that Joe was faced with. Be sure to include the effective ways in handling barriers. Culture Differences in the Business World Link: http://www.youtube.com/watch?v=HQw8KjCsgZc&list=PLxFsha7uj8TNOXSCvRihM6517rgUyVINa

PART TWO

Communication Skills Needed

CHAPTER 5

Listening and Feedback

STUDENT LEARNING OUTCOMES

Critical Thinking			Communication			Team Work		Social Responsibility	Personal Responsibility	Activity Measured
Creative Thinking/ Innovative	Analysis & Evaluation	Synthesis of Information	Writing	Visual	Oral	Differing Viewpoints	Work with Others	Intercultural Competence	Ethical Decision Making	Activity
X					X	X	X			5.0
X	X		X		X		X			5.1
					X		X			5.2
X	X		X	X	X					5.3, 5.4
		X		X	X	X	X			5.5
X	X	X	X	X		X	X	X		5.6
X	X		X	X	X	X	X			5.7

"LISTENING¹

Are you a good listener? Listening is a very important communication skill, yet we seldom receive special training for it in school. People often confuse listening with hearing. Some people play the game of listening by putting on a rubber reaction face along with occasional head nods and verbal sounds.

Listening requires time and effort. It involves much more than hearing. This chapter provides information about listening and activities that will help you learn about this most frequently used element of communication. You must have a desire to apply what you learn if you wish to improve as a receiver.

First, let us understand four very important terms:

Hearing

Definition: Hearing is necessary for listening, but is a separate process involving the reception of sound waves by the ear and brain.

Example: You may hear sounds but not necessarily pay any attention to them. Have you ever been guilty of staring at the speaker when she says, "You're not listening to me"?

Listening

Definition: A mental process of interpreting sound waves in the brain. We focus our hearing upon the stimuli we wish to attend to. Listening isn't passive. You must interpret this stimuli into meaning and action.

Example: Mother, in the kitchen, may be slightly aware of children's laughter and noise coming from the next room, yet can still concentrate on a meaningful task without distraction. But if some unusual sounds occur, they are then interpreted as being significant danger signals.

Empathic Listening

Definition: Listening to discover the sender's point of view. The speaker is encouraged to self-disclose. Establishing trust, the listener enters into that person's world and attempts to imagine the thoughts and feelings of the speaker. Empathic listening responses should be a willingness to understand, but not give advice.

Example: Let us imagine that a fellow student is sharing with a classmate that Professor Jones hates him, is out to get him, and will certainly fail him no matter how hard the student tries. An empathic response might be: "You don't feel Professor Jones is being fair with you?" To suggest that this person is irrational and should "talk it out" with Professor Jones is being judgmental and giving advice.

Feedback

Definition: Those verbal and nonverbal responses that affect the speaker in either a positive or negative way. Feedback may either strengthen or weaken communication. Feedback should express clearly what we want the speaker to know of our understanding about the message.

Example: A student speaker in a public speaking class would be more encouraged upon seeing affirmative head nods regarding a proposal than if he reads anger, negative body language, and glances at the clock.

LISTEN
(anonymous)

When I ask you to listen to me and you start giving advice,
you have not done what I asked.
When I ask you to listen to me and you begin to tell me
why I shouldn't feel that way,
you are trampling my feelings.
When I ask you to listen to me and you feel you have to
do something to solve my problems, you have failed me,
strange as that may seem.
So please, just listen and hear me. And if you want to talk,
wait a few minutes for your turn and I promise I'll listen
to you.

ACTIVITY 5.0 Listening Skill Exercise

PURPOSE
To practice the "Rogerian" Listening Techniques in order to improve listening skills.

PROCEDURE

1. Form listening triads and designate each participant A, B, or C. In each group, one person will act as referee (observe) and the other two will have a discussion, each alternating between being the listener and the speaker.

2. The discussion is to be unstructured, except that before each participant speaks she must summarize, in her own words and without notes, what the previous speaker said. If the summary is thought to be incorrect, the others are free to interrupt and clarify the misunderstanding. After about seven minutes, the participants switch roles and continue the process. The following topics may be used:

a. nuclear energy
b. Internet regulation
c. immigration
d. smoker's vs. nonsmoker's rights
e. pollution
f. Affirmative Action
g. death penalty
h. crime/criminals
i. gun control
j. drug abuse
k. violence in media
l. abortion
m. Education Standards
n. political parties
o. _____

DISCUSSION

1. Do we usually listen to all that the other person is saying?
2. Did you find that you had difficulty formulating your own thoughts and listening at the same time?
3. Were you forgetting what you were going to say? Not listening to others? Rehearsing your response?
4. When others paraphrased your remarks, did they do it in a more concise way?
5. How important is it to check out with the other person what you thought you heard her say?
6. Was the other's manner of presentation affecting your listening ability?
7. Does the way another person listens to you affect your self-concept? How?
8. Does the way a person listens to you affect your perception of that person's intelligence and personality? How?
9. What are some guidelines for good listening?

THE IMPORTANCE OF LISTENING

Most of us have, at one time or another, had the experience of talking with someone and getting the feeling that we weren't being listened to. At such times we may have felt frustrated or perhaps even angry. At other times we may have been in the role of the listener and experienced the embarrassment of being caught not listening. At these times, whether we have been the speaker or the listener, we may have become acutely aware that listening skills, whether someone else's or our own, were not as good as they could or should be. How many times have you made, or heard someone else make, the accusation, "You're not listening to me"? In trying to understand why we are not the listeners we could be, let's consider five questions essential to that understanding:

- How important is listening?
- How good are we as listeners?
- What are the various types of listening?
- What are the major barriers to listening effectively?
- How can we become better listeners?

Listening as a Basic Activity

How important is listening? Beyond our own awareness that it is important to have others listening to us when we are talking, research has indicated that listening is the most used basic communicating activity in our day-to-day lives. On the average, we spend about 70 to 80 percent of our time awake in some kind of communicating. Of that time, we spend approximately 9 percent writing, 16 percent reading, 30 percent speaking, and 45 percent listening. Furthermore, of all the information we come to know during our lifetime, we learn over 90 percent of it through our eyes and ears. In fact, some people have even suggested that the causes of some of the major disasters in history were due to poor listening.

In addition to being the most frequent communicating task that we perform, the importance of listening is further amplified when we consider that listening to someone is a form of recognizing and validating that person's worth. This is probably why we get angry or frustrated, or simply feel rejected when we are not being listened to. How often have you heard, or said, during an argument, "You're not listening to me"? Good, effective listening is a way of reducing hostility, while poor or withheld listening is a way of creating hostility. In fact, intentionally withheld listening has been used as a form of punishment during Victorian times and by primitive tribes. Withholding listening is also a major element in brainwashing techniques. Obviously then, being listened to is a very real need we all have!

Listening as a Skill

Finally, when looking at how important listening is, consider your attitude about people you know who are good listeners. You probably like them more than others who you feel are poor listeners. Research has revealed that being a good listener is considered the most important management skill. So it seems that listening is very important—it's the most used communicating skill. We depend on it heavily for most of the information we come to know. It's important for our success in school, on the job, and in relationships, as well as being vital to our own psychological wellbeing, and it's a key to having more friends.

How good are we as listeners? Listening ability is one communication skill that is relatively easy to measure, and when researchers have measured it, the results have been astounding. Studies have found that the average listening efficiency in this culture is 25 percent. This dismal figure was first discovered in research with college students listening to a 10-minute lecture. While we may wish that the percentage was higher, or even feel that we aren't as bad at listening as other people, the facts suggest that there is a great deal of room for improvement. To test out your own listening efficiency, ask yourself how often you repeat questions that have just previously been answered, ask someone to repeat something she said, write down the wrong information, or try to listen to someone while reading or watching television at the same time. None of us is perfect but when it comes to being a good listener, most of us don't even come close! The logical question to ask is, "Well, if we're such poor listeners, how did we get that way and what's keeping us from being better?" Before dealing with these two questions, let's consider the different kinds of listening that are possible.

ACTIVITY 5.1 Analysis of My Listening Effectiveness

This form is designed to give you an opportunity to evaluate your own listening effectiveness and for another to evaluate you. Ask another to complete it and return it to you within two days. The information provided will enable you to gain some important insight into your strengths and areas for improvement as a listener.

Part 1—Overall Estimate of my Listening Ability

Please rate my overall ability as a listener according to the following scale:

Poor	Fair	Average	Good	Excellent

Part 2—Assessment of Specific Listening Skills

Section A—For each of the following items, please indicate to the left of each item the frequency with which I demonstrate, to you, the behaviors indicated based upon the following scale:

0	1	2	3	4
never				always

Scale

_____ 1. Appear interested and concerned about what I have to say.

_____ 2. Appear energetic and anxious to listen.

_____ 3. Encourage me to continue communicating.

_____ 4. Indicate if you are confused or don't understand what I am saying.

_____ 5. Respond to what I am saying in a nonevaluative and nonjudgmental way.

_____ 6. Avoid interrupting me while I am speaking.

_____ 7. Look at me when I am speaking to you.

_____ 8. Don't try to change my mind when it's your turn to speak.

Section B—In your own words complete the following two items:

1. What do you consider to be my main strength as a listener?

2. What is the area I most need to work on as a listener?

ACTIVITY 5.2 Listening Activity

PURPOSE

To demonstrate how vital listening is to memorization.

PROCEDURE

1. Break into dyads.
2. Have one person in each pair read the following list to the other. The reader should first read item one, then items one and two, and so on through ten. The listener should try to repeat what she heard after each reading.
3. Read the following as directed:

    One pig.

    Two jaws.

    Three orange VWs.

    Four lively pacifiers.

    Five squelching jackasses.

    Six marinated chicks, prepared to perfection.

    Seven fox-trotters from Amazon County, New Delhi.

    Eight rusty outhouse seats unearthed from the tomb of King Tut.

    Nine dirty men, wearing purple tennis shoes, jogging to Lucretia's massage parlor in back of Mr. Yee's gas station.

    Ten amphibious, blubbery octopi legs from the northeast corner of the westernmost island of Mungula-Stikwee, two-stepping to "I Wanna Hug You All Night Long."

4. Get into a circle and see how many can repeat all ten lines.

DISCUSSION

1. What problems did you encounter as you got into this activity? Why?
2. How important is concentration to effective listening?
3. What part can verbal repetition play in acquiring good listening-memory skills?
4. Does the quality of the source's message affect receiver listening?

LISTENING TYPES

Listening is not just a single activity; rather it is a series of steps relating to a specific goal—what we wish to pay attention to. Just as there is more than one thing to which we can pay attention, there is more than one type of listening. For our purposes, listening can be classified into the following five types:

1. Listening for enjoyment
2. Listening for details
3. Listening for main ideas
4. Listening for overall understanding
5. Listening for emotional undertones

Listening for enjoyment is probably the easiest type of listening we are involved with because, rather than paying attention to someone else, we simply tune into our own emotional response to what we are listening to. This is the type of listening we do when we listen to our favorite radio station or a favorite tune. We enjoy the music for what it does to us, how it makes us feel.

Listening for details is one of the types most closely associated with school. This is the type we use when we are listening for the detailed information in a teacher's lecture. Here we are trying to pay attention to specific factual information that the speaker is trying to relate.

Listening for main ideas is also closely allied with the classroom. However, in this situation we are trying to identify the speaker's main point. What is he driving at? What is the point he is attempting to make? In this type of listening, we must pay more attention and attempt to tune in to the general main ideas.

Listening for overall understanding is even more difficult than the types previously mentioned. In this situation we are trying to piece together all of the speaker's information in an effort to get at the overall meaning in the message. What is the bottom line? In order to do this type of listening, we must attend to much more of the message and try to assemble it in much the same way that a child might assemble a puzzle in order to see the entire picture.

Listening for emotional undertones is yet another type of listening. This is probably the most difficult of all, because it requires the most attention and effort. In this type of listening, we shift our focus from what is being said to how the speaker is feeling. We are attempting to understand what is going on inside of her. Unlike listening for enjoyment, where we were concerned with tuning in to our emotions, in this situation we are concerned with the emotions of the other person. This is particularly difficult since emotions are often hidden beneath layer upon layer of verbal camouflage. Often the speaker may not be in touch with her own feelings. Here, great attentiveness to the emotion-laden words is vital along with the discipline to keep our own thoughts and comments quiet.

These, then, are the major types of listening. As we can see, this seemingly simple task is far more complicated than may have previously been thought. But why are we such bad listeners on the average? What keeps us from achieving our goal?

ACTIVITY 5.3 Active Listening

PURPOSE

To increase your active listening skills.

PROCEDURE

1. The first part is based on programmed instruction. Simply read and follow each step.
2. After completing the programmed section, role-play the situations suggested in the "Active Listening Exercise."
3. Try to determine the extent to which active listening is used in each of these situations.
4. Cover all sections, except 1, with a sheet of paper

---

1. This program is designed to help improve communication between people. You should be covering all of this page so that only this first instruction is exposed. Each printed instruction is called a frame. A black line, like the one below, means the end of a frame. After you have finished reading this frame, move the cover down to the black line below the next frame.

---

2. There are several reasons for attempting to improve communication. For one thing, in any relationship that the partners want to develop, situations will appear in which one person wants to talk about a problem and the other wants to listen. This session focuses on an approach to listening.

---

3. Experience has shown that people who work with others in solving problems typically go through specific stages of relating. At each stage they require new, more useful ways of looking at their problems, which leads them to better understanding and to new approaches to solutions. These new approaches come from changes in their awareness, thinking, feeling, and doing.

---

4. This program focuses on the first stage of relating to one another, that is, actively listening to the other so he can freely explore with you what is on HIS mind.

5. This is a step-by-step learning program. You will be learning from a series of brief exercises that involve YOU in DOING something. You will be learning from your own experience.

---

6. Now we can begin. I am going to describe an incident to you that involves you and another person in conversation. It ends with the other replying to you and waiting for your response. I will then give five possible responses. Imagine you are listening to the responses. Then read below and pick the ONE that is most likely to encourage the other to keep telling you what's on HIS mind, and to help you both explore the problem as HE sees it.

---

7. Here's the situation: A person in your class is telling you about how hard it has been lately for him to do the homework. You ask him why and he replies, "I don't know why, I just can't get to it. Frankly, I don't have any enthusiasm for doing it. I've lost interest in the class. I just stall around and then rush like mad to even get here on time every day."

---

8. Which of the following responses is most likely to encourage the other to keep talking about what's on his mind and what he is feeling?
    a. Don't you know that you are not going to get anything out of the class if you don't do your homework?
    b. You've just got to get it done or you'll flunk.
    c. What's happening? You been playing around too much?
    d. You shouldn't be late so much. It's not fair to the rest of us.
    e. It sounds as though you've lost your enthusiasm and interest in the class.

---

9. Write your answer here

---

10. Now let's continue. We will go through more steps before I tell you the answer I would give. It is not important whether your answer and mine agree; however, it IS important that you understand my answer. The purpose of the next few steps is to develop that understanding.

11. Now let's look at what the other is feeling. Pretend to be the other and speak his words aloud and with feeling. How do you feel as you speak the other's words? "I don't know why. I just can't get to it. Frankly, I don't have any enthusiasm for doing it. I've lost interest in the class. I just stall around and then rush like mad to even get here on time every day."

12. Write down some of your feelings as you spoke. Were you happy or sad? Were you angry? Write your feelings in the next frame.

13. 1 felt:

14. Many people report feeling discouraged, depressed, down, bummed out, dull, bored, listless, aimless, etc. Were the feelings you had generally the same, or were they different? (If your feelings were quite different, listen to the words again and try to feel them as having a discouraged, aimless feeling. The fact that you felt differently does not mean you were wrong, but that you just felt differently.)

15. The first possible response was: "Don't you know that you are not going to get anything out of the class if you don't do your homework?" Imagine that you are the other and are lacking in enthusiasm and have lost interest in your class. How do you feel when you hear this response? Write some of your feelings in the space below.

16. 1 felt:

17. Some people feel blamed, punished, criticized, resentful, misunderstood, annoyed, angry, etc. Other people feel blamed, regretful, bad, hurt, apologetic, sorry, etc. Were your feelings close to any of those?

18. Now react to each of the other responses as if you are the other. Remember that you have said: "I don't know why. I just can't get to it. Frankly, I don't have any enthusiasm for doing it. I've lost interest in the class. I just stall around and rush like mad to even get here on time every day."

19. Speaker's response to you: Your reaction to the speaker:

    a.   a.

    b.   b.

    c.   c.

    d.   d.

    e.   e.

20. In looking back over your reaction, remember that *what a speaker intends or means to say* does not necessarily affect a listener's feelings. The listener's feelings are affected by what he **hears** the speaker saying. With that point in mind, revise what you have written if you want to.

21. In our incident, the **other's** personal feelings are probably strong during the early part of this conversation and almost any response will move him AWAY from expressing what's on HIS mind. He may move away because he feels you are blaming, criticizing, or analyzing him. Even if you are supporting or approving, he is likely to move away from freely exploring what's on HIS mind, because he wants to keep getting the good feeling of your support and approval.

22. Now let's think about some different ways of responding to another person. The ones given in the exercise are evaluating, forcing, probing, directing, and accepting.

23. Each of the five responses you were given earlier is an example of a different way of responding by the respondent (R) to the speaker (S).

Response "a" says: "Don't you know that you are not going to get anything out of this class if you don't do your homework?"
These words are FORCING. They begin with "Don't you . . ." and the rest of the words express R's opinion about what S is doing. Look at the words again. The question FORCES S into agreeing with R's opinion and leaves S free only to admit that he "knows" or "doesn't know" that he's "letting himself down." The question shifts S's attention to what is on R's mind.

Response "b" says: "You've just got to get it done or you'll flunk."
These words are DIRECTING. They *tell* the other to *do* something. They also shift S's attention on what R considers important or interesting.

Response "c" says: "What's happening? You been playing around too much?"
These words are PROBING. They *ask for information* about a hunch the responder has. They focus S's attention on what R considers important or interesting.

Response "d" says: "You shouldn't be late so much. It's not fair to the rest of us."
These words are EVALUATING. They place blame on the other for the practice of unfairness.

Response "e" says: "It sounds as though you've lost your enthusiasm and interest in the class."
These words are ACCEPTING. They repeat the other's *key words* back to him without judging him. S knows that he has been heard and he is free to keep talking about what's on his mind.

---

24. In my experience, the response that is most likely to encourage the OTHER to keep telling you what's on HIS mind and to help you both explore the problem as HE sees it is the **accepting** response (e).

---

25. Later in a conversation, other kinds of responses can be helpful in (1) exploring the facts and feelings that are not at the surface of the other's mind, (2) in creating alternative solutions, (3) in evaluating alternatives, (4) in deciding, and (5) in motivating action.

26. Until the other gets **his feelings** off his chest and really feels you have understood and accepted his feelings, his communication will contain facts distorted by his feelings. Until you actively show your understanding and acceptance of his feelings, it is too soon for you to explore facts, create alternative solutions, or suggest action.

27. There is a logical sequence in working with another person to **solve a problem.**

ACCEPTING and UNDERSTANDING the other's way of seeing and feeling about things as being HIS, then
EXPLORING and PROBING for facts and feelings, then
CREATING alternative solutions, then
DECIDING on one solution, then
ACTING, then
FOLLOWING UP to see what is happening, . . . ETC.

This session focuses on the first step—developing your ability to respond in an **ACCEPTING** way when you feel it is appropriate.

28. Now we will look at another incident. A student in your class seems to be unable to do the work, and tells you, "I just can't seem to get the hang of things. I try to find out what I'm supposed to do on tells me. No one pays attention to me and I can't learn anything by just watching. Maybe I ought to quit."

29. Which of these responses is *accepting*?
     a. "Why don't you try harder? No one gets ahead without hard work."
     b. "If I were you, I'd ask the other people to help you."
     c. "Do you have any ideas why the others won't help you?"
     d. "Don't feel too bad. All of us have problems."
     e. "You feel that the others don't pay attention to you?"

30. Answer "e" is *accepting*. It reflects the other's main thinking and feelings.

31. Here's another incident. A student tells you, "That teacher! I've been here three years and no one ever told me before that I did a lousy job. So I made a few mistakes, but why does she blame me for everything?"

32. Which response is *accepting*?
    a. "All she wanted to do was to get you to be more thorough."
    b. "You think she expects too much of you?"
    c. "She really doesn't blame you for everything. She just wanted you to do it over again."
    d. "You feel she blames you for everything."
    e. "Are you really sure it's not all in your mind?"

---

33. Response "D" is *accepting*. It reflects the other's main thinking and feelings.

---

34. This time, you do the responding yourself. I'm going to say something to you and you will then write down an *accepting* response in the following frame.

---

35. I say, "I don't usually admit it, but I often have feelings of inadequacy when I'm asked to speak before a group of people. I'm sure they think I don't know what I'm talking about because I get so shaky and lose my train of thought."

---

36. You respond:

---

37. Now imagine that you are the person speaking. You have just said, "I don't usually admit it, but I often have feelings of inadequacy when I'm asked to speak before a group of people. I'm sure they think I don't know what I'm talking about because I get so shaky and lose my train of thought." Now listen to 10 possible responses. *Put a check in front of the responses that are **accepting** to you.*

    a. "You get shaky when you speak before a group?"
    b. "How do you know what the group thinks about you?"
    c. "Don't you realize that even the best speakers get a little shaky?"
    d. "When did this kind of thing first happen to you?"
    e. "Why are you afraid to admit to such a minor neurosis?"
    f. "You feel inadequate and lose your train of thought?"
    g. "I've had the experience many times. Have you tried taking deep breaths?"
    h. "Do you think this inferiority complex stems from your early childhood?"
    i. "Don't you think that this will hurt you in your activities as a leader?"
    j. "Wouldn't you like to sit in on the 'Speaking in Meetings' course I'm taking?"

38. Responses "a" and "f" are **accepting**.

---

39. Take a minute to look back at the responses you wrote down. Do they still seem accepting?

---

40. Now listen to a series of expressions. In the right hand column, write an accepting response.

Others say: *You say:*

"I don't think you understand some of the problems with this assignment."

"Sure I want to improve, but I think I'm doing all I can right now. After all, if I take time out to go to the lab sessions, my job will suffer."

"Do you really think I don't take enough initiative? I've always prided myself on my ability to really plunge into an assignment."

"I think you've got a fine idea there; however, I really doubt that the teacher will buy it."

(ANGRY) . . . "Most of the people in this class don't give a damn about it, so why should I?"

---

41. Some *accepting* responses that you might give to the aforementioned expressions are:

   a. "I don't understand some of the problems with this assignment." (And yet, I might say this with a tone of voice that says, "That's what YOU think, but I really DO understand." If I do say it this way, however, the other still won't feel understood or accepted.)
   b. "You want to improve but your work will suffer if you go to the study sessions."

c. "You feel that you really plunge into an assignment but I think you don't take enough initiative." (I would need to reassure him that I didn't see him. However, if I do reassure him, then I stop his talking about what is on HIS Mind.)

d. "You doubt that the teacher will buy it." (I would feel a need to start telling him how he could get the teacher to buy it. It might be that this is not the main thing on his mind. I won't find THAT out, though, unless I hear him out.)

e. "Why should YOU care when most of the people in this class don't give a damn about it." (I am just repeating his idea—not asking a question.)

42. Review your responses in frame 40 and revise them if you want to. As you revise them, think about the tone of voice in which you would say them. Think about how the other would react to your tone.

43. Experiment with ACCEPTING responses in your encounters with people for the next few days, and try to sense how people react. The only way to develop the skill of **accepting** is through practice. When you are really tuned into the other's world, you will find (if your experience is like mine) that the other becomes noticeably more interested in talking to you. YOU will enjoy it more, too.

44. a. As you listen, your main purpose is to ACTIVELY show the other that you are "with him," "in tune," "understanding him," and "caring about what he is trying to communicate to you." (If you don't honestly care, that will show through and the accepting responses will sound phony.)

b. You can show that you are "in tune" in other ways than accepting words. For example, there are times when the most helpful thing you can do is to be quietly attentive. Nodding your head, to let the other know you are with him, can help, too.

c. As the other continues talking to you, do more than just parrot his words. Try to capture the flavor of his ideas and his feelings, that is, try to be a mirror. If you are a clear mirror (and not a "judge" or a "critic"), he will feel free to change with you and in front of you. (And, if your experience is like mine, that can be a very satisfying experience.)

45. The next frame lists several statements. Try thinking of responses that catch the flavor or spirit of what the other is saying without just being repetitious of his words. Write your responses in the right hand column of the next frame.

46. *Others say:*   *You say:*

"It really gripes me when people say that. Ever since I was a kid in elementary school people have said I was stubborn. I'll be damned if I can see how being a 'wet mop' will help me to do a better job!"

(**INCREDULOUSLY**) . . . "You mean somebody said that about me?"

(**ANGRY**) . . . "One trouble with people in our class is that they never can see that we need answers now. I think too many of you have been concentrating on theories that still need to be proved."

"I doubt that it will work. I don't think you understand our problem. Our situation is completely different from anyone else's."

"It's hard to say where I would like to be five years from now. I certainly would like, gee . . . I don't know. I feel I could be doing a lot more than I am . . .; but, somehow, it doesn't seem worth it. Why bother trying?"

---

47. Answers I might give are:

    a. "It really gripes you when people call you stubborn."
    b. "You are surprised to hear that."
    c. "You are angry that we don't get answers for you right away."
    d. "You feel that I don't understand your situation."
    e. "Are you saying that life seems pretty overwhelming to you? That you feel like you'd like to do something—but why bother?"

---

48. As you practice using accepting responses, you may feel discomfort. If you do, remember that a new way of behaving is usually uncomfortable at first.

DISCUSSION QUESTIONS

1. When do you think Active Listening should be used?
2. Has anyone ever done this kind of listening with you? If so, how did it make you feel?
3. Since Active Listening is a skill and must be practiced to improve it, how do you think you could practice Active Listening?

ACTIVITY 5.4

PURPOSE

To practice creating Active Listening responses.

PROCEDURE

In small groups, discuss each of the following statements. What responses should be made? Why? If Active Listening is called for, suggest an appropriate Active Listening response.

1. I wonder if I ought to start looking for another job. They're reorganizing the company, and what with the drop in business and all, maybe this is one of the jobs they'll cut back on. But if my boss finds out I'm looking around, maybe he'll think I don't like it here and let me go anyway.
2. I said I'd do the collecting for him, but I sure don't feel like it. But I owe him a favor, so I guess I'll have to do it.
3. I've got a report due tomorrow, an exam the next day, rehearsals every night this week, and now a meeting this afternoon. I don't think I can even fit in eating and this has been going on all month.
4. Sure she gets better grades than I do. She's a housewife, takes only two classes, and all she has to do is study. I have to work a job and go to school too. And I don't have anyone to support me.
5. I can't understand why they haven't written. They've never been gone this long without at least a card, and I don't even know how to get in touch with them.
6. My daughter got straight A's this year and the high school has a reputation for being very hard. She's a natural student. But sometimes I wonder if she isn't all books. I wish I could help her get interested in something besides studying.
7. I worked up that whole study—did all the surveying, the compiling, and the writing. It was my idea in the first place. But he turned it into the head office, with his name on it, and he got the credit.

8. Boy, the teacher tells us he'll mark us off on our grade every time we're late, but it doesn't seem to bother him when he comes in late. He must figure it's his privilege.

9. I don't know whether I'm doing a good job or not. She never tells me if I'm doing well or need to work harder. I sure hope she likes my work.

10. She believed everything he said about me. She wouldn't even listen to my side; she just started yelling at me.

11. Look, we've gone over and over this. The meeting could have been over an hour ago if we hadn't gotten hung up on this one point. If we can't make a decision, let's table it and move on.

12. Look, I know I acted like a rat. I apologized, and I'm trying to make up for it. I can't do anymore, can I? So drop it!

DISCUSSION

1. Did your groups have difficulty in developing Active Listening responses?
2. Did the groups have any difficulty with responses to #6 and #12? Why?"

ACTIVITY 5.5

Listen and Follow: One should be able to concentrate and have a keen ear to effectively follow this activity. This is a classroom activity where the instructor will state the following:

- If the instructor hits the desk one time, the students should <u>stand</u>
- If the instructor hits the desk two times, the students should <u>lift their right foot</u>
- If the instructor hits the desk three times, the students should <u>sit down</u>

The instructor does not have to follow the order of the hits. The hits can be three, one, two etc. The students must be able to listen with complete concentration and follow through. The instructor can continue until one person is standing. The purchase left standing is the winner. As the instructor, you can add more commands than three for the students to follow.

"BARRIERS AND TO LISTENING AND STEPS TO BETTER LISTENING[2]

So why are we such bad listeners? While there are probably many causes to poor listening, four major factors can be identified that contribute in large part to the problem.

How then can we overcome these barriers and improve our listening? As mentioned earlier, listening actually consists of sets of skills that can be employed in different situations to meet different needs. However, there are six steps that actually underline all the different types of listening skills.

Physiological Factors

The first major factor is physiological in nature and, as such, is one we must learn to live with: the difference between the thinking and speaking rates. In essence, the brain works much faster than the mouth. Although the average speaking rate in our culture is about 125 words per minute, the brain processes language at the rate of approximately 800 words per minute. Since we can't slow the brain down, this gives us approximately 675 words per minute "free time" in our brain. So how do we use this "free time"? Well, we could use it to reinforce the message we are listening to, or we could use it to identify and organize the speaker's main points and supporting ideas. Unfortunately, most of us use this time to evaluate or criticize the speaker or message, prepare our rebuttal, or just daydream about a million things totally unrelated to the message. In short, we tune in to our own internal dialogue rather than tuning in to the speaker's message.

Some researchers have approached this problem from the other side. If we can't slow down the brain, perhaps we can speed up the message. Speech "compressors," which increase the rate without distorting the tone, have been developed and tested on subjects. Results have shown that it is possible to listen to rates two to three times normal without significant loss of comprehension. In fact, in some instances comprehension has been improved. Perhaps this is due to having less "free time" to allow distractions to creep in and divert the listener's attention. However, even though it sounds promising, "speed listening" is not practical in our day-to-day lives, so we must develop skill that enables us to use this "free time" constructively or we will surely continue to use it destructively.

Psychological Factors

The second major factor for poor listening is psychological. This is the tendency to treat listening as a passive, automatic activity. In other words, we confuse listening with hearing. Hearing is a physical process involving the reception of sound waves. It is passive and automatic. Listening, on the other hand, is an extremely active psychological process requiring attention and interpretation, and involving skills that must be learned. As we have seen, there is more than one kind of listening, and each involves a different set of skills suited to different needs or situations.

When we are actively involved in listening, our blood pressure and pulse rate increase and our palms tend to perspire. We actually burn more calories when we listen. (It might even be possible, but not too practical, to go on a listening diet.) Obviously, therefore, if listening takes work, it is important that we get our bodies ready to work in order to be better listeners, and that we employ the proper skills.

Educational Factors

The third major factor causing poor listening is educational. To understand this factor we must remember two concepts mentioned earlier: listening is the largest part of our daily communication, and listening is an active process. Yet in all the formal education we have received, we have spent major amounts of time learning how to read and write, two skills which total only 25 percent of our daily communication, little if any time learning how to speak in a formal way, and (for the vast majority of us) no time learning how to listen effectively. This is not to suggest reading and writing should not be taught, but when you consider the lack of emphasis that listening skills have received in our formal education, it is no wonder why our average listening efficiency is only 25 percent.

Some private corporations have come to realize the importance of teaching listening skills, and have developed their own listening programs. As the educational community increases its focus on the importance of listening education and more of us are taught proper listening skills, we will hope to see improvement in that 25-percent efficiency rate.

Social Factors

The last major factor relates to the previous one. Because we have not been taught how to listen effectively, *we often choose the wrong type of listening to do.* Have you ever found yourself tuning in to your own internal dialogue or emotions rather than trying to understand the meaning or emotion in the other person? Have you ever found yourself getting nice and comfortable, as if you were listening for enjoyment, when you were about to listen to a classroom lecture? Clearly, you may have wanted to listen, but you were doing the wrong type of listening.

STEPS TO BETTER LISTENING

How then can we overcome these barriers and improve our listening? As mentioned earlier, listening actually consists of sets of skills that can be employed in different situations to meet different needs. However, there are six steps that actually underlie all the different types of listening skills.

1. **Decide to listen.** Obviously, the commitment to listen is at the heart of being a better listener.
2. **Get your body ready to work.** Remember that listening is work. So it's important to get ready to do work by having an erect posture, being located close to the speaker, and creating some inner tension to combat the tendency to relax and daydream.
3. **Create a supportive climate.** Reduce or eliminate environmental distractions. Avoid statements or actions likely to create defensiveness.
4. **Put the other person first.** Focus on understanding what he/she has to say and use your brain's "free time" to that end.
5. **Select the appropriate type of listening.** Determine what your goal should be and focus on the appropriate part of the other person's message. Is the most important element your own feelings, the other person's details, main ideas, overall meaning, or underlying emotions?

6. **Communicate that you are listening.** Being a better listener is only half the job; you must also let the other person know that you are listening through eye contact, facial expressions, body posture, and feedback.

Because listening is a learned skill, changes won't occur overnight. As with any skill, "practice makes perfect." With the desire to become a better listener, knowledge of listening skills and a willingness to work, major improvements can be made. Then, no one will say to you, "You never listen to me!""

ACTIVITY 5.6 Suggestions About Listening Habits

10 Bad Listening Habits

1. Calling subject "uninteresting."

2. Criticizing speaker's delivery, personal appearance, etc.

3. Getting overexcited and preparing rebuttal.

4. Listening only for facts.

5. Trying to make an outline of everything you hear.

6. Faking attention to the speaker.

7. Tolerating distractions.

8. Avoiding difficult material.

9. Letting emotion-laden words affect listening.

10. Wasting difference between speech speed (words per minute) and thought speed (words per minute).

10 Good Listening Habits

1. Tuning in the speaker to see if there is anything you can use.

2. Getting the speaker's message, which is probably more important.

3. Hearing the person out before you judge her.

4. Listening also for main ideas, principles, and concepts.

5. Listening a couple of minutes before taking notes.

6. Good listening is not totally relaxed. There is a collection of tensions inside.

7. Doing something about the distractions, closing a door, requesting a person to speak louder, etc.

8. Learning to listen to difficult material.

9. Trying to understand your reaction to emotion-laden words, which might cause barriers.

10. Making thought speed an asset instead of a liability by:
   a. Anticipating the next point to be made.
   b. Mentally summarizing.

Ralph Nichols and Leonard Stevens, Are You Listening?

ACTIVITY 5.7

PURPOSE
The purpose of the assignments will help students and others understand listening barriers.

DIRECTIONS
When communicating and listening, one can listen and respond nonverbally, for example when nodding your head while listening in the United States, China, Mexico, and Canada it means *yes* or *you understand* but it may mean something else in another country. This may be a barrier to those who are not familiar with the nonverbal message for that country. Below is an exercise that will help you understand the listening barrier if you use the ok symbol.

1. Research the ok symbol for the following countries. Write the meaning for each.

    United Kingdom _____

    United States _____

    Japan _____

    Russia _____

    Brazil _____

    India _____

2. Jargon can be a barrier when listening. In the workplace, we may hear something but because the word is foreign to you the result may not be what was expected by the speaker. For example, *"think outside the box"* which means widening your limits of thought process where one can be more creative. List five workplace jargons that you have heard and write the meaning for each.

3. With social media we tend to text and chat with jargon. Below are computer jargon abbreviations. Write what they mean to you and discuss in class.

    BTW _____

    IMHO _____

    MOTD _____

    FAQ _____

    HTH _____

    LOL _____

    FYI _____

    PFA _____

    OMG _____

ENHANCING FEEDBACK

When one is in a working environment, school environment, or among peers, feedback is something we tend to want. For example, in order to give effective feedback you should first understand the message by using active listening skills, paraphrase what was stated for clarification, and use "I" to avoid the other person from becoming defensive. In order to enhance feedback avoid interrupting a person before he/she has completed the message, avoid making assumptions and give facts, be patient and if needed, cool off before giving feedback. This will prevent hasty decisions and can cause a better cohesive environment and communication flow.

Feedback as we know it may be given verbally, nonverbally, through social media, and through technology. Feedback can be either positive or negative. When exploring feedback, one will understand the different ways feedback is delivered.

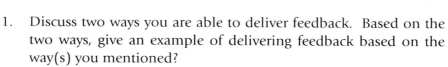

ACTIVITY 5.8

1. Discuss two ways you are able to deliver feedback. Based on the two ways, give an example of delivering feedback based on the way(s) you mentioned?
2. Brainstorm as many ways as you can on giving effective feedback. Discuss with a partner on why you feel that way is effective.
3. Role play on how one can deliver effective and negative feedback. State an example and role play it.

ENDNOTES

1 & 2 From *Communicate! A Workbook for Interpersonal Communication*, 7th Edition, by Communication Research Associates. Copyright © 2004 by Kendall Hunt Publishing Company. Reprinted by permission.

CHAPTER 6

Verbal and Nonverbal Communication

STUDENT LEARNING OUTCOMES

Critical Thinking			Communication			Team Work		Social Responsibility	Personal Responsibility	Activity Measured
Creative Thinking/ Innovative	Analysis & Evaluation	Synthesis of Information	Writing	Visual	Oral	Differing Viewpoints	Work with Others	Intercultural Competence	Ethical Decision Making	Activity
X	X		X		X	X				6.1
X	X	X	X							6.2
X	X		X		X	X	X			6.3
X	X		X							6.4, 6.5
X		X	X							6.6
X	X		X							6.7
X	X		X		X		X			6.8
X	X		X	X	X		X			6.9, 6.10, 6.11, 6.12
X	X		X	X	X		X	X		6.13
X	X		X				X			6.14

VERBAL AND NONVERBAL COMMUNICATION

The words that you use and the nonverbal behaviors that accompany them are critically important as you communicate, because they have the ability to clarify your ideas to others or to confuse them. In this section, you will learn about verbal language and nonverbal communication, to discover how they are used to create shared meaning.

"Using words to describe magic is like using a screwdriver to cut roast beef.[1]
—**Tom Robbins, twentieth century American author**

Better wise language than well-combed hair.
—**Icelandic Proverb**

All credibility, all good conscience, all evidence of truth come only from the senses.
—**Friedrich Wilhelm Nietzsche, nineteenth century German philosopher**

Eloquence is the power to translate a truth into language perfectly intelligible to the person to whom you speak.
—**Ralph Waldo Emerson, nineteenth century U.S. poet, essayist**

Get in touch with the way the other person feels. Feelings are 55 percent body language, 38 percent tone and 7 percent words.
—**author unknown**

The limits of my language means the limits of my world.
—**Ludwig Wittgenstein, twentieth century philosopher**

The eyes are the windows to the soul.
—**Yousuf Karsh, twentieth century Canadian photographer**

The difference between the right word and the almost right word is the difference between lightning and a lightning bug.
—**Mark Twain, nineteenth century American author**

Dialogue should simply be a sound among other sounds, just something that comes out of the mouths of people whose eyes tell the story in visual terms.
—**Alfred Hitchcock, twentieth century film director**

Through these quotations, you've just been exposed to the power of verbal and nonverbal communication to define our beliefs, expose our values, and share our experiences. The words that you use and the nonverbal behaviors that accompany them are critically important as you communicate, because they have the ability to clarify your ideas to others or to confuse them. In this chapter, you'll learn about verbal language and nonverbal communication, to discover how they are used to create shared meaning.

ACTIVITY 6.1 WHAT IS THE POWER OF VERBAL AND NONVERBAL COMMUNICATION?

Part One

There is power in verbal language. Language is a shared system of symbols and structures in organized patterns to express thoughts and feelings. Let's explore further the basic principles of language by identifying the following terms as they relate to how we use language.

Define the following:

Connotation

Denotation

Unbiased Language

Accurate Language

Jargon

Regionalism

Muted Group Theory

Phonological Rules

Regulative Rules

Semantic Rules

Slang

Cliché

Loaded Words

Empty Words

Equivocal Words

Part Two

Write a creative and engaging scenario about Shane and Kayla using the terms you have just defined. Indicate when you use each term by placing the term in parenthesis behind the example.

The story begins......

Shane and Kayla were in Precollege at Harmony University. They met at a pool party at Harmony gym when Shane walked over to Kayla and said "Hello, my name is Shane. What's up?" (semantic rules)

Be prepared to read your story to the class.

WHAT IS LANGUAGE?

So what do we know about language? Linguists estimate that there are about 5,000 to 6,000 different languages spoken in the world today; about 200 languages have a million or more native speakers. Mandarin Chinese is the most common, followed by Hindi, English, Spanish, and Bengali. However, as technology continues to shrink the communication world, English is becoming more dominant in mediated communication. According to Internet World Stats, which charts usage and population statistics, the top ten languages

Verbal language and nonverbal communication are used to create shared meaning.

used in the Web are English (31% of all Internet users), Chinese (15.7%), Spanish (8.7%), Japanese (7.4%), and French and German (5% each). English is one of the official languages of the United Nation, the International Olympic Committee, in academics and in the sciences. English is also the language spoken by air traffic controllers worldwide. Yet the English that we speak in the United States is really a hybrid, using vocabulary taken from many sources, influenced by media, technology, and globalization. Let's consider what all of this means for you as you try to share meaning with others.

Language is a shared system of symbols structured in organized patterns to express thoughts and feelings. **Symbols** are arbitrary labels that we give to some idea or phenomenon. For example, the word *run* represents an action that we do, while *bottle* signifies a container for a liquid. Words are symbols, but not all symbols are words. Music, photographs, and logos are also symbols that stand for something else, as do nonverbal actions such as "OK," and "I don't know." However, in this section, we're going to focus on words as symbols. Note that the definition of language says that it's structured and shared. Languages have a *grammar* (syntax, a patterned set of rules that aid in meaning). You've learned grammar as you've been taught how to write, and it's become an unconscious part of your daily communication. Take, for example, this sentence:

The glokkish Vriks mounged oupily on the brangest Ildas.

English is the language spoken by airline pilots and air traffic controllers all over the world.

Now, we can answer these questions:

>Who did something? The Vriks mounged.
>What kind of Vriks are they? Glokkish
>How did they mounge? Oupily
>On what did they mounge? The Ildas
>What kind of Ildas are they? Brangest

You might have difficulty identifying noun, verb, adverb, and adjective, but because you know the grammar of the English language, you're still able to decipher what this sentence is telling you because of the pattern, even if the symbols themselves lack meaning for now. That leads to the next part of the definition: *symbols must be shared in order to be understood.* George Herbert Mead's Symbolic Interaction Theory asserts that meaning is **intersubjective;** that means that **meaning** *can exist only when people share common interpretations of the symbols they exchange.* So if you were given a picture of Vriks and were told that these were ancient hill people of a particular region of the country, you'd have a start at meaning!

In order to get a grasp on language, this section will uncover basic principles about language, introduce to you a few theoretical perspectives, and then will suggest language strategies to enhance your communication."

"ACTIVITY 6.2 THE SLANG TEST[2]

PURPOSE
To examine the way words mean different things to different people, and the way slang changes with time.

PROCEDURE
Circle the letter for what you think is the correct answer for each term.

1. This food is dank.
   a. awful
   b. good
   c. cold

2. Let's bounce.
   a. dance
   b. play basketball
   c. leave

3. It's tight.
   a. doesn't fit
   b. good
   c. bad

4. Gimme the 411.
   a. Give me the phone number.
   b. Let me know the information.
   c. Give me the phone.

5. Can I get your digits?
   a. measurements
   b. address
   c. phone number

6. What a Betty!
   a. a good cook
   b. good looking girl
   c. a bad gambling debt

7. He got game.
   a. He has the girls.
   b. He's good at sports.
   c. He lies.

8. That's off the chain.
   a. wild
   b. stupid
   c. cool

9. Why you trippin?
   a. Why are you stumbling?
   b. Why are you acting stupid?
   c. Why are you dressed that way?

10. That's burned out.
    a. ugly
    b. ridiculous
    c. over-cooked

11. Dang, you got years.
    a. intelligence
    b. experience
    c. nice clothes

12. Pimp my ride.
    a. Give me a ride.
    b. Fix up my car.
    c. Pick up my girlfriend and me.

13. You so fly.
    a. You're busy.
    b. You're a pest.
    c. looking good

14. Chicken head
    a. You like to eat chicken.
    b. ugly girl
    c. stuck-up girl

15. I give you props.
    a. money
    b. You need help.
    c. positive reaction

16. Let's cheese-it.
    a. eat
    b. get out of here
    c. rest

17. He's got a six-pack.
    a. gun
    b. well-developed abs
    c. beer

18. Throw up your set.
    a. Show your gang signs.
    b. Put up your fists.
    c. Bet your car.

19. Are you down?
    a. in a bad mood
    b. placed your bet
    c. in favor of it

20. He's a big timer.
    a. ex-con
    b. rich person under 30
    c. famous

21. That's pimp.
    a. nice or cool
    b. cheap
    c. sleazy

22. You're bling-blinging.
    a. not making sense
    b. talking too much
    c. wearing a lot of gold

23. Nice kicks.
    a. shoes
    b. moves
    c. dancer

24. What's the skuttlebut?
    a. drugs
    b. rumor
    c. food

25. Her idea was a real boondoggle.
    a. creative
    b. good
    c. poor

26. Let's boogie.
    a. have sex
    b. dance
    c. leave

27. She's a snazzy dresser.
    a. stylish
    b. sexy
    c. tasteless

28. He's a Jackson.
    a. criminal
    b. good dancer
    c. good looking

29. She's got ice.
    a. bad personality
    b. diamonds
    c. stuck up

DISCUSSION

1. Were you surprised at the number of questions you had to guess at?
2. What causes words to change meaning?
3. Why don't meanings stay the same?
4. How has slang changed over the years?"

"WHAT ARE THE BASIC PRINCIPLES OF LANGUAGE?"[3]

There are some basic principles of language. It is arbitrary, it changes over time, it consists of denotative and connotative meanings, and it is structured by rules. Let's look at these more closely.

Arbitrary

"Language is arbitrary" means that *symbols do not have a one-to-one connection with what they represent.* What is the computer form that you use if you take a test? Is it a bubble sheet? A scantron? An opscan? Each of these names has no natural connection to that piece of paper, and it's likely that at different universities, it's called different names. Because language is arbitrary, people in groups agree on labels to use, creating private codes. That's why your organization might have specialized terms, why the military uses codes, and why your family uses nicknames that only they understand. The language that you create within that group creates group meaning and culture. The arbitrary element of language also adds to its ambiguity; meanings just aren't stable. To me, a test is the same as an exam; to you, a test might be less than an exam. If you say to me, "I'll call you later," how do I define the term *later*? We often fall into the trap of thinking that everyone understands us, but the reality is, it's an amazing thing that we share meaning at all!

Changes over Time

Language *changes* over time in vocabulary, as well as syntax. New vocabulary is required for the latest inventions, for entertainment and leisure pursuits, for political use. In 2007, the top television buzzwords included surge and *D'oh,* while in 2006, they were *truthiness* and *wikiality.* How many of those words play a role in your culture today? Words like *cell phones* and *Internet* didn't exist fifty years ago, for example. In addition, no two people use a language in exactly the same way. Teens and young adults often use different words and phrases than their parents. The vocabulary and phrases people use may depend on where they live, their age, education level, social status, and other factors. Through our interactions, we pick up new words and phases, and then we integrate them into our communication.

How is your language different from your parents' and grandparents'?

Consists of Denotative and Connotative Meanings

Denotative meanings, the literal, dictionary definitions, are precise and objective. **Connotative meanings** reflect your personal, subjective definitions. They add layers of experience and emotions to meaning. Elizabeth J. Natalle examined this dichotomy in a case study of urban music, examining how our language has evolved over the years to include more negative connotation regarding talk about women as compared to talk about men. Think about *chick, sweetie, sugar pie* and *old maid,* versus stud, *hunk, playboy,* and *bachelor.* Do you get a different image? Using a study of rap music, she attempted to clarify how urban music names a particular world, creates male community, and has implications for power and gendered relationships.

A simpler way to consider denotative and connotative meanings is to examine the terms President Bush used to describe the terrorists who crashed the planes on Sept. 11, 2001. Bush's labels on that day in various locations began with "those folks who committed this act" (remarks by the president when he first heard that two planes crashed into World Trade Center) to "those responsible for these cowardly acts" (remarks by the president upon arrival at Barksdale Air Force Base) to "those who are behind these evil acts" and "the terrorists who committed these acts" (statement by the president in his address to the nation). Consider how the connotative meaning shaped the image of the perpetrators.

David K. Berlo provided several assumptions about meaning:

- Meanings are in people.
- Communication does not consist of the transmission of meanings, but of the transmission of messages.
- Meanings are not in the message; they are in the message users.
- Words do not mean at all; only people mean.
- People can have similar meanings only to the extent that they have had, or can anticipate having, similar experiences.
- Meanings are never fixed; as experience changes, so meanings change.
- No two people can have exactly the same meaning for anything.

These ideas echo the idea that when you use words, you need to be aware of the extent to which meaning is shared. For example, when an adoptive parent sees those "adopt a highway" locator signs, it's probable that that person sees something different than others might. "Adopt a" programs might be seen as confusing and misleading others about the term *adoption.* An adoptive parent might say that you don't adopt a road, a zoo animal, or a Cabbage Patch doll. Adoption is a means of family building, and it has a very subjective, emotional meaning. To the town official who erected the sign, it's a representation of the good work being done by some group to keep the highway clean.

STRUCTURED BY RULES

As we understand and use the rules of language, we begin to share meaning. Think of rules as a shared understanding of what language means, as well as an understanding of what kind of language is appropriate in various contexts. Many of the rules you use weren't consciously learned; you gathered them from interactions with other people. Some, however, were learned aspects of your culture.

Phonological rules *regulate how words sound when you pronounce them.* They help us organize language. For instance, the word lead could be used to suggest a behavior that you do (you *lead* the group to show them the way) or a kind of toxic metallic element (*lead* paint in windows is harmful to children). Do you enjoy getting a *present,* or did you *present* one to someone else? Another example of phonological rules is demonstrated by your understanding of how letters sound when they're grouped in a particular way. Take for instance the letters omb. Now put a t in front of them, and you have *tomb.* Put a c in front, and it becomes *comb.* Put a b in front, and you have *bomb.* See how the sounds shift?

What does this sign's language mean to you?

The way we make singular nouns plural is also phonological. It's not as simple as adding the letter s to the end of a word. The sound changes too: dog/dogs (sounds like a z at the end); cook/cooks (sounds like an *ess*); bus/buses (sounds like *ess-ez*). English has many inconsistent phonological rules like these, which makes making errors quite typical, especially for nonnative English speakers.

Syntactical rules *present the arrangement of a language, how the symbols are organized.* You saw that earlier in the "glokkish Vriks" example; you're usually unaware of the syntactical rules until they're violated. In English, we put adjectives prior to most nouns: I live in a red house. In French, you live in a house red (the adjective follows the noun).

Semantic rules *govern the meaning of specific symbols.* Because words are abstractions, we need rules to tell us what they mean in particular situations. Take, for example, the headline, "School Needs to Be Aired." What does that mean? Is the school so smelly that it needs to be refreshed? Or are the needs of the school going to be broadcast or spoken in a public forum? Words can be interpreted in more than one way, and we need semantic rules to lead us to shared meaning. Although these three kinds of rules help us to pattern language, there are also rules that help us guide the entire communication event.

Regulative rules *tell us when, how, where, and with whom we can talk about certain things.* You know when it's OK to interrupt someone; you know when turn-taking is expected. You may be enrolled in classes where you are expected to express your opinion; in other classes, you know to hold your tongue. How do you feel about public displays of affection? When is it OK to correct your boss? These regulative rules help us to maintain respect, reveal information about ourselves, and interact with others.

Constitutive rules *tell us how to "count" different kinds of communication.* These rules reveal what you feel is appropriate. You know that when someone waves or blows kisses, that person is showing affection or friendliness. You know what topics you can discuss with your parents, friends, teachers, co-workers, and strangers. You have rules that reveal your expectations for communication with different people; you expect your doctor to be informative and firm with advice, and you anticipate that your friend will compliment you and empathize. As we interact with others, we begin to grasp and use the rules. For instance, when you start a new job, you take in the rules on whom to talk with, how to talk with supervisors and co-workers, and what topics are appropriate, along with the mechanics of how to talk and the meaning of job-specific words. Interestingly enough, you might not even be aware of the rules until they're broken!"

You can count on a close friend for comfort when you have a problem.

ACTIVITY 6.3 Sexist Language Activity

PURPOSE

To explore the words used to describe both sexes that prompt both negative and positive reactions in the people described.

PROCEDURE

1. Divide into same-sex small groups.
2. Each group should brainstorm a list of words that they use to describe members of the opposite sex in a negative, demeaning way.
3. Each group should then list the demeaning words that they have heard the opposite sex use for them, and their reactions to these words.
4. Each group should then develop a list of words they would prefer to be called by the opposite sex.
5. As a full class, discuss each group's list and the feelings about the words

DISCUSSION

1. How do the negative words make generalizations about the people they describe?
2. How do the negative words dehumanize the people they describe?
3. What are the differences between the negative and the preferred words?
4. How can the words we use to describe people influence their self-concept and their behavior?
5. How accurate do the words we use describe our perceptions?
6. What can we do to avoid sexist language when talking about our perceptions?

ACTIVITY 6.4

When looking at connotative (your feelings and emotions that is associated with words) and denotative (dictionary definitions) words you may have different means based on how you interpret the word(s). Below are words that may be positive, neutral, or negative words. In the box below, write how you see the word. If you are not sure, you can look the word up in a dictionary.

		POSITIVE	NEUTRAL	NEGATIVE
1.	House, Dump, Home			
2.	Car, Automobile, Jalopy			
3.	Attractive, Ugly, Stunning			
4.	Slender, Skinny, Thin			
5.	Relaxed, Lazy, Inactive			
6.	Modest, Shy, Mousy			
7.	Self-confident, Proud, Conceited			
8.	Woman, Broad, Lady			
9.	Fat, Curvy, Overweight			

"HOW DO THEORISTS DESCRIBE LANGUAGE AND MEANING?"[4]

Can you picture a book, a pen, a laptop, and a horse? Your ability to conjure up these images means that you've been exposed to the symbols that represent them in the English language. How about the picture shown on the right? What do you see? If you said "keys," then that shows how you have acquired language; you've been taught that these things are associated with the symbol "keys." How are you able to do those connections? There are a great number of perspectives related to language, meaning, and symbols. In this section, you'll be exposed to three models that present varying perspectives on the way that meaning is created.

Semantic Triangle

One of the models that demonstrate how words come to have meaning is the **semantic triangle.** Ogden and Richards suggest that a major problem with communication is that we tend to treat *words* as if they were the *thing*. As a result, we confuse the symbol for the thing or object.

At the bottom right hand of the triangle is the **referent,** the thing that we want to communicate about that exists in reality. As we travel up the right side, we find the **reference(s),** which consist of thoughts, experiences, and feelings about the referent. This is a causal connection; seeing the object results in those thoughts. Another causal connection exists as you travel down the left side of the triangle, to the *symbol,* or *word.* That's the label we apply to that referent.

The problem is that there is not a direct connection between a symbol and referent; it's an indirect connection, shown by the dotted line. According to this model, it's that indirect link between *referent* and *symbol* that creates the greatest potential for communication misunderstandings. We assume that others share our references, and we think that they must use the same label or symbol because of that shared state of being. A simple example should help.

A mom is teaching her son words by reading simple children's books—books about tools, farms, trucks, zoos, and dinosaurs. Usually, this reading activity happens on the front porch. One day, the mom sees the neighbor's cat sneaking up on her birdfeeders, and under her breath, she mutters something about the "stupid cat." The next day, the toddler goes off to day care, and when mom comes to pick him up, she's met by the teacher. She laughingly tells how she was reading a book about animals that day, and when she got to the page with cute kittens on it, the little boy yelled out, "Stupid cat." The embarrassed mother just learned a lesson about the semantic triangle. For her, the referent (cat) evokes images of bird-murdering, allergy-causing felines (references). She creates the label "stupid cat." (symbol). When the boy sees a picture of one, he naturally thinks that is what those things are called. Unfortunately, that's not the universal name!

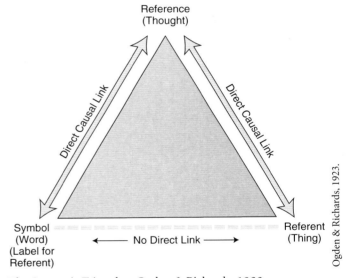

The Semantic Triangle—Ogden & Richards, 1923.

You can experience the same thing: If you tell others that you own a dog, what referent do you think they apply the label to? The semantic triangle is a practical tool that helps us to understand the relationship of referent, references, and symbol, or thing, thoughts, and word. It reminds us that one word doesn't necessarily evoke the same meaning in any two people.

Sapir–Whorf Hypothesis

Another theoretical approach to language is the *Sapir–Whorf hypothesis* (also known as the theory of linguistic relativity). According to this approach, your perception of reality is determined by your thought processes, and your thought processes are limited by your language. Therefore, language shapes reality. Your culture determines your language, which, in turn, determines the way that you categorize thoughts about the world and your experiences in it. If you don't have the words to describe or explain something, then you can't really know it or talk about it.

For example, researchers Linda Perry and Deborah Ballard-Reisch suggest that existing language does not represent the reality that biological sex comes in more forms than female and male, gender identities are not neatly ascribed to one's biological sex, and sexual orientation does not fit snugly into, "I like men, I like women, I like both, I like neither," choices. They also assert that evolving new language such as the word *gendex* (representing the dynamic interplay of a person's sexual identity, sex preference, sexual orientation, and gender identity) can work against biases and discrimination. Another example is the concept of *bipolar disorder*. It used to be called manic depressive, and it refers to a mood disorder characterized by unusual shifts in a person's mood, energy, and ability to function. But if you don't know what that illness is, you might just agree with a family member who says, "You're just going through a phase." The lack of language restricts our ability to perceive the world. Reality is embedded in your language.

Muted Group Theory

As these perspectives suggest, the *words* that you use are powerful. They have the ability to express attitudes and to represent values. Communication scholar Cheris Kramarae developed *the muted group theory* to suggest that power and status are connected, and because muted groups lack the power of appropriate language, they have no voice and receive little attention. Kramarae noted, "The language of a particular culture does not serve all its speakers, for not all speakers contribute in an equal fashion to its formulation. Women (and members of other subordinate groups) are not as free or as able as men are to say what they wish, when and where they wish, because the words and the norms for their use have been formulated by the dominant group, men." She asserts that language serves men better than women (and perhaps European Americans better than African Americans or other groups) because the European American men's experiences are named clearly in language, and the experiences of other groups (women, people with disabilities, and ethnic minorities) are not. Due to this problem with language, muted groups appear less articulate than men in public settings.

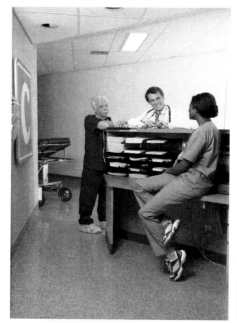

The muted group theory suggests that language serves men better than women.

The task of muted groups is to conceptualize a thought and then scan the vocabulary that is suited to men's thinking for the best way to encode the idea. The term sexual harassment is an example. Although the act of harassment has existed for centuries, it wasn't until sex discrimination was prohibited by Title VII of the 1964 Civil Rights Act. It also took the Clarence Hill–Anita Thomas hearing in 1991 to make the term *gender discrimination* part of the popular dialogue, as the media focused attention on the workplace issue.

Because they are rendered inarticulate, muted groups are silenced in a variety of ways. Ridicule happens when the group's language is trivialized (men talk, women gab). Ritual creates dominance (the woman changes her name at the wedding ceremony but the man doesn't). Control happens as the media present some points of view and ignore others (we don't hear from the elderly or homeless). Harassment results from the control that men exert over public spaces (women get verbal threats couched as compliments when they walk down the streets). This theory affirms that as muted groups create more language to express their experiences and as all people come to have similar experiences, inequalities of language (and the power that comes with it) should change.

Each of these perspectives demonstrates how language impacts meaning. They show how we believe meaning comes into being, how we are limited by the language we possess, and how language wields power. By now, you should be sensitive to the many ways that you can miscommunicate, or at least communicate ineffectively through language choices. How can you become more sensitive to strategic language choices?"

"ACTIVITY 6.5 Choosing Appropriate Language[5]

OBJECTIVE
Public speakers must be able to captivate and hold the attention of their audiences. Good communication depends upon clear articulation and correct wording. In order to properly communicate your thoughts and ideas to others, there are some words, phrases, and habits speakers should avoid.

1. Terminology and References Used in Specific Fields

These include medical, educational, computer, legal, etc. . . . These are terms not understood or used by the common public.

1.

2.

How can you explain these terms to your audience to make communication clearer?

2. Emotionally Charged Words

These words may offend your audience, or your audience may feel threatened by the use of these words.

    1.

    2.

What words could be used to replace emotionally charged words?

3. Words Used Out of Context or Mispronounced

    1.

    2.

For help, use a dictionary or thesaurus.

4. Verbal Fillers

These words are often used in informal conversations or social settings. However, they are inappropriate when giving a public speech or presentation. These include: "so, like, you know, ya'll, you guys, uh, uhm, err, yeah," and more.

    1.

    2.

Replace verbal fillers with transitional words or leave a moment of silence.

ACTIVITY 6.6 Language Exercise

DIRECTIONS

In the list below left are male referents. Across from each term, see if you can fill in the blank with a female equivalent. Once you have listed the female equivalent follow the directions below.

Male Referents	Female Equivalent
1. Gentleman	1. _____
2. Guy	2. _____
3. Mister (Mr.)	3. _____
4. Man	4. _____
5. Brother	5. _____
6. Father	6. _____
7. Boy	7. _____
8. Boyfriend	8. _____
9. Husband	9. _____
10. Don Juan	10. _____
11. Playboy	11. _____
12. Cock	12. _____
13. Hunk	13. _____
14. Stud	14. _____
15. Bachelor	15. _____
16. Governor	16. _____
17. Landlord	17. _____
18. King	18. _____
19. Prince	19. _____
20. Bastard	20. _____
21. Sir	21. _____
22. Gigolo	22. _____
23. Master	23. _____
24. Wolf	24. _____

Now, **circle** those terms which have sexual connotations. Also **write a P** for those having **positive** connotations. **Write an N** for those with **negative** connotations. Be sure to follow these directions for both sets of terms."

"HOW CAN I USE LANGUAGE EFFECTIVELY?"[6]

Communication scholar Julia T. Wood says that the single most important guideline is to engage in a dual **perspective**, recognizing another person's point of view and taking that into account as you communicate. Wood suggests that you should understand both your own and another's point of view and acknowledge each when you communicate. You'll see that concept played out throughout this text; you need to consider your audience's beliefs, attitudes, and values as you create your message. Here are some strategic tips for effective language use to maintain that dual perspective.

Use Accurate Language

Make sure you are using the term correctly, and if you're unsure if the audience will understand your meaning, define it. You'll learn about defining in the chapter on informative speaking. Remember, what makes perfect sense to you may be gobbledygook to me. When the doctor tells you that you have a rather large contusion, do you know what that is?

Use Appropriate Language

Appropriate means that the language you use is suitable for the context, for the audience, for the topic, and for you. Some occasions call for more formal language (proposals to a client), while others will let slang pass (texting a friend). Some audiences expect technical language, while others need simple terms. Off-color humor might work in certain instances and with specific groups, but you probably shouldn't choose to use it at a church gathering. You need to consider if your audience utilizes regionalisms (words or phrases that are specific to one part of the country) or jargon (specialized professional language) as you speak with them.

Your topic also can determine suitable language. Some topics call for lots of vivid language and imagery, while others are better suited to simplicity. If you are honoring your boss upon his retirement, then the topic probably calls for words that evoke appreciation and emotion. But if you're telling someone how to put together a computer table, then simple explanatory words are expected. Finally, you need to use words that are appropriate to you. You have developed your own style of language over the years; do you use the same words as your parents? Don't try to use words that just don't flow easily from your mind; it's not going to sound like you.

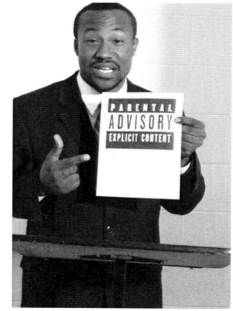

It's important to use appropriate language for the occasion.

Use Unbiased Language

Biased language includes any language that defames a subgroup (women; people from specific ethnic, religious, or racial groups; people with disabilities) or eliminates them from consideration. Even if you would never think about using language that defames anyone else, you can fall into using language that more subtly discriminates. Sexist language is replete with this: We use the masculine pronoun (he, him) when we don't have a referent. So if you personify "the judge," "the executive," "the director," as male by using the pronoun *he*, you eliminate one whole subgroup from consideration.

The same holds true when you use the word *man* in occupational terms, when the job holders could be either male or female. Examples are fireman, policeman, garbage man, chairman; they're easily made nonsexist by saying firefighter, police officer, garbage collector, and chair or presiding officer. Finally, while the generic use of *man* (like in mankind) originally was used to denote both men and women, its meaning has become more specific to adult males. It's simple to change the word to be more inclusive: mankind becomes people or human beings; man-made becomes manufactured; the common man becomes the average person.

The Associated Press *Stylebook* has a lengthy entry on "disabled, handicapped, impaired" terminology, including when to use (and not to use) terms such *as blind, deaf, mute, wheelchair-user,* and so on. A separate entry on *retarded* says "mentally retarded" is the preferred term. The World Bank advises using *persons with disabilities and disabled people,* not handicapped.

Use appropriate labels when referring to sexual orientation. The terms *lesbians, gay men,* and *bisexuals or bisexual women and men* are preferred to the term *homosexuals* (because the emphasis on the latter is on sex, while the former all refer to the whole person, not just the sex partner he or she chooses). In general, try to find out what the people's preferences are, and be specific when applicable. For instance, if all the subjects are either Navajo or Cree, stating this is more accurate than calling them Native Americans.

Avoid Verbal Distractions

If you divert the audience from your intended meaning by using confusing words, your credibility will be lowered and your audience may become lost. The following are distractions:

- **Slang** *consists of words that are short-lived, arbitrarily changed, and often vulgar ideas.* Slang excludes people from a group. Internet slang was usually created to save keystrokes and consists of "u" for you, "r" for *are*, and "4" for for. Poker slang includes *dead man's hand* (two pair, aces, and eights); to act (make a play); and *going all* in (betting all of your chips on the hand). *Daggy* means out of fashion or uncool; *fives* means to reserve a seat.

- **Cliches** or **trite words** *have been overused and lose power or impact.* The Unicorn Hunters of Lake Superior University keeps a list of banished words that is regularly updated. In 2007, it listed words such as combined celebrity names (*Brangelina* and *Tomcat*), *awesome* (because it no longer means majestic), and *undocumented alien* (just use the word illegal).

- **Loaded words** *sound like they're describing, but they're actually revealing your attitude.* When speaking of abortion, consider the different image created by the terms *unborn child* or *fetus*. Are you *thrifty* but your friend is *cheap*? How about your brother; is he one of those *health-*

nuts who is dedicated to the cult of marathoning? Colorful language is entertaining, but if it distorts the meaning or distracts the audience, then don't use it.

- **Empty words** *are overworked exaggerations.* They lose their strength because their meaning is exaggerated. How many products are advertised as *new and improved or supersized*? What exactly does that mean?

- **Derogatory language** *consists of words that are degrading or tasteless.* If you use degrading terms to refer to ethnic groups (*Polack* for a person of Polish descent; *Chink* for someone from China; Spic for an Italian) then you are guilty of verbal bigotry.

- **Equivocal words** *have more than one correct denotative meaning.* A famous example is of a nurse telling a patient that he "wouldn't be needing" the books he asked to be brought from home. Although she meant that he was going home that day and could read there, the patient took that to mean that he was near death and wouldn't have time to read. One time while evaluating a debate, an instructor encountered students arguing the issue of the legalization of marijuana. The side arguing for the legalization used the Bible, citing chapter and verse and asserting that God created the grass and said, "The grass is good." This sent the other side into a tailspin as they tried to refute the biblical passage. This simple equivocal use of the term grass lost the debate for the opposition!

WHAT SHOULD YOU TAKE FROM THIS SECTION ON LANGUAGE?

Because our language is arbitrary and evolving, it's easy to be misunderstood. You can attempt to enhance shared meaning by remembering that language is a shared system of symbols; through language, you share ideas, articulate values, transmit information, reveal experiences, and maintain relationships. Language is essential to your ability to think and to operate within the many cultures (community of meaning) that you travel through. You should be sensitive to the words you choose as you attempt to connect with others. Now let's turn our attention to the other means by which you create meaning: your nonverbal communication behaviors.

WHAT IS NONVERBAL COMMUNICATION?

Pretend you are hoarse and the doctor has told you not to speak at all for the next three days. Nor can you IM or text or do any other computer-related communication. How would you do the following?

- Let your friend know that you can't hear her. Or tell her that she's talking too loudly.

- Tell your lab partner that you want him to come where you are.

- Show the teacher that you don't know the answer to the question she just asked you.

- Let a child know that he needs to settle down; his play is getting too rough.

- Tell your significant other that you're not angry, and everything is OK.

- Express disappointment over a loss by your team, which always seems to lose the lead in the last two minutes.

- Signify that you're running late and have to leave.

How hard would it be to make yourself understood? What you've just attempted to do without verbal language is present a message nonverbally. We all constantly send nonverbal messages, giving our receivers all types of cues about ourselves. An awareness of nonverbal communication is important: your nonverbal behaviors present an image of yourself to those around you. They tell others how you want to relate to them, and they may reveal emotions or feelings that you either are trying to hide or simply can't express.

In the remainder of this chapter, you will be introduced to some of the elements of the study of nonverbal communication in the hopes of creating a greater awareness of these elements of the message. You will examine *definitions* of nonverbal communication, its *functions*, and *types* of nonverbal communication. Along the way, we will provide examples and illustrations to help you understand the applications of various nonverbal behaviors and how they can be used to help you interpret the messages of other people. You should also gain some insight into how to use nonverbal behaviors to enhance your own communication.

WHAT IS THE NATURE OF NONVERBAL COMMUNICATION?

Although nonverbal communication is a complex system of behaviors and meanings, its basic definition *can be* fairly straightforward. Here are four definitions for comparison:

1. All types of communication that do not rely on words or other linguistic systems

2. Any message other than written or spoken words that conveys meaning

3. Anything in a message besides the words themselves

4. Messages expressed by nonlinguistic means

Taking these definitions and the body of related research into consideration, we propose a very simple definition: nonverbal communication is *all nonlinguistic aspects of communication*. That definition covers quite a lot of territory. Except for the actual words that we speak, *everything* else is classified as nonverbal communication. The way you move, the tone of your voice, the way you use your eyes, the way you occupy and use space, the way you dress, the shape of your body, your facial expressions, the way you smell, your hand gestures, and the way you pronounce (or mispronounce) words are all considered nonverbal communication. Some of these behaviors have meaning independent of language or other behaviors; others have meaning only when considered with what is said, the context and culture in which a communication event takes place, and the relationship between the communicators.

Maybe you're getting a hint of the richness of nonverbal expression. Without any formal training, you already are able to interpret messages that others send nonverbally. Your skill level, however, may not be as strong as you think, so keep in mind the goal of increasing strategic communication as you continue. Researchers have also been fascinated with the extent to which nonverbal communication impacts meaning, and their findings provide glimpses into the impact of nonverbals on shared meanings and culture. If nothing else, by the end of this section, you will discover that the study of nonverbal communication has come a long way since it was referred to only as *body language!*

WHAT ARE THE CHARACTERISTICS OF NONVERBAL COMMUNICATION?

Ambiguous

Most nonverbal behaviors have no generally accepted meaning. Instead, the connection between the behavior and its meaning is vague or *ambiguous,* leaving understanding open to various interpretations. The meaning we apply to words is fairly specific, but the meaning we give to nonverbal communication is nonspecific. The meanings you attribute to nonverbal behaviors are heavily dependent on the relationship between you and the others you're interacting with, the nature of the communication event, the content of the words that accompanies it, and the culture in which the event takes place. For example, consider the ubiquitous "thumbs up" hand gesture. In the United States it means, "OK" or "very good." In some eastern cultures, however, it is considered an insult and an obscene hand gesture. In Great Britain, Australia, and New Zealand, it could be a signal used by hitchhikers who are thumbing a lift; it could be an OK signal; it also could be an insult signal meaning "up yours" or "sit on this" when the thumb is jerked sharply upward. In Indonesia, the thumb gesture means "good job" in response to someone who has completed an excellent job, or "delicious" when great food is tasted. In another context, if you smile at a joke, that's understood in an entirely different way than if you do it after someone misses a chair and falls to the ground. A smile could also show affection, embarrassment, or even be used to hide pain or anger. As you can see, it is possible to find several meanings for the same nonverbal behavior, and it is possible to find several nonverbal behaviors that mean the same thing.

What can you say about his nonverbal communication?

Continuous

With verbal communication, if you stop speaking, listeners can't attribute any more meaning to your words. Nonverbal communication, by contrast, is so pervasive and complex that others can continue to gather meaning, even if you are doing absolutely nothing! The mere act of doing nothing can send a message; you might blush, stutter, wring your hands, or sweat unintentionally, causing others to react to you. You might not mean to send a message, but your lack of intention to communicate doesn't prevent other people from assigning

In the United States, a thumbs-up is appropriate for celebrating.

meaning to your behavior. In addition, your appearance, the expression on your face, your posture, where (or if) you are seated, and how you use the space around you all provide information that is subject to interpretation by others.

Sometimes Unplanned and Unconscious

Nonverbal communication can be either unconscious or intentional, but most of our nonverbal behaviors are exhibited without much or any conscious thought. You rarely plan or think carefully about your nonverbal behaviors. When you are angry, it is naturally expressed on your face as well as elsewhere in your body. The same is true for how your voice changes when you're nervous, how your arms cross when you're feeling defensive, or how you scratch your head when you're unsure of something. These expressions and behaviors are rarely planned or structured; they just happen suddenly and without conscious thought.

Sometimes Learned and Intentional

Saying that some nonverbal behaviors are natural or occur without conscious thought doesn't mean that people are born with a complete inventory of instinctive nonverbal behaviors. Much of your nonverbal behavior is learned rather than instinctive or innate. You learn the "proper" way to sit or approach, how close to stand next to someone, how to look at others, how to use touch, all from your experiences and your culture. You have been taught their meaning through your experience in interactions with other people. As a result, you can structure some nonverbal behaviors to send intentional messages, such as disapproval when you shake your head from side to side or give a "high five" to show excitement. However, unlike the formal training you received in reading, writing, and speaking, you learned (and continue to learn) nonverbal communication in a much less formal and unceremonious way, and you use it in a much less precise way than spoken language. But *because* many of these behaviors are learned, you can actively work to improve your nonverbal skills. There is a debate as to whether unintentional nonverbal behaviors really count as communication. Since others incorporate their understanding of our nonverbals as part of shared meaning, we're going to say that intentional and unintentional nonverbals both are worth recognizing here. Our position is that it's nearly impossible not to communicate nonverbally.

More Believable than Verbal

Communication textbooks have been saying for years that, when verbal and nonverbal messages contradict each other, people typically believe the nonverbal message. Because nonverbal is more spontaneous and less conscious, we don't or can't manipulate it as easily as we can control verbal communication. When you were younger and your parents thought that you might be lying to them, they would say, "Look me in the eye and say that again." Your face was more believable to them than what you were saying verbally. Your nonverbal messages would tell them the truth. How could this be so?

What can you tell by this boy's expression?

Research suggests that between 65 percent and 93 percent of the meaning people attribute to messages comes from the nonverbal channel. There is a small fudge factor in those percentages, however, because the Mehrabian and Ferris study assumed up to 93 percent of meaning came from nonverbal messages in situations *where no other background information* was available. The reality is that many factors affect the meaning given to messages, including how familiar the communicators are with the language being spoken, cultural knowledge, and even individual differences in personality characteristics.

Regardless of the exact percentage of meaning that comes from the verbal or nonverbal channels, we still appear to get more meaning from the nonverbal channel. Unless you are very good at controlling all your nonverbal behaviors, your parents can probably still know when you are not telling the truth.

WHAT ARE THE FUNCTIONS OF NONVERBAL COMMUNICATION?

Types of nonverbal communication will be described a little later in the chapter, but you first need to understand what part nonverbals play in the communication process. Nonverbal communication performs six general functions that add information and insight to nonverbal messages to help us create meaning. Those functions are complementing, substituting, repeating, contradicting, regulating, and deceiving.

Complementing Verbal Messages

If someone shakes your hand while saying "Congratulations" at your college graduation, the handshake gives added meaning to the verbal message. Gestures, tone of voice, facial expressions, and other nonverbal behaviors can clarify, reinforce, accent, or add to the meaning of verbal messages. For instance, if you are angry with a friend and are telling him off, pounding your hand into your fist would add depth to your meaning. These nonverbal behaviors are usually not consciously planned, but they are spontaneous reactions to the context and the verbal message.

Substituting for Verbal Messages

You can use a nonverbal message *in the place* of a verbal message. A substituting behavior can be a clear "stop" hand gesture; it can be nodding the head up and down to say yes; or it can be a shoulder shrug to indicate "I don't know." When you use this kind of gesture, you don't have to supply any verbal message for the meaning to be clear to others. However, keep in mind that your nonverbals may be interpreted differently, given what you have learned from your context and culture. As an example, someone in Japan might act in a controlled fashion, while someone from the Mideast might seem more emotional, even when both are feeling the same intensity of emotion. Your interpretation of those postures, without accompanying verbals, might lead you to the wrong conclusions.

Repeating Verbal Messages

If a stranger on your college campus asks you for directions to the administration building, you might reply, "Carty Hall is two blocks south of here." While you are delivering the verbal message, you also *repeat* the message by pointing to the south. The gesture reinforces the meaning of the verbal message and provides a clear orientation to listeners who are unfamiliar with the campus.

Contradicting Verbal Messages

Nonverbal messages sometimes *contradict* the verbal message. It can be done by accident, such as when you say "turn right" but you point to the left. Or it could be done without thinking (unconsciously), such as when you have a sour expression on your face as you tell your former girlfriend how much you "really like" her new boyfriend. Finally, you could use planned nonverbal behaviors, such as a wink of the eye and a sarcastic tone of voice, to contradict the verbal message, "Nice hat!" A famous example of this contradiction happened in September 1960, when 70 million U.S. viewers tuned in to watch Senator John Kennedy of Massachusetts and Vice President Richard Nixon in the first-ever televised presidential debate. The so-called Great Debates were television's first attempt to offer voters a chance to see the presidential candidates "in person" and head to head. Nixon was more well known, since he had been on the political scene as senator and two-term vice president. He had made a career out of fighting communism right in the midst of the Cold War. Kennedy was a relative newcomer, having served only a brief and undistinguished time as senator; he had no foreign affairs experience. Expectations were low for Kennedy; there seemed to be a huge reputation disparity between them.

During the debate, their points were fairly even. But it was the visual contrast between the two men that was astounding. Nixon had seriously injured his knee, had lost weight, and had recently suffered from the flu. When the first debate came, he was underweight and pasty looking, with a murky 5:00 shadow darkening his lower face. He wore a white, poorly fitting shirt and a gray suit that nearly blended into the background set, and he refused to wear make-up, even though he was advised to do so. Kennedy supplemented his tan with make-up, wore a dark suit, and had been coached on how to sit and where to look when he wasn't speaking. Kennedy's smooth delivery made him credible, because he came off as confident, vibrant, and poised. Nixon looked tired, pasty, and uncomfortable (he sweated heavily).

Polls taken after the first debate showed that most people who listened to it on the radio felt that Nixon had won, while most who watched it on television declared Kennedy the victor. Those television viewers focused on what they saw, not what they heard.

© 2008, JupiterImages.

© 2008, JupiterImages.

Nonverbal messages can substitute for verbal messages. What specific messages are being sent by the people in these photos?

Contradictory messages can be difficult for others to interpret, so it's important to monitor your nonverbal behaviors. People have a tendency to prefer the meaning of the nonverbal message when it conflicts with the verbal, so when you say turn right, you should try to point to the right. Or if you don't want your former girlfriend to know how jealous you are of her new boyfriend, try to guard against making that sour face. Most adults, however, will interpret the "Nice hat" comment as sarcasm and clearly understand the message.

Regulating the Flow of Communication

Nonverbal behaviors help us to control the verbal messages we're presenting. To prevent chaos when two are more people are engaged in conversation, we use a system of signals to indicate whose turn it is speak. Think about that. How do you know when it is appropriate for you to begin speaking in a group or in a classroom? When you're talking, no one is there saying, "Now, it's your turn." You might use tone of voice to indicate that you want to speak and silence to show that you're ready to yield the floor. If you don't want to be interrupted, you might not make eye contact with the potential interruptor. If you expect an answer, you might directly look at the other person. You probably also use nonverbals to let others know that you're trying to control their talk. Have you ever started to put your computer or lecture materials away before the professor is done speaking? You use nonverbal behavior to indicate that you want to speak, that you are finished speaking, that you want to continue speaking, or that you do not want to speak at all. The nonverbal signals include tone of voice, posture, gestures, eye contact, and other behaviors.

Gestures are very important in establishing speaker credibility in debates.

Courtesy of Kendall Hunt Publishing

Deceiving Listeners

Sometimes, your nonverbal behaviors are attempts to mislead somebody or hide the truth. This deception doesn't have to be malicious or mean. If you're a poker player, you might wear sunglasses in order to shield your eyes; pupils dilate when you're excited, and you want to keep that excitement close to your vest. Sometimes, you deceive to protect yourself or the other person, like when you pat someone on the back and say, "Everything will be all right," even when you know it won't.

There are many movies based on the premise that you can learn to nonverbally behave like someone you're not in order to deceive others. In *Tootsie* (1982), Dustin Hoffman becomes the female star of a television soap opera. Robin Williams stars as *Mrs. Doubtfire* (1993), dressing as a woman so he can see his children. In *The Birdcage* (1996), Robin Williams attempts to teach Nathan Lane how to do an exaggerated John Wayne walk to disguise his effeminate stroll. *Mulan* (1998) is a young woman wanting to fight the Huns in the place of her father, so she poses as a male to join the army. Big *Momma's House*

Is there sarcasm detected in the "nice hat" comment?

© 2008, JupiterImages.

(2000) stars Martin Lawrence, who plays an FBI agent who goes undercover and dresses as a heavy-set woman. In *White Chicks* (2004) Shawn Wayans and Marlon Wayans are sibling FBI agents who must protect two cruise line heiresses from a kidnapping plot. Finally, in *The Lord of the Rings: The Return of the King* (2004), Éowyn dresses as a soldier to be allowed to fight with the men.

A great deal of research on deception has practical implications. For instance, some occupations, such as lawyers and actors, require you to act differently than you might feel. Research has found that they are more successful at deception than the rest of the general population. People who monitor themselves have been found to be more effective in hiding deception cues than are people who are not as self-aware. Just think about the last time you told someone a "white lie." Were you a little nervous? How did you show that? Did the words come easily? Did you stammer or have to search for words? When you fib, you have to weigh the consequences of being caught versus the need to fib (telling a child that Santa or the Easter Bunny exists). You have to look and act sincere and believable, even though you're churning inside. If you can look composed and natural, then you are more likely to be a successful liar. In fact, research tells us that people with a greater social skills repertoire and more communication competence will generally be more proficient, alert, confident, and expressive, and less fidgety, nervous and rigid, making them more skilled at deception than others.

Now that you see the many roles that nonverbals can play in communication, let's turn from the functions to the categories of nonverbal communication.

WHAT ARE THE TYPES OF NONVERBAL COMMUNICATION?

Although many types of behaviors can communicate, available space and the focus of this book limit our discussion of nonverbal communication to body movement (kinesics), the use of space (proxemics), dress and appearance, and eye contact (occulesics). Vocalics, or paralanguage (the use of the voice), is covered in the chapter on delivery.

Body Movement/Kinesics

(Birdwhistell first identified kinesics, or the study of our use of the body to communicate. It includes gestures, posture, facial expressions, and other body movements. Five research themes have emerged in kinesics: the use of emblems, illustrators, regulators, affect displays, and adaptors. A brief look at all five themes will provide a good orientation to the complex ways that we can use our bodies to send messages.

Emblems. An emblem is a nonverbal behavior that has a distinct verbal referent or even a denotative definition, and it is often used to send a specific message to others. The verbal referent is typically one or two words of a short phrase. For example, the "thumbs-up" hand gesture is listed in many dictionaries and is defined as a *gesture of approval*. There is a high level of agreement about the meaning of an emblem within cultures, but not usually across cultures.

Most emblems are created with the hands, but we can create them in other ways. For example, a shoulder shrug suggests "I don't know," or a wrinkled nose indicates that "something stinks." But the emblems we are most familiar with are usually hand gestures. Try to make the gesture that goes with each of the following meanings:

- "Sit down beside me."
- "Follow me."
- "I can't hear you."
- "Be quiet!"
- "Shame on you!"

- "OK."
- "I promise."
- "What time is it?"
- "Good bye!"

In addition to everyday conversation, emblems are used by divers while under water, by police officers directing traffic, by construction workers, and by catchers, pitchers, and managers during baseball games. Don't forget the very familiar and more or less universal signal some people use to indicate displeasure with other drivers! Keep in mind, though, that the emblems you know are not always shared. The hand gesture we use for "come here," with the hand palm up with the index finger extending in and out three or four times, has a very different meaning in Latin America. It means that you are romantically interested in the person, and is considered a solicitation. Emblems can replace the verbal or reinforce it.

Illustrators. An illustrator is a gesture that is used with language to emphasize, stress, or repeat what is being said. It can be used to give directions, show the size or shape of something, and give clarification. Can you imagine trying to explain to a new parent how to "burp" a baby without using illustrators? Can you give directions to the campus library with your hands in your pockets? Sure you could, but the illustrators add much meaning and clarification to your directions or instructions; they help with that function of clarifying. In a study done several years ago, speakers were found to be more persuasive when they used illustrators than when they did not. More recent research has even extended the importance of illustrators. Robert Krauss found that gestures do more than amplify or accent verbal communication. They also help people retrieve ideas and words, such as when you try to define a term with a spatial meaning such as underneath, next to, and above, which Krauss calls *lexical retrieval*. If not done to excess, "talking with your hands" can be a very good thing!

Regulators. A regulator is a turn-taking signal that helps control the flow, the pace, and turn-taking in conversations, and you learned about their coordinating role earlier. If a group of people are talking and trying to share meaning, they must take turns speaking, and taking turns requires cooperation among the communicators. To accomplish this cooperation, along with the content of the conversation, participants must also communicate about who will speak next and when that turn will begin. Regulators help us with this task.

Weimann and Knapp and Argyle identified four categories of turn related signals in a typical conversation:

1. *Turn requesting* signals: These are used by a nonspeaker to take the floor. Nonverbal regulators used to request a turn include rapid head nods, forward leaning posture, and increased eye contact with the speaker.

2. *Turn yielding* signals: The speaker uses these to give up the floor. Nonverbal regulators used to yield a turn include increased eye contact with a nonspeaker, leaning back from a forward posture, or a sudden end to gesturing used while speaking.

3. *Turn maintenance* signals: These are used by the speaker to keep the floor (i.e., continue speaking). Nonverbal signals used to keep the turn include speaking louder or faster (increasing volume or rate of speech), continuing to gesture, or avoiding eye contact with the person requesting the turn.

4. *Back channel* signals: Nonspeaker refuses a turn that has been offered by the speaker. Nonverbal signals used to refuse a turn include nodding the head and avoiding eye contact with the person exhibiting a turn-yielding signal.

Affect displays. An **affect display** is a form of nonverbal behavior that expresses emotions. Although this behavior is most often associated with facial expressions, affect can also be expressed through posture and gestures. These behaviors cannot only express the type of emotion being experienced, but can also express the intensity of the emotion. A smile suggests that you are happy. A slumped-over posture and a scowl on your face can suggest that you are unhappy, while your clinched fists and tense muscles can communicate just *how* unhappy you might be.

The emotions communicated by your face and body can affect the way you are perceived by other people. People who smile spontaneously are often considered by others to be more likable and more approachable than people who do not smile or people who just pretend to smile.

Adaptors. Adaptors are behaviors that can indicate our internal conditions or feelings to other people. We tend to use these behaviors when we become excited or anxious. Think about the kind of things that you do in communication situations when you feel nervous or excited. Do you scratch your head? Bite your nails? Play with your glasses? Rub your nose? You might not know, because most people are not aware of displaying these behaviors.

Bikers use emblems when manuvering in traffic.

Affect displays express emotion.

© 2009. Courtesy of JaxonPhotoGroup.

© 2007. Courtesy of Jaxon-PhotoGroup.

© 2009. Courtesy of Jaxon-PhotoGroup.

© 2009. Courtesy of Jaxon-PhotoGroup.

Can you make judgments about the nature and intensity of the emotions expressed on these faces?

Adaptors are generally considered the least desirable type of nonverbal communication. Self-touching in this way could be a distraction to the audience, and it is often perceived as a sign of anxiety. One study found that deceivers bob their heads more often than people who tell the truth. Cultural guidelines may prohibit these behaviors, too. Wriggling your nose or having a disgusted facial look to show that you're repulsed seems to have a universal meaning.

However, in some cultures, people are socialized to mask emotional cues, and in others they're taught to emphasize them. Latin Americans will usually greet friends and relatives more personally than do Americans. Everyone hugs, including the men. Men usually also greet woman with *besitos*, meaning they touch cheeks while making a kissing noise with their lips. Women also greet other women with *besitos*. These little kisses are purely friendly and have no romantic meaning. Maslow and colleagues suggested that the anxiety displayed by adaptors can be interpreted by other communicators as a sign of deception; you are anxious because you are not being honest with the others and you fear being discovered!

Use of Space/Proxemics

The study of proxemics is typically divided into two applications: The use of personal space and how people claim and mark territory as their own. Most of us don't even think about the impact of space on our relationships, but research has shown that your use of space can influence shared meaning and impact your relationship. Knapp and Hall found that our use of space can seriously affect our ability to achieve desired goals. Both applications can be used and managed by people to communicate fairly specific messages, and they can provide evidence to help us make judgments about person using the space.

Personal space. When you consider the idea of **personal space,** think of a small amount of portable space that you carry around with you all the time. You control who is and who is not permitted inside of that space. Permission to enter that space is granted based on the relationship you have with that person, the context of the encounter, the culture in which you live, and your own personal preferences and tolerances. For example, you would be likely to allow business and professional

What do these adaptors tell you about the internal feelings of the people in the photos?

colleagues to be reasonably close to you; you would allow good friends to be very close to you; and you would allow romantic partners to be closer still, even to the point of touching. In addition, you might allow people that you don't know to be very close to you in the appropriate context, like a crowded elevator or a busy airport.

When someone enters your space without permission, you can interpret it as a lack of courtesy, or even as a threat. You will feel uncomfortable, so you can either wait for the trespasser to move out of your space, or you can move away until you feel comfortable again.

The range of personal space varies across cultures. The box describes spaces typical to the culture in the United States. If you visit the United Kingdom, you will notice that these spaces are slightly expanded; that is, the British prefer just a bit more distance between people. By contrast, many Eastern cultures, including Asia and the Middle East, prefer a smaller distance. When these cultures meet, people from the United States often feel "crowded" by people from Asian cultures, while people from Japan might think that Americans are "cold" or "stand-offish" because of the increased interpersonal distances. As you can see, there is no shortage of opportunities for misunderstanding! Burgoon suggests that we want to stay near others, but we also want to maintain some distance—think about the dilemma this causes! Try to be sensitive to cultural norms when you assign meaning to the use of personal space.

Territoriality. We also have a tendency to claim space as our own. We have just looked at personal space, which is portable space that you carry around with you. Territory, by contrast, is not mobile; it stays in one place. You can think of territory as a kind of extension of you that is projected on to space or objects. Space that you occupy or control, and objects that belong to you or that you use regularly, are all important to you. If any person not authorized by you occupies that space or touches those objects, you feel violated and threatened. To help describe this kind of attachment to places and things, we turn to Altman, who classified territory into three categories: primary, secondary, and public.

PERSONAL DISTANCES

Hall recognized characteristic distances maintained between people in the U.S. culture, depending on their perceived relationships. The distance categories are *intimate, personal, social,* and public.

Type	Distance	Who Is Permitted/Context
Intimate Distance 	touching to 18 inches	**Who:** Spouses and family members, boyfriends and girlfriends, and very close friends. **Context:** A date with your spouse.
Personal Distance 	18 inches to 4 feet	**Who:** Good friends and people you know well **Context:** Having lunch with a good friend or co-worker.
Social Distance 	4 feet to 12 feet	**Who:** Business associates, teachers, and people you know but with whom you have a professional but less social relationship. **Context:** A business meeting, small group discussion, or an employment interview.
Public Distance 	12 feet and beyond	**Who:** A person you don't know; a stranger on the street. **Context:** Giving a presentation to a large group; walking downtown on a public sidewalk.

© 2007. Courtesy of Jaxon-PhotoGroup.

© Kendall Hunt Publishing

© Kendall Hunt Publishing

© Kendall Hunt Publishing

Relationships affect the way we use space. Based on the use of space, describe the relationships in these photos. Be specific about the nonverbal clues that indicate the relationship.

Primary territory is space or those items that you personally control. This includes personal items that only you would use, like your clothes and your toothbrush. It also includes the private spaces in your house like your bathroom and bedroom. Many people treat still other places as primary territory such as their car, their office at work, and even their refrigerator!

Secondary territory is not your private property. That is, it is not owned by you, but it is typically associated with you. Examples of secondary territory include the desk you always use in class, the seat you always sit in at the office conference table, your favorite fishing spot at the lake, or your usual table at the library.

Public territory is available to anyone, so any space that you try to claim is only temporary. You might define your space on the beach by using markers such as blankets, beach chairs, or umbrellas. Or you might spread out your books and notes at the library to claim space on a work table. Our use of the territory lasts as long as we are using it, or as long as other people respect our markers.

Most of us pay little attention to these claims of space, and we probably don't even realize that we do it. However, these claims come clearly to our attention when they are violated. It seems like there is almost nothing worse than walking into the classroom on the day of the big exam to find someone else in your seat! Sure, any seat will work just as well, but that is *your* seat where you feel most comfortable and confident. We tend to feel violated whenever any unauthorized person uses our space or touches our stuff!

Lyman and Scott identified three levels of **intrusion of territory**: violation, invasion, and contamination. A *violation* happens when your space or your stuff is used without your permission, like when a neighbor borrows one of your tools without asking first. An *invasion* occurs when an unauthorized person enters the territory

Sometimes we allow our personal space to be violated.

© 2008, JupiterImages.

© 2008, JupiterImages.

People mark their territory in many ways.

that you have claimed with markers. They might move your books and notes at the library (while you were looking for a book) and take over your space at the table, or they could cut in front of you in a check-out line at the grocery store. Finally, a *contamination* occurs when space that you claim is used without your authorization, but your evidence of the use is not the presence of the user but objects left behind. For example, you arrive at your office in the morning to find cups and fast food wrappers on your desk. There is nobody in your office, but you know somebody *was* there, and he or she was eating at your desk. Territory that you claim as your own should not be used by anyone without your permission. How you respond to territory depends very much on who invaded the territory and why it was invaded, which you'll see explained in expectancy violations theory, which follows later in this chapter.

Dress/Appearance

Your appearance, along with the way you dress, influences the way other people respond to you. In some situations, your appearance can be the primary factor that determines the response of others. *Physical attractiveness*, as well as personal grooming and hygiene, weigh heavily on judgments that are made about you every day. If that's not enough pressure, along with protecting you from the environment and fulfilling cultural requirements for modesty, *clothing* is also a potent source of nonverbal information about you. Morris tells us that clothing sends continuous signals about us and who we think we are. For example, watch the scene in the 1990 movie *Pretty Woman* when the character played by Julia Roberts first enters a "high-class" clothing store and is treated poorly by the staff. What about her appearance led to that treatment?

Among other qualities, clothing can suggest social and economic status, education, level of success, or trustworthiness and character. Morris suggests that clothing can be a cultural display and one that communicates something special about the wearer. People have a tendency to express certain values central to their belief systems that indicate the kind of people they perceive themselves to be.

Katz tells us that we hold and express particular attitudes to satisfy this need and that those attitudes reflect a positive view of ourselves. Clothing and appearance are consistent with this concept. For example, if you consider yourself to be the "artistic" type, or a successful business person, or a talented athlete, your clothing choices will likely reflect that self image.

Gordon et al., suggests that clothing fulfills a number of symbolic functions:

- Traditional and religious ceremonies often involve specific clothing.

- Self-beautification (real or imagined) is often reflected in clothing.

- Clothing expresses cultural values regarding sexual identity and practice.

- Clothes differentiate roles and levels of authority.

- Clothing is used in the acquisition and display of status.

Think about the way you dress and why you make those clothing choices. What are you trying to say? Are you trying to fit in? Are you trying to identify yourself with a particular group? Are you trying to show respect for an occasion or person?

Clothing is not the only aspect of appearance to consider. Think of the other personal choices people make with tattoos, body art, and personal grooming. What are the impacts of blue hair, black nail colors, Mohawks or dreadlocks, multiple piercing and colorful tattoos? You have the right to communicate about yourself in any way you want, but remember that if you go against cultural norms, you may be creating perceptual barriers that impede communication. Your appearance is a prime source of information that others use to make judgments about you. Try to use some care when making choices about how you should look in particular situations. You can always maintain your individuality, but you should also dress to show respect for the occasion and the people that you will be coming into contact with. If you have to give a presentation for a business group, for example, you can show your respect for the group by dressing in more formal attire. Wearing jeans with ripped out knees may say a lot about who you think you are, but wearing the suit for the business group also communicates who you think you are. You are someone who combines your own needs with a respect for the needs of other people!

Is there ever a time when you should allow your territory to be violated?

Eye Movement/Occulesics

In many Western cultures, including the United States, making **eye contact** with another person is considered a sign of sincerity, caring, honesty, and sometimes power or status. Pearson found that men sometimes use eye contact to challenge others and to assert themselves. Women tend to hold eye contact more than men, regardless of the sex of the person that they're interacting with. Some Eastern cultures view eye contact with others as an impolite invasion of privacy and they especially disapprove of eye contact with a person of higher status. In another study, it was found that inner-city African-American persuaders look continually at the listener, and African American listeners tend to look away from the persuader most of the time. The opposite is true of middle-class Whites; as persuaders, they look only occasionally at the listener, and White listeners look continuously at the persuader. This could explain why the two groups could have incorrect inferences about the amount of interest the other has when they communicate.

We consider the use of eye contact to be an essential tool for achieving communication goals. In U.S. culture, how does it make you feel when someone will not make eye contact with you? Do you trust this person? Do you suspect his or her motives?

Eye contact helps us communicate in at least four ways: It can open a channel of communication, demonstrate concern, gather feedback, and moderate anxiety.

Open a communication channel. You can let others know that you would like to communicate with them by simply looking at them. A brief moment of eye contact can open a channel of communication and make other messages possible.

Demonstrate concern. Engaging other people in eye contact during conversations shows a concern for them, as well as your commitment that they understand your message. In addition, eye contact can be used to communicate liking and attraction.

Gather feedback. If you would like information about what other people are thinking, take a look at their eyes. You won't be able to read thoughts, but you can certainly find clues to indicate that they are listening, that they understand the message, and perhaps that they care about what you are saying. The old adage that speakers should look at the back wall of the room when giving a public speech is pretty bad advice; you will miss out on critical information about the frame of mind of audience members, as well as other feedback essential to achieving your goals.

Moderate anxiety. When speakers get nervous or anxious during a public presentation, they have a tendency to avoid eye contact with the listeners by either looking at the floor, the back wall of the room, or at their notes. As they continue to stare at the floor, anxiety (fear of unknown outcomes) continues to build. Occasionally, but rarely, anxiety can build to the point at which it completely takes over, and the speaker freezes.

How could her tattoos impact others' perceptions?

You can avoid this scenario through *careful preparation* for the event, and by allowing the listeners to provide you with support. By *establishing eye contact* with members of your audience, you will see listeners smiling at you or expressing support with their posture, head nods, or other behaviors. Not looking at the audience or conversational partners removes your opportunity to get or give supportive feedback. When others notice your anxiety, they usually want to help you. Look at the audience, feel the support and try to relax, and then refocus on your communication goals.

By making eye contact with others, you can find clues about their level of understanding and interest.

HOW DOES THEORY DESCRIBE NONVERBAL BEHAVIOR'S IMPACT ON RELATIONSHIPS?

Have you ever played elevator games with strangers? You know, you enter an empty elevator and take the "power position" by the buttons. At the next floor, someone enters and either asks you to push the button for a floor or reaches in front of you to select a floor and then retreats to the opposite corner away from you. There's no further talk or eye contact. The next person who enters does the same thing, finding a corner. Everyone faces the doors, anticipates its opening, watching the numbers change as if by magic. If others enter, their volume drops to a hush, or they stop talking until they leave. Now, have you ever tried *this*? Get on an elevator and keep walking until you face the back wall. After all, that's how you entered, right? Go stand right next to the power person, real close. Keep talking real loud. Sit down on your backpack or luggage. What do you think will happen? How will others react to you?

One theory that attempts to explain the influence of nonverbal communication on meaning and relationships is **expectancy violations theory.** Judee Burgoon said that "nonverbal cues are an inherent and essential part of message creation (production) and interpretation (processing)." Expectancy violations theory (EVT) suggests that we hold expectations about the nonverbal behavior of others. It asserts that when communicative norms are violated, the violation may be perceived either favorably or unfavorably, depending on the perception that the receiver has of the violator. Burgoon's early writing on EVT integrated Hall's ideas on personal space (which you read about earlier) as a core aspect of the theory. EVT says that our *expectancies* are the thoughts and behaviors anticipated when we interact with another.

We have expectations of how others ought to think and behave. Levine says that these expectancies are a result of social norms, stereotypes, and your own personal idiosyncrasies, and these expectancies cause us to interact with others. We have both preinteractional and interactional expectations.

Preinteractional expectations are made up of the skills and knowledge you bring to an interaction; *interactional expectations* are your skills and knowledge that let you carry out the interaction.

Another basic idea of EVT is that we learn our expectations from our cultures: You've learned what kind of touching is appropriate with whom, how to greet a stranger, and where to stand in relationship with another, for example.

Finally, EVT says that we make predictions about others based on their nonverbal behavior. So how does this work? Let's say you're standing in line at the grocery store, and the person in front of you looks at what you're about to buy and then makes eye contact with you. At first, you might be uncomfortable, thinking that the person is judging you by the way she is eyeing your groceries. If she then gives you a warm smile and points to her big pile containing the same things, you might feel a bit more comfortable. You've made predictions based on nonverbal behavior: The person is not threatening or judging you negatively.

But EVT is about *violations* of our expectations. Burgoon says that when people deviate from expectations, that deviation is judged based on the other's ability to reward us. A reward could be something as simple as a smile, friendliness, or acknowledgment of competence. This potential to reward is called *communicator reward valence*, which is the interactants' ability to reward or punish and the positive and negative characteristics they have. Someone in power, like your professor for instance, may have more communicator reward valence than a stranger, because the professor has the power of grades and probably has more credibility for you. If someone violates our expectations, these deviations cause *arousal*, an increased attention to the deviation. Cognitive arousal is mental awareness of the deviation; physical arousal involves physiological heightening. For instance, if a person stares at you, you might wonder why he's doing that (cognitive arousal) or you might start to sweat (physical arousal). Once arousal happens, threats occur. Your *threat threshold* is the tolerance you have for deviations; how threatened do you feel? Maybe you don't mind if another person stands too close; maybe you can't put up with someone staring at you. The size of your threat threshold is based on how you view the person who is deviating from your expectations; what is that other's communicator reward valence? Then you add in the *violation valence*, which consists of your positive or negative value placed towards the deviations from your expectations.

When someone violates one of your expectations (for instance, he touches you when you didn't expect it), you interpret the meaning of that violation and decide if you like it or not. If you don't like it, then the violation valence is negative; if the surprise was pleasant (even though you didn't expect it), then the violation valence is positive. The theory predicts that if a violation is ambiguous, then the communicator reward valence will influence how you interpret and evaluate the violation. If the person is someone you like, then you'll positively evaluate his violation; if you don't like him, then you'll negatively evaluate his violation. Take a simple example of how someone is dressed. On an interview, there are certain expectations of how you should look. If you go in wearing jeans and a t-shirt and the company wants its workers to wear suits, then you've violated expectancies. It's pretty likely that you don't have any power here, or any way to reward the company for hiring you. Thus, the interviewer will evaluate you negatively, feeling aroused that you didn't understand such a basic concept like appropriate attire. However, what if you are a highly sought-after, uniquely imaginative individual that the company has been pursuing? Your violation of the dress code might be seen positively; you're bold and creative, just like they thought. EVT is an interesting theory that focuses on what we expect nonverbally in conversations, as well as suggesting what happens when our expectations aren't met. It's very practical in applications across many contexts."

ACTIVITY 6.7 Owning My Communication

PURPOSE

To demonstrate that substituting the word "I" for the word "you" (changing the frame of reference) can improve communication.

PROCEDURE

Read the sentences below, which contain the word "you." Note the critical tone that the sentence assumes because of the use of the word "you."

Rewrite the sentences, substituting the word "I" and changing the phrase where necessary, and see if that neutralizes the tone of the sentence.

"YOU" Messages

1. You always give me another job do before I finish the one I have.
2. You never pick up your clothes

3. You don't make an effort to get along with my friends.
4. You never show up on time.
5. Your tests are unreasonable.
6. You wasted your money on that.
7. You expect too much from me.
8. Why can't you communicate?
9. Why are you so angry?
10. You hurt my feelings.

"I" Messages

ex: *I need a break between projects.* to

ex: *I am frustrated with the mess from these clothes.*

DISCUSSION

1. What makes changing the frame of reference difficult?
2. Why do we tend to use "you"?
3. Consider some recent situations where you could have changed the frame of reference. How would the outcome have changed?

"ACTIVITY 6.8 "I" Statements[7]

PURPOSE

Practice credibility and descriptive language versus evaluation.

DIRECTIONS

In groups, choose 3–4 of the following statements. Turn the following statements into "I" statements which places accountability and responsibility upon the "self." Once completed, discuss your results in a whole group setting.

1. You are unfair.

2. You are too emotional.

3. You are disrespectful.

4. You never let me speak.

5. You ignore what I say.

6. You always want your own way.

7. You only receive and never give.

8. You are always late.

9. You are careless.

10. You always break promises.

10. You make me mad.

12. You complain about everything I do.

13. You never hear me.

14. You oppose me on every issue.

15. You never want to go anywhere I want to go."

"ACTIVITY 6.9[8]

Nonverbal Communication is all nonlinguistic aspects of communication. The types of nonverbal communication include: Body movement, eye messages, space and distance, dress and appearance. Give a brief definition of each. Then, visit one of the sites listed below and record examples of each as you observed the nonverbal "types" in action. Record your time and place on the sheet attached and be very specific with your observations.

Choose one site: Student Center

                          Cafeteria

                          Local fast food restaurant

                          Library

                          A dorm lobby

NAME _____ PLACE _____

TYPE OF NONVERBAL BEHAVIOR	DEFINITION	OBSERVATION
Body Movement		
Eye contact		
Space and Distance		
Dress and Appearance		

Be prepared to share your observations with the class."

"ACTIVITY 6.10 Nonverbal Cafeteria Exercise[9]

PURPOSE
To demonstrate that nonverbal communication sends "clues, not facts."

PROCEDURE

1. With the following worksheet, select an interesting looking individual (whom you do not know) to observe. Try to pick someone who does not seem ready to move on, and station yourself far enough away so that you can see your subject but not hear what she is saying.
2. Observe the individual for as long as possible, remembering to be discreet, and record your impressions.
3. When the person looks as though she is getting ready to leave, approach her with a smile, confess your "spying," and check your observations. You'll be surprised how friendly a stranger can be when she discovers she's helping you with classwork.
4. When you return to class, compare your observations with your classmates

NONVERBAL CAFETERIA OBSERVATION FORM

BASIC DESCRIPTION	APPEARANCE	ACTUAL
Gender		
Age		
Major		
Bilingual		
Live with parents		
Political Party		
Sports		
Activities		
Veteran of military service		
Children		
Brothers, sisters		
Relationship to others at table		
Mood		
From out of state		
Type of car		
Name		
Type of employment		

ACTIVITY 6.11 Personal Space (Proxemics)

PURPOSE

To determine what your personal space is, and to explore your feelings about your personal space when it is invaded.

PROCEDURE

1. With your partners, perform the following exercise. As you perform the exercise, examine your "feelings' or emotional responses.

2. Have a person of the same sex approach you from each of the given directions. Stop the partner when the distance between you is comfortable. Measure the approximate distance.
   a. Directly from the front.
   b. Directly from the left.
   c. Directly from the right.
   d. From a 45-degree angle from the left.
   e. From a 45-degree angle from the right.
   f. From the rear.

3. Repeat the same exercises with a person of the opposite sex.

4. From the front position allow the person to come too close. At this distance, engage the person in a conversation for at least one minute.

5. Again, take time to examine your feelings or emotional responses.

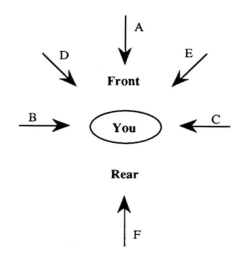

DISCUSSION

1. What differences in your body space and in your emotional responses did direction make?
2. What difference did the sex of your partner make?
3. What other factors could influence the size of your "body bubble"?
4. How did you feel when your personal space was invaded?
5. How did you and your partner react when your space was invaded?
6. How can differences in the size of personal space affect communication between people and cultures?

ACTIVITY 6.12 Eye Contact and Body Position Activity

PURPOSE
To determine feelings associated with too much and too little eye contact, to find what is "normal" eye contact and to examine feelings associated with "talking down" versus "talking up."

PROCEDURE

1. Select a partner and carry on a discussion for about one minute in each of the following positions; note your feelings associated with each.
   a. side by side with *no eye contact*
   b. face to face with *no eye contact*
   c. face to face with *constant eye contact*
   d. one standing and one sitting facing each other with "normal eye contact."
   e. reverse the standing and sitting positions again with "normal eye contact."

DISCUSSION

1. Which did you find more difficult: no eye contact or constant eye contact? Why?
2. Which felt more uncomfortable: talking "down" or talking "up?" Why?
3. In what kinds of situations might you find yourself talking "down" or "up," and what can you do about it?
4. What is "normal" eye contact? When do you look at the other person and when do you look away?

ACTIVITY 6.13 Nonverbal Rules

PURPOSE

To compare and contrast nonverbal behaviors and expectations in a variety of social settings.

PROCEDURE

Read the following scenario below and then list the appropriate nonverbal behavior as understood by *your own cultural background*.

Scenario: You are about to have a foreign exchange student stay with you: they have asked you for some guidelines regarding the following situations. Remember, provide direction as you understand what is appropriate from *your cultural background*. Write down all acceptable variations.

1.   Greetings/introductions:

   a.   boss

   b.   senior citizen

   c.   "new person" at a party

   d.   stranger in a public place

2.   Saying goodbye to your partner/spouse in a public place:

3. Clothing for:

    a. school

    b. religious ceremony

    c. dinner at a good friend's house

4. Dressing for a funeral:

    a. women

    b. men

5. Seating:

    a. a group of men at the movies

    b. a group of women at the movies

DISCUSSION
Form groups of 4–6 and compare and contrast your answers.

1. What was similar? What was different?
2. Were there differences based on gender?
3. What might these nonverbal expectations say about cultural values such as formality, informality, modesty, status, etc?
4. Were there any generational differences?"

UNDERSTANDING NONVERBAL BEHAVIORS

How Does Theory Describe Nonverbal Behavior's Impact on Relationships?

Have you ever played elevator games with strangers? You know, you enter an empty elevator and take the "power position" by the buttons. At the next floor, someone enters and either asks you to push the button for a floor or reaches in front of you to select a floor and then retreats to the opposite corner away from you. There's no further talk or eye contact. The next person who enters does the same thing, finding a corner. Everyone faces the doors, anticipates its opening, watching the numbers change as if by magic. If others enter, their volume drops to a hush, or they stop talking until they leave. Now, have you ever tried this? Get on an elevator and keep walking until you face the back wall. After all, that's how you entered, right? Go stand right next to the power person, real close. Keep talking real loud. Sit down on your backpack or luggage. What do you think will happen? How will others react to you?

One theory that attempts to explain the influence of nonverbal communication on meaning and relationships is **expectancy violations theory**. Judee Burgoon said that "nonverbal cues are an inherent and essential part of message creation (production) and interpretation (processing)." Expectancy violations theory (EVT) suggests that we hold expectations about the nonverbal behavior of others. It asserts that when communicative norms are violated, the violation may be perceived either favorably or unfavorably, depending on the perception that the receiver has of the violator. Burgoon's early writing on EVT integrated Hall's ideas on personal space (which you read about earlier) as a core aspect of the theory. EVT says that our expectancies are the thoughts and behaviors anticipated when we interact with another.

We have expectations of how others ought to think and behave. Levine says that these expectancies are a result of social norms, stereotypes, and your own personal idiosyncrasies, and these expectancies cause us to interact with others. We have both preinteractional and interactional expectations. Preinteractional expectations are made up of the skills and knowledge you bring to an interaction; interactional expectations are your skills and knowledge that let you carry out the interaction.

Another basic idea of EVT is that we learn our expectations from our cultures: You've learned what kind of touching is appropriate with whom, how to greet a stranger, and where to stand in relationship with another, for example.

Finally, EVT says that we make predictions about others based on their nonverbal behavior. So how does this work? Let's say you're standing in line at the grocery store, and the person in front of you looks at what you're about to buy and then makes eye contact with you. At first, you might be uncomfortable, thinking that the person is judging you by the way she is eyeing your groceries. If she then gives you a warm smile and points to her big pile containing the same things, you might feel a bit more comfortable. You've made predictions based on nonverbal behavior: The person is not threatening or judging you negatively.

But EVT is about violations of our expectations. Burgoon says that when people deviate from expectations, that deviation is judged based on the other's ability to reward us. A reward could be something as simple as a smile, friendliness, or acknowledgment of competence. This potential to reward is called communicator reward valence, which is the interactants' ability to reward or punish and the positive and negative characteristics they have. Someone in power, like your professor for instance, may have more communicator reward valence than a stranger, because the professor has the power of grades and probably has more credibility for you. If someone violates our expectations, these deviations cause arousal, an increased attention to the deviation. Cognitive arousal is mental awareness of the deviation; physical arousal involves physiological heightening. For instance, if a person stares at you, you might wonder why he's doing that (cognitive arousal) or you might start to sweat (physical arousal). Once arousal happens, threats occur. Your threat threshold is the tolerance you have for deviations; how threatened do you feel? Maybe you don't mind if another person stands too close; maybe you can't put up with someone staring at you. The size of your threat threshold is based on how you view the person who is deviating from your expectations; what is that other's communicator reward valence? Then you add in the violation valence, which consists of your positive or negative value placed towards the deviations from your expectations.

When someone violates one of your expectations (for instance, he touches you when you didn't expect it), you interpret the meaning of that violation and decide if you like it or not. If you don't like it, then the violation valence is negative; if the surprise was pleasant (even though you didn't expect it), then the violation valence is positive. The theory predicts that if a violation is ambiguous, then the communicator reward valence will influence how you interpret and evaluate the violation. If the person is someone you like, then you'll positively evaluate his violation; if you don't like him, then you'll negatively evaluate his violation. Take a simple example of how someone is dressed. On an interview, there are certain expectations of how you should look. If you go in wearing jeans and a t-shirt and the company wants its workers to wear suits, then you've violated expectancies. It's pretty likely that you don't have any power here, or any way to reward the company for hiring you. Thus, the interviewer will evaluate you negatively, feeling aroused that you didn't understand such a basic concept like appropriate attire. However, what if you are a highly sought-after, uniquely imaginative individual that the company has been pursuing? Your violation of the dress code might be seen positively; you're bold and creative, just like they thought. EVT is an interesting theory that focuses on what we expect nonverbally in conversations, as well as suggesting what happens when our expectations aren't met. It's very practical in applications across many contexts.

"ACTIVITY 6.14 Behavioral Descriptions[10]

DEFINED

Language that describes the behavior observed. Specific, behavioral language will enhance clarity and understanding and will reduce miscommunications that can lead to serious problems.

METHOD

1. **Identify who is involved.**

   "If you are talking to another person, consider whether your appreciation, complaint, or request is directed solely at him or her or whether it also involves others (Adler-Towne, 201)."

2. **In what circumstances does the behavior occur?**

   Who – What – When – Where

3. **State what behaviors are involved.**

   What have you observed? State it specifically.

EXAMPLE
- **Vague statement:** John's full of action.
- **Behavioral description:** John rode his bike for an hour and then mowed the lawn.

PRACTICAL APPLICATION

Rewrite the following statements using the method above.
1. Connie is so much fun.
2. My teacher is boring.
3. Janice is a very hard worker.
4. My boyfriend is a jerk."

ENDNOTES

1, 3, 4, 6, & 8 From *Communication: Principles of Tradition and Change* by Wallace, et al. Copyright © 2009 by Kendall Hunt Publishing Company. Reprinted with permission.

2 & 9 From *Communicate! A Workbook for Interpersonal Communication*, 7th Edition, by Communication Research Associates. Copyright © 2004 by Kendall Hunt Publishing Company. Reprinted by permission.

5, 7, & 10 From *The Competent Communicator Workbook for Communication*, 2nd Edition, by Cristina Doda Cardenas and Connie Duren. Copyright © 2013 by Kendall Hunt Publishing Company. Reprinted with permission.

CHAPTER 7

Conflict

STUDENT LEARNING OUTCOMES

Critical Thinking			Communication			Team Work		Social Responsibility	Personal Responsibility	Activity Measured
Creative Thinking/ Innovative	Analysis & Evaluation	Synthesis of Information	Writing	Visual	Oral	Differing Viewpoints	Work with Others	Intercultural Competence	Ethical Decision Making	Activity
X	X		X	X	X	X	X			7.1
X		X	X	X	X	X	X			7.2, 7.2
X	X		X	X	X	X	X			7.4

"CONFLICT[1]

Managing Conflict

The subject of conflict introduces some interesting dichotomies into the study of human communication. While the existence of conflict is a fact of life, we tend to treat conflict, whenever and wherever it is encountered, as something bad that should be avoided, sometimes at all costs. We therefore doom ourselves and our interactions to a nonproductive, negative cycle of avoidance and denial. This view of conflict generally arises, not so much from the conflicts themselves, but rather from the ways in which we try to manage, or more accurately, avoid managing them. In fact, it will be the contention of this section that conflict is neither good nor bad. It simply is! It is our preconceptions and ways of confronting conflicts that cause not only our overall negative attitude about them but also the nonproductive ways in which we attempt to manage them.

The Nature of Conflict

In order to begin a better and more constructive outlook toward conflict, let's begin by understanding that conflict is really not a thing. Rather, conflict is a condition. It is a state of imbalance existing within an individual. Later we will consider the reason for the imbalance and the different types of conflict. But in order to see better what conflict is, it is necessary to define it.

By now, it is no surprise to you that many concepts in communication do not have a common, agreed-upon definition. As with the definition of communication itself, conflict has almost as many definitions as there are people to define it. However, for our purposes, let's consider a working definition.

A Definition

Conflict may be defined as *the perception of two or more, apparently mutually exclusive, objectives, choices, or courses of action that motivates the person, or persons, to seek to resolve the situation.* To begin to understand more about the nature of conflict, let us look more closely at the above definition. First of all, as was mentioned earlier, conflict is a condition—the perception of a situation. As soon as we label conflict a perception, we should remember what we have already learned about the process of perception, namely, that it is a highly subjective, incomplete, and inaccurate process that has been learned. Therefore, our perceptions of conflicts are always going to carry these subjective, incomplete, and inaccurate traits. Furthermore, it matters little to attempt to prove or disprove in some objective sense whether or not a conflict really exists, as one might try to prove or disprove who won the Super Bowl in a given year. The perception that a conflict exists makes it real to the person or persons sharing that perception, and that is where we must begin—with that perception.

This perception has some special qualities about it that get us closer to an understanding of the nature of conflict. It is the element of exclusivity that begins to lead us down the path toward feeling or experiencing conflict. The idea here is based on one generally agreed principle of communication and psychology: Humans prefer a state of balance—a consistency within ourselves, our beliefs, our attitudes, and our view of the world. Just as we seek to maintain or restore this balance, we seek to avoid or eliminate imbalance.

An example might be helpful here. If I have two good friends who like me and also like each other, I can be said to be in a state of balance in this situation. However, if these two friends suddenly begin to dislike each other, I begin to experience imbalance. Or perhaps to put the example somewhat differently, what would happen if you were engaged to be married to someone but your parents, presumably people you like, dislike your future mate? We have all probably been in some kind of situation where this kind of imbalance existed and it is precisely this imbalance and the discomfort associated with it that motivate us to seek to resolve the situation, or, as we are defining it, the conflict.

This imbalance need not involve our feelings for people; this same condition can be prompted by having to choose between two equally appealing alternatives such as two or more places to go on vacation, items to order from the menu at your favorite restaurant, or two dates for the same evening. The issue is the same: Which do I choose? At this moment, I am in a conflict. Granted, some of these conflicts are quickly and easily resolved, but others can exist for long periods of time and cause us to be miserable. But in each, the goal is the same: to eliminate the imbalance in our perceptions.

One way to eliminate the imbalance is to make the choice, if choice is involved in the situation. Another way to manage the conflict is to have the imbalance resolved by another person or by the situation itself. For instance, if I am applying for a new job, there is a natural conflict occurring between me and all the other applicants for that same position. Once the choice has been made by the employer, that conflict is over. Sometimes another conflict surfaces, as we shall see a bit later on, but the specific conflict over who will be chosen will cease to exist.

Another way to eliminate a conflict is to discover that our perception is wrong, that is, that the items in apparent conflict are not really mutually exclusive. I don't have to choose between steak and lobster, I can order a combination of the two!

Still another approach is to separate the conflict items altogether by simply realizing that no balance can be achieved or perhaps even expected. In this situation, we can simply agree to disagree. This last situation is most often the case when people encounter conflicts with one another involving their values. If I like jazz and my wife likes opera, is it reasonable for us to try to resolve this apparent conflict? In fact, I am perhaps not even likely to view this situation as a conflict unless I take the position that there is only one type of music that both of us can like.

The Recipe Approach:

One way to look at the nature of conflict, and the nature of conflict management in particular, is to view the above definition as though it were a recipe. Each element of the definition is an ingredient which, when combined together, makes conflict. Therefore, all I have to do is eliminate one of the ingredients and I no longer have a conflict. This may seem overly simplistic but it is at the heart of productive conflict management.

ACTIVITY 7.1 Feelings about Conflict

PURPOSE
To allow you to examine how we feel about conflicts.

PROCEDURE
Identify a recent conflict you have had.

1. What was it about?

2. Who was it with?

3. How did you handle it?

4. How satisfied are you with the results?

General feelings about conflict.

5. How do you feel when you know you are facing a conflict situation?

6. When you come away from a conflict feeling as though you won, how do you feel?

7. When you come away from a conflict feeling as though you lost, how do you feel?

8. When you experience a conflict that is not resolved, how do you feel?

9. Generally, when you experience a conflict, what do you do?

DISCUSSION

1. Form a small group and compare your responses to the above questions.
2. What general conclusions can you make about people's feelings regarding conflict?
3. What, if any, barrier to resolving conflicts can these feelings produce?

CHARACTERISTICS OF CONFLICT AND TYPES OF CONFLICT

We have already discussed one of the essential characteristics of conflict-it is a *condition*, not a thing. However, there are several other characteristics that would be helpful to understand at this point. First, conflicts are generally neither productive not nonproductive. Rather, it is the ways in which they are approached and managed that make the outcomes either productive or nonproductive.

Second, conflicts can be experienced *intrapersonally* or *interpersonally*. While it is true that as perceptions, all conflicts are really intrapersonal, to whatever extent that you and I share a similar perception of a conflict in which we perceive ourselves, it can be said that we are involved in an interpersonal conflict. It is important to be able to distinguish between these two in order to know how to go about resolving or managing the conflict. I cannot resolve an interpersonal conflict on my own. I must resolve it interpersonally. It is also important to recognize when I am experiencing an intrapersonal conflict. It is often the case that individuals misanalyze a conflict and attempt to deal with an intrapersonal conflict as if it were really an interpersonal one, resulting in behaviors that attempt to put blame on others rather than realizing that the conflict and the resolution of it rest with us.

A third characteristic of conflict deals with its structure or context. In this sense we can classify conflict as either formal or informal. *Formal* conflict is characterized by rules, an acknowledged structure such as time limits, order of presentation of arguments, and so on, and usually by the fact that a third party usually determines the resolution of the conflict. Conflicts involving the courtroom, ballot box, and debating area are types of formal conflict. The important thing with these types of conflicts is to understand the structure and rules and to realize that the other person or opponent is not the one to be convinced but rather the third party. I have often judged intercollegiate debates in which the conflicting sides tried endlessly to convince one another of the correctness of their own viewpoint, while ignoring the fact that I was the one who would ultimately decide who won!

Informal conflicts, on the other hand, have no formal rules or structure and the resolution must come from the ones in conflict. These are the ones in which we find ourselves daily and that usually present the most challenge. If you and I are in a conflict and it is up to us to come to mutual agreement as to its resolution, our communication skills are truly put to the test. We cannot turn to others to decide for us; we cannot appeal to some unseen judge; we must rely on each other and ourselves.

Types of Conflict

With the above concepts in mind, let's examine the kinds of conflicts that can occur, and how they can be characterized according to the above classifications. Conflicts can generally be classified into one of the following seven categories:

1. Content
2. Decisional
3. Material
4. Role
5. Judgmental

6.   Expectancy
7.   Ego

Content conflicts arise over perceived differences in facts or information. For example, if you and I are in a conflict over who won the Super Bowl in a given year, we are experiencing a "content" conflict. This type of conflict is almost always interpersonal. It can be either formal, as in the case of whether or not a defendant is guilty, or informal, as in the case of who won the Super Bowl. Content conflicts are perhaps the easiest to resolve, in that all that is needed is more information or a re-examination of existing information. There is generally little room for compromise here. The attempt is to determine who is right.

Decisional conflicts revolve around decisions that an individual or individuals must face. Sometimes these decisions involve simply ourselves and can therefore be classified as intrapersonal. In this case the conflicts often arise from alternatives that appear equally attractive or unattractive. A decision over which car to buy can confront an individual with equally attractive alternatives. On the other hand, a decision over whether to quit your job and risk unemployment or stay in your job and continue to be dissatisfied would be an example of equally unattractive alternatives. In either case, the approach toward resolution is the same—resolve the conflict by unbalancing the alternatives. In this case it is important to be honest with yourself regarding your feelings and to be as thorough as possible in investigating the alternatives.

The important steps in this process are to identify the alternatives, to evaluate each along with the outcomes each is likely to produce, and then to role-play the option you are considering taking. Acting as if you have made the decision in a particular way will allow you to see how the decision "feels." This will help you discover how easy it will be to live with the decision once you actually make it. It is also important to realize that few decisions, even once they are made, are irrevocable. If a decision turns out to be wrong, it is better to recognize that fact and then change it than to continue to live with the stress and dissatisfaction of a decision with which you are unhappy.

Interpersonal decisional conflicts simply compound the variables. Now more than one person's feelings and reactions must be considered. The steps, however, remain the same. Analyze, evaluate, and role-play the decision to determine how it feels. It is virtually impossible to live emotionally with a decision made on purely rational grounds. In the case of interpersonal conflicts of this type it is also important to look for compromise alternatives that may be more satisfactory to all parties.

Material conflicts are exclusively interpersonal, and involve competition for a limited resource, such as money, a job, property, food, or any other limited resource. The more of a limited resource one person gets, the less there is for someone else. The first step in dealing with this type of conflict is to determine if the resource in conflict is really limited. People often find themselves competing for things that are actually not in limited supply. Conflicts over love or esteem are examples of this misinterpretation. Once the resource has been determined to actually be in limited supply, it is then important for the parties in conflict to seek a "win-win" solution so that each leaves the conflict with more than they had previously but less than if there had actually been a "winner" and a "loser." "Win-lose" solutions invariably result in hard feelings and a desire on the part of the "loser" to get back at the other person the next time. When this occurs, such damage is done to the relationship that "win-lose" conflicts usually disintegrate into "lose-lose" conflicts.

Role conflicts are another type of conflict. These involve disagreements in role expectations between two people, or conflicting role expectations in the case of intrapersonal role conflict. As with decisional conflict, the steps to resolve this type of conflict involve a thorough analysis of the role expectations in conflict, a willingness to be open and honest about these expectations, and a willingness to negotiate a "win-win" solution. Couples having conflicts over their expectations of one another's behavior are prime examples of role conflicts. Sometimes the intervention of a third party, such as a marriage counselor, is necessary to encourage people to identify their expectations of one another and freely share those expectations with the other person. It is important here for an individual to be assertive and to be a "clean fighter."

The remaining three types of conflicts—*judgmental, expectancy,* and *ego*—are always destructive. *Judgmental* conflicts revolve around conflicting value statements as to the worth of something. Conflicts about whether or not a particular movie, book, or political candidate is good or bad are examples of this type of destructive conflict. In managing these conflicts it is important to remember that value judgments reflect an individual's value system and will always be to some degree different between people. Rather than continue to fight over whose judgment is correct, it is far more productive to acknowledge the right of each person to feel the ways he or she does and simply "agree to disagree." Once a person adopts this position, the alternatives are no longer mutually exclusive and, as stated earlier in this article, once we remove one of the elements in the definition of what conflict is, we no longer have conflict.

Expectancy conflicts are intrapersonal in nature, and deal with the expectations we set regarding the things and people in our world. It is a natural part of living to make expectations about people and situations, but if these expectations are unrealistic, the "reality" can never measure up and we doom ourselves to increasing amounts of dissatisfaction with life. Statements such as "that's not fair" or "that shouldn't have happened" are symptomatic of expectancy conflict. To deal more productively with our expectations it is important to try to perceive the world as accurately as possible and to realize that statements about the fairness or unfairness, or incorrectness of some happening ignore the reality that life is not fair nor correct; it simply is.

Finally, *ego* conflicts are the last type of conflict in which an individual can find himself or herself. These are the most destructive of all conflicts and can cause the most damage to relationships. In this type of conflict, the competition is over which person is the better person. Once our ego defense mechanisms come into play, good communication goes out the window and people begin attacking each other. There is no hope for resolution here. The rule is simply not to get into arguments over the worth of yourself compared to someone else. The unfortunate thing is that other types of conflicts often escalate into ego conflicts if they are not correctly identified and dealt with in a productive way. It is important here to learn to recognize "dirty fighting" behaviors, avoid using them yourself, and avoid others who insist on using them.

In order to begin to deal constructively with our conflicts it is important to first come to grips with what is in conflict; that is, what are the mutually exclusive objectives? Once these can be determined, applying the appropriate skills will lead to constructive and productive behaviors. Another valuable question to ask is "Who owns the conflict?" Many times we inadvertently buy into someone else's conflict and begin to think that it is actually ours. This mistake can doom us to frustration, since we cannot resolve a conflict to which we are not actually a party.

Now that we have examined in general what conflict is, and discussed the different types of conflict along with various characteristics of it, let's look at some of the barriers to handling conflict productively.

ACTIVITY 7.2 Identifying Conflicts Activity

PURPOSE

To help you identify the types of conflict we encounter in our daily lives.

PROCEDURE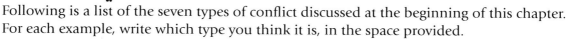

Following is a list of the seven types of conflict discussed at the beginning of this chapter. For each example, write which type you think it is, in the space provided.

CONFLICT TYPES

CONTENT—disagreement over "facts"

DECISIONAL—decision about different courses of action to take

MATERIAL—competition for material goods such as money, job, etc.

ROLE—disagreement over role expectations and/or behavior

JUDGMENTAL—disagreement over the value or worth of something

EXPECTANCY—difference between our expectations of something and the perceived reality

EGO—disagreement over the worth of yourself or someone else

EXAMPLES

1. You are disagreeing with your boy friend/girl friend over which movie to see.
    _____

2. You are arguing with your brother or sister over who gets use of the family car on Friday night. _____

3. Your boss and you disagree about how you should act around the other employees in your area of responsibility. _____

4. You have had plans for a vacation in Hawaii for several months. You have arrived and now feel upset at how it is turning out. _____

5. You and your father or mother are having an argument over what time you need to be home from a date. _____

6. You are having a disagreement with a friend over who won the Oscar for Best Picture in 1988. _____

7. You are having an argument with a co-worker about the new sick leave policy that has been enacted. _____

8. You have decided to show another player on the team that you are better than him/her. _____

9. You are having a disagreement with your instructor about your study habits.
_____

10. You and another employee are competing for the same promotion.
_____

DISCUSSION

1. Compare your answers with others in the group.
2. As you identified these conflict types, what personal examples did you think of?

ACTIVITY 7.3 Nonproductive Conflict Styles

PURPOSE

To help you explore the nonproductive ways we manage conflict.

PROCEDURE

1. Read the following descriptions of nonproductive styles, and try to identify those of which you may be guilty.
2. Form groups and answer the discussion questions below. Indirect conflicts often result in games because the individuals involved do not openly and directly acknowledge the real conflict. These games are called "crazymakers" or "dirty fights" by George Bach and they lead to a worsening of the conflict rather than to a satisfactory solution. There are three basic "crazymakers" styles:

A. *The Avoider.* This person denies the conflict by refusing to face up to it directly and assertively.

Typical Behaviors:

*   pretending there is nothing wrong
*   refusing to fight (falling asleep, leaving, pretending to be busy)
*   changing the subject whenever conversation approaches the area of conflict
*   hinting at the conflict or talking in generalities but never quite coming out and expressing self
*   kidding around when another person wants to be serious, thus blocking expression of important feelings
*   attacking other parts of other person's life rather than dealing with real problem

B. *The Manipulator.* This person wants to "win." She attempts, in an indirect way, to get the other person to behave as she wants them to, rather than dealing in a direct way.

Typical Behaviors:

*   trying to change other person's behavior by making them feel guilty or responsible ("It's OK, don't worry about me . . .")
*   going into character analysis by explaining what's wrong with the other person or what the other person really means rather than allowing them to express themselves directly
*   refusing to allow the relationship to change from what it once was

C. ***The Avenger.*** This aggressive behavior often results from nonassertive behavior. Because of an unwillingness to deal with the conflict openly and directly, this person attempts to get back at the other person in a number of indirect ways. An especially dirty fighter, he creates fights because he experiences second-order conflicts for which he wants to "pay back" or get even.

Typical Behaviors:

- storing up resentment and dumping it all on the other person all at once
- doing things to upset them
- finding fault by blaming other person for things
- bringing up things in an argument that are totally off the subject (other behavior, bad breath, etc.)
- attempting to punish partner by withholding
- encouraging others to ridicule or disregard partner

DISCUSSION

1. Which of the preceding styles have you been guilty of?
2. What were your feelings when employing any of these styles?
3. What were the results when you used these styles?

BARRIERS TO CONFLICT MANAGEMENT

Some barriers to managing conflict in a productive way are:

- **Avoidance**—As was mentioned at the outset, people tend to have a negative attitude about conflict and therefore tend to avoid dealing with conflicts once they are perceived, hoping that the conflict will simply go away.
- **Nonassertiveness**—Not being willing to speak your own mind and allow others the same opportunity increases frustration and distorts communication.

Let's work this out!

Source: Mickey Tillman (MJRT)

- **Misanalysis**—Buying into someone else's conflict or failing to analyze what is actually in conflict causes inappropriate behavior and may cause us to apply the wrong management strategy. Not being able to correctly determine who owns the problem is also an example of misanalysis.
- **Escalation**—Becoming defensive and thereby escalating the situation to an ego conflict produces disastrous effects.
- **Dirty fighting**—Using strategies associated with nonassertive, passive-aggressive, or aggressive behavior promotes poor communication and leads to escalation.
- **Competing**—Failing to recognize that interpersonal conflict management requires cooperation and good will between the parties generally brings about competition among the individuals involved in a conflict. Rather than cooperatively seeking a "win-win" solution, people go after a "win-lose" answer and ultimately everyone loses.

By understanding the true nature of conflict, developing a positive outlook about it, learning to recognize the types of conflicts in which we find ourselves, and avoiding destructive types of conflicts and the barriers to effective conflict management, we can begin to deal with our conflicts in a far more constructive and productive manner."

"ACTIVITY 7.4 Conflict Scenario Dialogues[2]

DIRECTIONS

Work with a partner to role play the scenarios below. Each partner will choose which side of the conflict style he/she wishes to demonstrate. After each skit, the class will identify which type of conflict style was evidenced.

- **Win-Lose SCENARIOS** (The competitive paradigm: if I win, you lose! The authoritarian leadership style is shown in this conflict dialogue. In relationships, both people aren't winning, both are losing.)
  1. Spouses disagreeing over whose television program should be watched.
  2. An intimate couple, disagreeing about where they will take their vacation.

- **Lose-Lose SCENARIOS** (When people become obsessed with making the other person lose, even at their own expense. This scenario represents adversarial conflict, war, or highly dependent persons.)
  3. A student and teacher disagreeing about the teacher's decision to drop the student due to excessive absences.
  4. Two fans at a ball game disagreeing about who should get the last beverage a vender has to sell.

- **Compromise-Compromise SCENARIOS** (Both parties change their goals to make them compatible. Both often abandon part of their original desires.)
  5. A parent and daughter or son disagreeing about which college to attend.
  6. Two motorists who have just had a minor collision, disagreeing about who is at fault for the accident.

- **Win-Win SCENARIOS** (People can seek mutual benefit in all human interactions.)
  7. A cashier and a customer disagreeing about whether the customer gave the cashier a ten or one dollar bill.
  8. An elderly parent and his or her adult child disagreeing about whether the parent will go to a nursing home or come to live with the adult child.
  9. Two friends disagreeing over both wanting to date the same person.

- **Accommodate-Compromise SCENARIOS** (One person abandons their own goals and both parties come to a compatible goal.)
  10. A home remodeling professional disagreeing over the amount of the construction cost with the customer."

ENDNOTES

1 From *Communicate! A Workbook for Interpersonal Communication*, 7th Edition, by Communication Research Associates. Copyright © 2004 by Kendall Hunt Publishing Company. Reprinted by permission.

2 From *The Competent Communicator Workbook for Communication*, 2nd Edition, by Cristina Doda Cardenas and Connie Duren. Copyright © 2013 by Kendall Hunt Publishing Company. Reprinted with permission.

PART THREE
Understanding Relationships

CHAPTER 8

Relational Communication

STUDENT LEARNING OUTCOMES

Critical Thinking			Communication			Team Work		Social Responsibility	Personal Responsibility	Activity Measured
Creative Thinking/ Innovative	Analysis & Evaluation	Synthesis of Information	Writing	Visual	Oral	Differing Viewpoints	Work with Others	Intercultural Competence	Ethical Decision Making	Activity
X	X		X	X	X	X	X			8.1, 8.2, 8.3, 8.4

"RELATIONAL COMMUNICATION[1]

We share a large part of our lives with other individuals in what we call "relationships." All relationships involve elements of interpersonal communication; however, the study of relational communication focuses specifically on the communicating that occurs between two people who are in the process of beginning, continuing, or ending a relationship with each other. Although we have many relationships (i.e., with neighbors, our boss, teachers), this section will address the intimate communication between family members, close friends, or significant love relationships. In order to gain an understanding of the communication process that occurs in these relationships, we will define several terms that will be used in this section:

Definition of Relationships

➢ Relationships

Definition: The context in which continuing social interaction occurs.

Example: Whenever we communicate with anyone in an ongoing way, we, do that within a relational framework.

We share a large part of our lives with other individuals in what we call "relationships." All relationships involve elements of interpersonal communication; however, the study of relational communication focuses specifically on the communicating that occurs between two people who are in the process of beginning, continuing, or ending a relationship with each other. Although we have many relationships (i.e., with neighbors, our boss, teachers), this chapter will address the intimate communication between family members, close friends, or significant love relationships. In order to gain an understanding of the communication process that occurs in these relationships, we will define several terms that will be used in this chapter:

➢ Relationships

Definition: The context in which continuing social interaction occurs.

Example: Whenever we communicate with anyone in an ongoing way, we, do that within a relational framework.

➢ Relational Communication

Definition: Communication that affects our willingness, and that of others, to initiate, continue, or terminate our relationships.

Examples: Greeting people, handshakes (initiating), expressing our commitment to the relationship (continuing), telling someone we no longer want to be friends (terminating), and so on.

➢ Relational Identity

Definition   The perception of two individuals in a relationship as something different from who they are as individuals.

Examples: We may see ourselves as a "couple," "twosome," or a "duo." We begin to refer to ourselves as "we" or "us" instead of "you and me."

➢ Intimacy

Definition: According to Adler, Rosenfeld, and Towne in their book Interplay, this can be classified in three areas: intellectual, emotional, and physical intimacy. Intimacy is characterized by extended and concentrated communication in any of these areas. It is also not the goal in all relationships.

Examples: We may share our life philosophies with a friend (intellectual), our feelings of love with a parent (emotional), and a sexual relationship with a girl friend or boy friend (physical).

➢ Self-Disclosure

Definition: Sharing information about oneself that the other individual is unlikely to find out by other means.

Examples: Sharing secrets, discoveries, confidential information, past history, and experiences or information that we do not commonly express.

THE IMPORTANCE OF RELATIONAL COMMUNICATION

Imagine for a moment that you are suddenly alone in the world. You woke up this morning and found that the people you share your home with are gone. You stepped outside and your neighborhood was void of the sounds of people awakening and preparing for a new day—no car engines running or doors closing as other individuals go about their daily routines. You leave for work or school only to find the streets empty. Every store, school, or business you see is the same: deserted. As far as you know, you are the only person left in the world!

This is not a very pleasant scene but it does allow us to examine how we feel about those who share our lives. Whether it be a parent, a roommate, or a spouse, we would sorely miss the company of others if we suddenly found them absent from our lives. The reality is that we are social creatures by nature and our relationships provide the foundation of our daily lives. Understanding how and why we establish these relationships, and what barriers we face in successfully maintaining them, can help us avoid the "disappearance" of important relationships from our lives. And, most importantly, the more we understand about how we communicate in these relationships, the greater the opportunity we have to make them work well.

Relationships Are Inevitable

Relationships are, fortunately, unavoidable. From business contacts to friendship to intimate love, relationships pervade our lives. We begin by being born into families where we learn the basics of communication in relationships. Babies learn, through nonverbal communication with their parents, that certain people are more important to their experience than others. Toddlers discover that developing more relationships makes life more interesting. Brothers, sisters, grandparents, and others provide social opportunities and stimulation.

Relationships also fulfill basic human needs. Simply communicating with others is not enough. We need to know that significant people share a future with us. We need companionship, love, and a sense of belonging. And we don't fulfill these needs in any one relationship. Instead, we often have several or many relationships that serve us differently. We may socialize with one friend and confide in another. And we fulfill others' needs as well. This is the reciprocal nature of relationships. As long as we are both having our needs met we can be quite satisfied with each other. However, as soon as one person starts to expect more than the other person is willing to give, or if one person feels she is giving more than she is receiving, then we have a "needs" imbalance and the relationship may suffer as a consequence.

ACTIVITY 8.1 Relationship Expectations Activity

PURPOSE

To enable you to explore the expectations that males and females have for relationships with one another.

PROCEDURE

1. Divide into same-sex small groups.
2. Each group should make a list of the expectations that they have for a relationship with the opposite sex.
3. Once this list is put together, the group should pick its top 5 expectations.
4. As a group, discuss what are you willing to do or give up to get these expectations met.
5. Next, each group should put together the list of expectations that they think the opposite sex has for them, and identify what they think will be the top 5 expectations that the opposite sex will have.

DISCUSSION

1. As a class, discuss each group's list of expectations, and what they would be willing to do or give up to achieve their expectations.
2. Compare your guesses about the opposite sex's expectations to the expectations identified by the opposite sex. How accurately did your group guess the expectations of the opposite sex?
3. How similar are the expectations that the two sexes have for one another?
4. How can all of these expectations affect initiating and maintaining a relationship?
5. With respect to expectations, what can you do to establish healthy and satisfactory relationships?

RELATIONSHIP STAGES

Effective relationships need to be carefully created and constructively maintained. The path a relationship takes does not happen by accident; we can exercise some degree of control by understanding how communication influences the development of relationships. According to researcher Mark Knapp in the book *Interpersonal Communication and Human Relationships*, relationships develop through the following 10 stages:

- **Initiating.** In this stage we want to create the impression that we are an interesting person worth knowing. At the same time we are evaluating the other individual's reaction to us. Initiating is often characterized by communication such as a handshake or "nice to meet you." If we are really interested in initiating a relationship, we often strategically plan our approach. Being "accidentally" in the same place as the same time, smiling, or nodding may gain us the entrance we desire.

- **Experimenting.** At this point we try to find things that we have in common with the other person. We often engage in "small talk." Now, you may be one of those people who find small talk to be superficial and useless, but at this early stage of a relationship it serves an important communication function. Besides finding out if we have anything in common, it helps us determine if we want to pursue the next step.

   For instance, Anthony had wanted to meet Brenda for a long time. When he finally got the courage to introduce himself, he suddenly started telling his life story, including some intimate details. When he asked her out to dinner, she turned him down. Little did he know that she was very uncomfortable with what he had told her. Brenda felt that Anthony was either insecure or moving "too fast!" Small talk would have broken the ice for Anthony and allowed the relationship to develop along a more natural path.

- **Intensifying.** At this point we begin to develop a relationship that will, hopefully, meet our needs. This stage is characterized by informal communication. We start referring to each other as "we" rather than "I" or "you." We begin disclosing more about ourselves as the potential for growth becomes obvious. It is here that we find the courage to start expressing our feelings about commitment. Sheri, a college student, stated in class, "I have a friendship that has become very important to me. Yesterday my friend told me that we're going to be friends forever! I can't tell you how nice it is to know I can count on her."

- **Integrating.** In this stage a relational identity is developed. We are recognized by others as a "couple," "partners," or "buddies." We begin interacting with each other based on this new identity called "us." For example, Matthew canceled an appointment so he could go to his girl friend's company picnic with her. When we integrate, we often make rational commitments rather than continue to follow our individual schedules.

- **Bonding.** Now we make our commitment known through public rituals. A wedding is an example of such a ritual. Research in psychology indicates that public commitments create in us a stronger desire to make the relationship work. We decide to let the "world" know that we are having a relationship.

- **Differentiating.** We reach a point where the relational identity may be too restricting and we want to re-establish our own identities. Often this is a reaction to conflict in the relationship.

For instance, a wife may stop referring to the family automobile as "our car" and start calling it "my car" in an effort to communicate her individuality. This doesn't mean that differentiation cannot have a positive outcome. Recognizing the other person's need for individuality and personal space can strengthen the original commitment to each other.

- *Circumscribing.* Hopefully all relationships will have happy endings, but we all know this is not realistic. At some point what we have with another person begins to deteriorate. The first stage of this disintegration is circumscribing, wherein we reduce the quantity or quality of time and energy we put into the relationship. For example, Tony and Sophie became a clear case of a relationship in this stage when they both started spending more time with other friends, avoiding each other's phone calls, and responding to each other by saying "you wouldn't be interested" or "it doesn't concern you." The sad part is that, while avoiding each other, we often avoid the fact that we are both contributing to the disintegration of what we called us.

- **Stagnation.** Here we really begin to live life in a rut! The relationship has no novelty or excitement and we react to it in a very routine way. Have you ever had a job that you disliked but you continued to perform? It becomes robotic, repetitive, and boring. The same thing happens to a relationship if we allow it to stagnate. We become the stereotypical picture of the old couple living in the same house and never speaking a word to each other.

- **Avoiding.** Stagnation may develop to the point that we cannot handle any contact with each other, so we go out of our way to avoid one another. For example, Angela, who dated Mario for two months, wanted so badly to avoid him that she dropped out of two classes that they attended together. Avoiding is a clear sign of the death of the relational identity. We no longer talk about "us"; rather we communicate in terms "you" or "me."

- **Terminating.** This is, of course, when one or both parties involved end the relationship can be brought on by the death of one of the individuals or a decision that staying together is no longer beneficial. This is one of the most difficult stages, for it can often be painful to the parties involved. How it occurs often depends on how intimate the relationship was. A casual friendship may end, but a marriage or cutting the ties with a family member may take more negotiation and expressing of feelings.

Most communication researchers agree that all relationships follow a systematic development. However, that doesn't mean that every time we get involved with someone it is destined for termination. What is important is that we discover how to stop the pattern when we've reached a stage where both participants are happy, and maintain the relationship at that level.

ACTIVITY 8.2 Figuring Out Who to Talk To

PURPOSE

To learn to identify nonverbal signals that tell us if a person is willing
to have a conversation.

PROCEDURE

1. For three days observe people you do not know but to whom you are attracted (as a possible friend or love interest).
2. Identify nonverbal signals that communicate to you whether a person is approachable or not (state specifically what the person is doing that makes you feel this way).
3. Describe the communication behavior below.

Not Approachable	Approachable
1.	1.
2.	2.
3.	3.
4.	4.
5.	5.
6.	6.
7.	7.

DISCUSSION

1. What did the "approachable" people do that made you feel this way? The "unapproachable?"
2. Which person seemed to be the most approachable, and why?
3. Which person seemed to be the most unapproachable, and why?
4. How approachable do you think other people perceive you, and why?
5. How will these observations help you in your future relationships?

ACTIVITY 8.3 The Art of Small Talk

PURPOSE

To examine the value of small talk as a way to initiate communication in a new relationship.

PROCEDURE

1. Select someone you do not know very well and initiate a conversation on one of the following topics: the weather, your favorite foods or hobbies, your jobs, a TV program or movie you've recently seen, a current news event, or the surrounding environment.

2. Carry on the conversation for at least 15 minutes, changing subjects if necessary to maintain dialogue.

DISCUSSION

1. How comfortable/uncomfortable were you using small talk?
2. Did small talk help you find areas of common interest?
3. Did small talk lead to any in-depth conversation? Explain.
4. How can small talk help you start a relationship with someone you're interested in?
5. How can small talk be used in your current significant relationships?

OVERCOMING BARRIERS TO DEVELOPING RELATIONSHIPS

Initiating Relationships

There are many barriers to maintaining good communication in a relationship. However, the first major barrier is how to begin a relationship, how to initiate contact. We have probably all experienced the desire to meet someone and the uncertainty about how to go about communicating with them. Regardless of the kind of relationship we're interested in establishing (we may want a new friend or a new love), we face the barriers of overcoming our own shyness, having our advances rejected, and taking the risk of putting ourselves on the line. But if a relationship is going to exist, someone has to make the first move.

Arthur Wassmer, in his book *Making Contact*, recommends the SOFTENS Techniques to help make the initial contact more productive. He uses each letter of the word "softens" to represent nonverbal behaviors that we can use when breaking the ice with someone new. Taking these nonverbal signals into consideration can help us overcome the fear we often feel on the initial contact. The technique is as follows:

- Smiling—genuinely done, helps establish a positive climate
- Open posture—communicates interest
- Forward lean—communicates involvement
- Touching by shaking hands—establishes physical contact

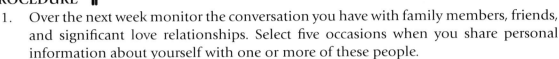

ACTIVITY 8.4 Sharing Yourself—More In-Depth Conversations

PURPOSE
To explore the value of sharing personal information as a means of encouraging in-depth conversation.

PROCEDURE
1. Over the next week monitor the conversation you have with family members, friends, and significant love relationships. Select five occasions when you share personal information about yourself with one or more of these people.
2. If you do not normally share personal information, then select five opportunities to do so.
3. For each occasion, describe the following:
   a. My partner was:
   b. The information I shared was:
   c. His/her response was:

DISCUSSION
1. Did the personal information encourage more conversation? Why or why not?
2. How did the person respond? How did you feel about his/her response?
3. How can sharing personal information enhance your relationships?

- Eye contact—communicates interest and listening, and builds rapport
- Nodding—communicates listening and can help you focus on what the other person is saying
- Space—can promote closeness depending on culture and the kind of relationship you want to encourage

Maintaining a Relationship

The second barrier we face is communicating within the relationship in such a manner that we maintain the relationship. The more intimate the relationship is, the more complex it may become to maintain, whether it is with a family member, a friend, or a lover. Intimacy, whether physical, emotional, or intellectual, can enhance the relationship by allowing two people to bond to each other through this closeness, or it can drive them a-part if-one or the other is not ready or prepared to maturely deal with the intimacy.

Intimacy involves vulnerability and therefore requires trust in each other. If we feel like we are being manipulated or played with, we often find it difficult to be intimate with someone. This can happen when we encounter "control factors." Control factors are any issues in a relationship that cause one or more participants to feel a lack of balance in the relationship. In other words, these factors set things out of control. Several major communication control factors that surface in many relationships are:

- Unequal participation. Teresa feels she puts out a lot more effort in the marriage than her husband, Chris. She is feeling very dissatisfied with this imbalance and wants him to contribute his share to the relationship.
- Simultaneous Relationships. Rod and Mike have been friends for a long time. Recently, Mike became involved in a club at school and has been spending a lot less time with Rod. Rod, who has no interest in the club's activities, has made a request for more of Mike's time. Mike feels a tremendous imbalance. He wants to see Rod, but also continue developing his new relationships. He feels like he's doing a juggling act with friends.
- Incompatibility. Jennifer and Troy are very attracted to each other. They feel there is a real chemistry between them. However, as they start to spend time together, they find they have little in common. They want to see each other because of the interpersonal attraction, but when together, they have a tendency to argue over opposing viewpoints. They want to resolve this imbalance but don't know how.
- Game Playing. Matt feels confused about his relationship with his father. They can be getting along one day, but the next day his father is putting "some guilt trip on me." He would like to spend more time at home but the emotional "yo-yo" is getting to be more than he can handle.
- Control. Jesse is realizing that she is tired of being considered a "little girl" by her parents. Granted, they controlled her life when she was small, but she wants to make her own decisions now. She does not want the scales to lean go heavily in her parents' favor.

In each of these situations, the individuals involved feel an imbalance in their relationships. Each one has a choice: they can continue to feel the lack of satisfaction, they can reduce the amount of involvement in the relationship, or they can try to resolve the conflict by communicating with their partners about the factor causing the problem. The last option is necessary if the relationships are going to be maintained at a positive stage. But this step also requires willingness to self-disclose feelings in an honest and supportive fashion. If they are willing to take the risk of disclosure, then they have the chance to bring balance back to the relationship.

But disclosure must be given in appropriate amounts. We can overwhelm another person with our inner feelings and literally chase them away. If handled sensitively, self-disclosure has two benefits for relationships: it encourages reciprocal disclosure (I will be more motivated to share if you are equally willing), and it can increase the intimacy of the relationship.

Lastly, it is important to be aware of the influence self-disclosure has in our lives. It is not only important in maintaining healthy relationships, but it is also one of the first things to diminish as the relationship begins to deteriorate. Relationships that are stagnating are often characterized by a lack of disclosure—the individuals just won't share!

Ending a Relationship

The last barrier we'll address here deals with ending a relationship. For most of us this is one of the most difficult communication situations. Few of us want to play the "bad guy." Yet, if our partner is the one ending the relationship, we may suffer feelings of rejection and a loss of self-esteem. It is very rare to have an outcome where both parties are happy; however, this can happen. For example, Raul was tired of his girl friend, Janie, playing games; Janie was fed up with Raul continually trying to control her time. So they mutually agreed to call it quits and both were happy.

Most of us, however, suffer a feeling of loss when we lose relationships, whether they be through the death of a family member or the breakup of a love relationship. We are literally in mourning for the relational identity, that element that was composed of ourselves and another. We not only miss the other person but we miss that identity that was "us." As in any mourning situation, acknowledging our grief and allowing it to run its course is one of the best treatments to the pain of an ended relationship.

Knowing why we need relationships in our lives helps us understand the way we communicate within them. We are striving to start and maintain them, but sometimes find ourselves in one that is ending. Relationships, like life, work in a cycle. And, like life, how much we gain from them. The activities in this Chapter are designed to help you determine the kind of relationships you want and how to improve the ones you are currently involved in, and aid you in acquiring the skills to start new ones. With this information you will, hopefully, never find yourself alone in the world."

ENDNOTES

1 From *Communicate! A Workbook for Interpersonal Communication*, 7th Edition, by Communication Research Associates. Copyright © 2004 by Kendall Hunt Publishing Company. Reprinted by permission.

CHAPTER 9

Relationship Challenges

STUDENT LEARNING OUTCOMES

Critical Thinking			Communication			Team Work		Social Responsibility	Personal Responsibility	Activity Measured
Creative Thinking/ Innovative	Analysis & Evaluation	Synthesis of Information	Writing	Visual	Oral	Differing Viewpoints	Work with Others	Intercultural Competence	Ethical Decision Making	Activity
X	X		X	X	X		X			9.0
X	X	X	X		X					9.1
X	X		X							9.2
X		X	X	X	X					9.3

As we experience the different stages of relationships, we may also face challenges that relationships may have. The relationship challenges may consist of lying, jealousy, stalking, and being obsessed. These are a few challenges which are also called the *"dark side"*. The next section will focus on recognizing the dark side of communication and to understand the motivation behind the behaviors.

"ACTIVITY 9.1 Relationship Expectations Activity[1]

PURPOSE

To enable you to explore the expectations that males and females have for relationships with one another.

PROCEDURE

1. Divide into same-sex small groups.
2. Each group should make a list of the expectations that they have for a relationship with the opposite sex.
3. Once this list is put together, the group should pick its top 5 expectations.
4. As a group, discuss what are you willing to do or give up to get these expectations met.
5. Next, each group should put together the list of expectations that they think the opposite sex has for them, and identify what they think will be the top 5 expectations that the opposite sex will have.

DISCUSSION

1. As a class, discuss each group's list of expectations, and what they would be willing to do or give up to achieve their expectations.
2. Compare your guesses about the opposite sex's expectations to the expectations identified by the opposite sex. How accurately did your group guess the expectations of the opposite sex?
3. How similar are the expectations that the two sexes have for one another?
4. How can all of these expectations affect initiating and maintaining a relationship?
5. With respect to expectations, what can you do to establish healthy and satisfactory relationships?

ACTIVITY 9.2 Relationship Roles

PURPOSE

To examine the different purposes that different significant relationships serve in our lives.

PROCEDURE

1. For each situation below, list three people whom you would select to meet the situation.
2. List these people in the order of whom you would call on first, second, and third.
3. Explain why you picked each person.

SITUATION

You are stranded 200 miles from home and need someone to drive your brand new sports car to you. Whom would you ask?

Person   **Reason**

1.

2.

3.

SITUATION

You are going out of town for two weeks and need someone to stay at your house and take care of your pets. Whom would you ask?

Person   **Reason**

1.

2.

3.

SITUATION

You have been offered another job and feel very uncertain about taking it. With whom would you discuss this offer?

Person   **Reason**

1.

2.

3.

SITUATION

You just broke up with a person whom none of your friends or family likes very well. With whom would you share the news?

Person   **Reason**

1.

2.

3.

SITUATION

You have just been informed that you are the winner of the Readers' Digest Sweepstakes. Whom would you tell?

Person   **Reason**

1.

2.

3.

DISCUSSION

1. Was it difficult selecting people for any of the situations? Why or why not?
2. How does the situation change the way we communicate with others?
3. What did you learn about these relationships and the roles they play in your life?"

"THE DARK SIDE[2]

The dark side of communication is defined as, "an integrative metaphor for a certain perspective toward the study of human folly, frailty and fallibility" (Cupach and Spitzberg 1994, 240). Some examples of dark communication that have been studied are: deception or lying, conflict, jealousy, intentionally hurtful messages, relationship termination, embarrassment, loneliness, co-dependency, and obsession, or stalking (Spitzberg 2006). This section recognizes that interpersonal relationships are abuse power, and cheat in all types of relationships.

The goal of this chapter is to recognize the dark side of communication and to understand the motivation behind these behaviors. Although we cannot possibly attempt to discuss all of the communication behaviors that have been identified as potentially negative or dark, we have selected a few which most students in interpersonal communication are likely to encounter. Specifically, we will explore the how and why individuals in romantic or platonic relationships deceive each other, become jealous, deal with social embarrassment, engage in aggressive behavior, and abuse relationships. Further, we will discuss the role that dark communication plays in online interactions. To assist you in understanding how these concepts have been examined, we will discuss various studies that provide a clearer picture of these destructive forms of communicating. We will also provide suggestions on how to cope if you encounter these circumstances.

DECEPTION AND INTERPERSONAL RELATIONSHIPS

In 2004, a study conducted by Britain's *That's Life!* magazine examined the prevalence of lies in relationships. The magazine surveyed 5,000 women and discovered that ninety-four percent of them admitted to lying. While thirty-four percent of them reported that they tell "white lies" daily, seventy-six percent of the women revealed to researchers that they have told life-changing lies (Knox, Schact, Holt, and Turner 1993). While your initial reaction may be one of shock at the high percentage of women who admitted to lying, stop for a minute and recall the last time that you failed to tell the complete and honest truth. Perhaps your significant other asked what you thought about a meal he had cooked or how she looked in an outfit. Or maybe you lied to your boss about why you called off work or needed to switch shifts. What do we lie about? Most people admit to lying about everything from what they ate for breakfast to why they were late for work. Married couples may even lie to one another about their finances. In 2006, the *New Zealand Herald* reported results of a poll taken by a bank which discovered that forty-two percent of women and thirty-five percent of men lie to their partners about their financial situation. **Deception** is defined as, "a message knowingly transmitted by a sender to foster a false belief or conclusion by a receiver" (Buller and Burgoon, 1996, 209). While we would like to believe that our relationships are built on truth and honesty, the reality is that friends, family members, and romantic partners deceive each other from time to time. Consider this scenario:

Jack has been in love with Shawna since their freshman year of college. He was always extremely nervous about speaking with her and he came to terms with the fact that they would probably never be together. In the meantime, Jack started dating Shawna's roommate, Tina. After three months, Jack really started to fall for Tina. One evening, Shawna asked Jack for a ride to the library. He agreed. In the car, Shawna started expressing feelings for Jack. Jack was stunned. He just could not believe that this day had come. His heart raced as he tried to think of an appropriate reply. However, out of respect to his relationship with Tina, he reluctantly told Shawna that he did not have feelings for her.

In this example, Jack protects his current relationship with Tina by deceiving Shawna about his true feelings. Of course, we know that not all deception is done with such honorable intentions. David Buller and Judee Burgoon (1996) proposed **Interpersonal Deception Theory** (IDT) to explain the strategic choices made when engaging in deceptive communication (1996). While a person may attempt to be strategic in creating a deceptive message, there are cues that alert the other person that the individual is being less than honest. At the same time, the receiver of the message attempts to mask, or hide, his knowledge of the deception. Rather than directly accuse the person who is lying, the person may nod their head, offer verbal prompts ("I see!" or "So what else happened?"), and generally behave in ways designed to keep the source from seeing his suspicion. In essence, it is a back-and-forth game between relational partners. The source tries to mask the deception and the receiver tries to hide his suspicion of the deception. Now, consider this example:

Julie and Robbie have been dating for two years. During the fall semester of their junior year, Julie decided to study abroad in Scotland. Although, Robbie was not happy that Julie was leaving, he was excited for her. At first, Julie was extremely homesick and spoke with Robbie every evening. As time passed, she met several new friends in Scotland and enjoyed going out dancing every night. Some evenings she had a little too much to drink and would end up kissing other men on the dance floor. Robbie continued to call Julie each night. He was becoming increasingly suspicious of Julie's behavior abroad. One evening he asked Julie, "Have you been with anyone since you have been there?"

There are three potentially deceptive responses that Julie can give. She can tell an outright lie or resort to **falsification**: "No, I have been completely faithful." Oftentimes this requires the source to create a fictional story to explain the lie. Alternatively, Julie might partially tell the truth while leaving out important details. This refers to **concealment**: "Well, when I go out I do dance with other guys." We typically do this when we want to hide a secret. Or Julie could engage in **equivocation,** or be strategically vague: "Just because I go out dancing does not necessarily mean I have to hook up with someone." This type of response is used to avoid the issue altogether.

In addition to managing the deceptive responses discussed previously (falsification, concealment, equivocation), Interpersonal Deception Theory also suggests that deceivers manipulate their verbal and nonverbal behavior to appear more credible (Burgoon et al. 1996). This manipulation is accomplished by varying the message along five fundamental dimensions.

Completeness

First, deceivers may vary on the **completeness** or extent of message details. The deceiver knows that an appropriate amount of information needs to be provided in order to be perceived truthful by the receiver. The more practiced deceiver also realizes that specific details are probably best kept to a minimum; there is less for the receiver to challenge. When interpreting the completeness of a message, receivers may become suspicious if the information provided is too brief or vague.

Relevance/Directness

A second fundamental dimension on which deceptive messages are manipulated is its **relevance** or **directness**. This refers to the extent to which the deceiver produces messages that are logical in flow and sequence, and are pertinent to the conversation. The more direct and relevant the message, the more it is perceived as truthful. Two indicators of potential deception are when a person goes off on a tangent in response to a question or is cautious in his or her response.

Clarity

The extent to which the deceiver is clear, comprehensible, and concise is a third dimension of message manipulation. The **clarity** dimension varies along a continuum from very clear to completely ambiguous. The more evasive or vague a message is, the more cause there is for a receiver to probe for additional information and clarification.

Personalization

A fourth dimension involves the **personalization** of the information. The extent to which the deceiver takes ownership of the information may vary. If the deceiver relies on verbal distancing or non-immediate communication, he will be perceived as less truthful. For example, the suggestions "everyone goes out during the week here" and "I just miss you so much that I am just trying to keep myself busy," are two examples that disassociate the deceiver with the behavior.

Veridicality

The last dimension is the extent to which the deceiver appears to be truthful, or the **veridicality** of the message. This dimension is twofold. First, the message is constructed based on the objective truth value reported by the source. In other words, to what extent does the deceiver believe the message is truthful? Next, the believability of the message is judged by the receiver. In evaluating the truthfulness of a message, receivers often rely on nonverbal cues that are the result of our body language. Examples of behaviors believed to signal deception include increased blinking, speech errors, higher voice pitch and enlarged pupils (Zuckerman and Driver 1985). Although these behaviors are believed to signal deception, there is no evidence that they help us discriminate between truth tellers and liars. Remembering back to our discussion of myths in Chapter Two, nonverbal cues are not good sources of information about whether someone is lying or not.

WHY DO WE LIE?

Based on the high percentage of people who report engaging in deception, the question becomes, why are we so prone to lying? When asked, most people suggest that they lie to make themselves appear more admirable. In Chapter Eight we discussed the role of physical attraction in initiating relationships. Thus, it comes as no surprise that one study revealed that we lie to attract an attractive date (Rowatt, Cunningham and Druen 1999). In the study, participants reported lying about their own personal attri-butes such as appearance, personality, income, career, grades and past relational outcomes in an attempt to attract another person. In fact, twenty-five percent of respondents indicated that they engage in this type of deception in initial encounters with someone they are attracted to.

People often tell lies to make themselves seem more attractive to someone new.

Consider the following conversation from the *Friends* episode "The One the Morning After." Ross debates whether he should be honest with Rachel about sleeping with another woman during the time that he and Rachel were apart.

Ross tells Chandler and Joey that Rachel wants to work on their relationship and worries about how she will react to hearing that he slept with another woman. They can't believe Ross is even considering telling Rachel about it . . . how stupid can he be?

But Ross believes that he needs to be completely honest with Rachel if there is any hope to rebuild their relationship. Joey agrees that being honest is best, as long as it doesn't cause any problems! And Chandler points out that it will only hurt Rachel. There won't be anything left to save if Ross tells her.

Ross still isn't completely convinced that he should keep quiet. Chandler concedes, saying that at least Ross should wait until the time is right to tell Rachel . . . and that would be when he's on his deathbed.

According to the deception literature, there are three types of lies that people tell (Camden, Motley, and Wilson 1984; DePaulo, Kashy, Kirkendale, Wyer, and Epstein 1996). These include lies to: (1) harm others, (2) protect self, and (3) spare others.

Lying to Harm Others

The first type of deceptions, lying to harm others, is often the most damaging type of lie in interpersonal relationships. These types of lies are done to intentionally hurt others by distorting information, fabricating stories, or deliberately omitting important information. Perhaps the best example of lies designed to harm others are those seen during political campaign ads. Specific information about one's opponent is strategically distorted and manipulated in an attempt to damage their candidacy.

Lying to Protect Self

A more egotistical goal refers to lying to protect self. The goal of this type of lie is to make oneself look good. This can be accomplished by exaggerating praise and/or omitting weaknesses. In a study that examined sexual lies among college students, lying about the number of previous sexual partners emerged as the most frequently told lie (Knox et al. 1993). Regardless of whether the number of sexual partners was inflated to appear more experienced, or reduced to appear more "pure," the goal of the lie was to enhance one's image.

Spare Others

The most common type of lie is to spare others. In the movie *A Few Good Men*, Jack Nicholson's character, Colonel Nathan R. Jessep, states, "You can't handle the truth." In this situation, Col. Jessep emphasizes that sometimes we lie in order to spare or protect others from the truth. Perhaps we want to avoid hurting the other person's feelings or damaging his self-esteem. At other times we may "stretch the truth" or omit details for the good of the relationship. Consider the earlier example of Ross' lie to Rachel. Joey and Chandler try to help justify the deception by pointing out that the truth would end up hurting Rachel and would eliminate any chance of a potential future together.

ARE THERE GOOD REASONS FOR LYING?

While the definition of deception indicates that a source intentionally designs the message with the goal of instilling a false belief in the receiver, it is important to take a step back and consider the potential benefits of deception in relationships (Knapp and Vangelisti 2006). Dan O'Hair and Michael Cody (1994) distinguish between positive or negative deceptive strategies. They suggest that strategies that enhance, escalate, repair, and improve relationships can be considered **positive relational deceptive strategies.** These include responses to the inevitable questions, "How do you like my new outfit?" or "What do you think of my new haircut?" In these situations we often respond with a white lie in order to foster liking, or positive affect. In other words, we are motivated to deceive to preserve the relationship, to avoid hurting the other person's feelings, to avoid a conflict, or even to protect a third party. In other instances, we may decide that the deception is not worth the risk. Consider the following example when it was determined that the potential consequences of deception outweighed the benefits. In the film *The Pursuit of Happyness*, Will Smith portrays a homeless man who is seeking an internship with a stock brokerage firm. After spending the night in jail for unpaid parking tickets, Smith rushes to his interview at Dean Witter. As he enters the room in a t-shirt and jeans spattered with paint, he says, "I've been sitting outside trying to think up a good story of why I would show up for such an important interview dressed like this. And I couldn't think of a good story. So I finally decided it was probably best to just tell the truth." In the end, his character's honesty impresses the interviewers, and he is offered the internship.

DETECTING DECEPTION

Understanding the ways in which messages are manipulated is one way to enhance your ability to detect deception. Earlier we described some of the nonverbal cues associated with deception. But there are several verbal cues that can tip us off about lies as well. In a recent study on deceptive communication practices (Park et al. 2002), 202 college students were asked to recall a time when they had caught another person being deceptive. While a variety of discovery mechanisms were identified in the study, the three most prominent ones include the strategies labeled third party information, physical evidence, and confessions.

Have you ever lied about a friend's appearance to avoid hurt feelings?

© Simone van den Berg, 2007, Shutterstock.

Third-Party Information

Third-party information involves information being revealed by a person outside the relationship. Suppose a teenager wants to go to a party while his parents are out of town, but he knows his parents would not approve. He lies to his parents and tells them that he is spending the night at his friend's house in case they call home while he is at the party. When his mother speaks with the friend's mother a few days later and thanks her for allowing him to stay at their house, the friend's mother reveals that he never spent the night. Thus the lie is revealed by an outside party.

Physical Evidence

Sometimes we are able to detect deception by doing our best Sherlock Holmes impression and looking for physical evidence. For instance, on an episode of *Grey's Anatomy*, Addison, Dr. Shepherd's wife, discovered a pair of black panties that clearly did not belong to her in her husband's tuxedo pocket. The physical evidence swiftly revealed Derek's betrayal and finally ended the fragile marriage. The classic lipstick-on-the-collar shtick is another familiar Hollywood portrayal of deception detection.

Confessions

Another method by which deception is detected is via confessions made by the deceiver. **Solicited confessions** are often offered as the result of direct questioning or confrontation. Suppose you heard that your best friend went on a ski trip with a group of people the same weekend that the two of you had planned to go to a professional hockey game. Initially, he told you that he could not go to the game because he was swamped with homework. When you follow up and tell him that you heard he had gone skiing that same weekend, he feels guilty and confesses his lie. While some confessions are solicited, at other times these declarations come from out of the blue. Suppose your significant other spontaneously confesses that she has been reading your emails without your knowledge. Nothing caused you to suspect that she was engaging in this behavior, yet she decided to make an **unsolicited confession.** An important point to note is that we are often able to detect deception using a combination of cues—in fact, many people report a combination of verbal and nonverbal signals as tipping them off about dishonesty.

TO LIE OR NOT TO LIE: THAT IS THE QUESTION

Deception and lying are multidimensional constructs. Key components to consider when analyzing a deceptive message include: the importance of the relationship, the importance of the information to the relationship, and the costs and rewards associated with the lie. When deciding whether it is to your benefit to tell a lie, consider the following three sets of questions posed by Knapp and Vangelisti (2006):

1. What is the potential outcome of the lie? Can it potentially benefit our relationship, or one of us, individually?

2. Based on the rules we have established for our relationship, is it reasonable and just for me to tell a lie? Or am I violating one of the spoken or unspoken expectancies that we have for our relationship? What lies would we agree upon that are acceptable versus unacceptable?

3. Am I telling a lie in an attempt to protect my partner from being harmed? If I were to be caught telling the lie, would my partner understand my justification for telling the lie?

What is the most important determinant in ending a relationship as a result of deception? Knapp and Vangelisti (2006) state that the more importance the receiver attaches to the information being lied about, the greater the chance that he or she will decide to end the relationship.

Now that you have a better understanding of the concept of deception and of the reasons why people lie, it is our hope that you will be strategic in your analysis of the appropriateness of deceptive messages.

EMBARRASSMENT: WHY DID I SAY THAT?

Can you remember a time when you had a huge crush on someone, and when you finally had the opportunity to talk to them and make that great first impression, something went horribly wrong and you ended up putting your foot in your mouth? Or have you ever told a joke at a party and nobody laughed? In these types of situations, we often experience social embarrassment. Recall our discussion in Chapter Three regarding the role of self-presentation in relationships. When we perceive that our self-esteem has been threatened or if we have presented what we perceive to be a negative view of the self to others, **embarrassment** occurs. Our sense of identity is at stake if the response to our behavior is not what we expected. Gross and Stone (1964) proposed that embarrassment emerges as the result of three factors that occur in social interactions. First, misrepresentations or cognitive shortcomings may cause us to feel embarrassment. Have you ever called someone by the wrong name or forgotten how you know someone? Losing confidence in our role or ability in a social situation can also cause us to experience discomfort. Sometimes we script out an interaction, such as the all-important first phone call to an attractive person, and the conversation does not turn out like we had anticipated. Finally, a loss of dignity, or composure, can cause us to become "red-faced." Examples of this may include tripping as you are making your big entrance into the campus hangout, or discovering that your pants are unzipped after you have just had a conversation with your boss.

Our Role in Embarrassment

It is easy to see why we would be embarrassed in any of these situations, even as we were in control of our own behavior. We can just as easily become uncomfortable in those situations where we are the silent observer. Sattler (1965) identified three roles that exist in embarrassing social situations: agent, recipient, and observer. As an **agent,** we are responsible for our own embarrassment, perhaps by accidentally swearing in front of your grandmother or unexpectedly burping during an important interview lunch. In other situations, we are the **recipients,** or targets, of embarrassing communication. Examples of this type of embarrassment might include your best friend revealing to your secret crush that you are attracted to him and your mother telling your friend about the time you ran naked around the neighborhood when you were three years old. Finally, it is likely that you can recall a situation where you were simply a bystander, or **observer,** of another's embarrassment and experienced feelings of discomfort yourself. In these situations, we often offer an awkward comment, express a reassuring remark, or simply attempt to ignore the situation.

Responding to Embarrassment

Building on Goffman's theory of face-saving and identity management, Edelmann (1985) identified three primary types of messages individuals use in response to embarrassing encounters. These include accounts, apologies, and jokes. **Accounts** provide a potential explanation for the cause of the embarrassing situation. Suppose you arrive at class only to discover that you forgot an important assignment that was due. You decide to speak with your instructor and explain that you have been overwhelmed with group projects in two other classes and with searching for a job. In some instances, we may feel the need to apologize for the embarrassing behavior. **Apologies** are attempts to identify the source of blame for the incident. Suppose you accidentally revealed to your friend that she has not been included in the group's plans for the weekend. As you stumble over your words, you might comment, "I'm sorry. I didn't realize until now that you weren't invited," or "I didn't make the plans. They invited me along and I just assumed you were included." These responses are made with the hope that your friend will forgive you for the non-invitation. **Joking** involves using humor to create a more light-hearted response to a situation. At the 2006 Academy Awards, Jennifer Garner tripped over her dress as she approached the podium. To cover her embarrassment, she joked, "I do all my own stunts." According to arousal relief theory (Berylne 1969), use of humor in embarrassing or difficult situations often evokes positive affective responses which can help individuals diffuse anxiety or stress.

The next time that you find yourself becoming embarrassed in a social situation, remember—everyone experiences this discomfort at one time or another. While at the time it may appear to be a black cloud that hangs over your head, it is likely that these feelings will be temporary and short-lived. However, there are other dark aspects of interpersonal communication whose impact may not be so minimal on our interactions and relationships.

JEALOUSY IN INTERPERSONAL RELATIONSHIPS

Another aspect of interpersonal relationships that has received a lot of attention in the literature is jealousy. Chances are that you have heard jealousy described as the "green-eyed monster." In the movie *Terms of Endearment*, a mother's jealousy over her daughter's relationships wreaks havoc in their own relationship. Jealousy causes us to experience a variety of emotions and sometimes causes us to communicate or react in ways that we normally would not. Consider some of the things that can cause us to experience jealousy:

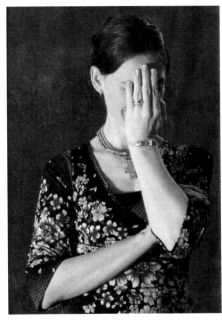

Sometimes one embarrassing moment seems like it will last forever.

- Your best friend recently went away to college. He sends you text messages describing all the fun he is having with his new roommate and other friends he has made in the dorm.

- A co-worker talks about all the activities that she does with her young children. You wonder how she is able to find the time to finish her work and spend so much time with her kids, especially because you see yourself as a neglectful parent.

- Your relationship partner has been spending a great deal of time lately with a new friend and has expressed repeatedly how much he likes this friend.

In situations like those described in the scenarios above, it is normal to experience feelings of anger or sadness. Maybe we even feel a little bit envious or resentful. **Jealousy** has been defined as, "a protective reaction to a perceived threat to a valued relationship, arising from a situation in which the partner's involvement with an activity and/or another person is contrary to the jealous person's definition of their relationship" (Hansen 1985, 713). It is important to point out that this definition addresses the fact that jealousy can be experienced in various types of relationships, not just romantic, and can be induced by various issues or situations.

Types of Jealousy in Relationships

Jennifer Bevan and Wendy Samter (2004) used this definition as the foundation for their study, which examined six different types of jealousy, three that are experienced as a result of the type of the relationship, and three that are based on the issues experienced between partners. The types identified in this study include: (1) friend jealousy, (2) family jealousy, (3) romantic jealousy, (4) power jealousy, (5) intimacy jealousy, and (6) activity jealousy. The first two types, **friend jealousy** and **family jealousy,** are typically the result of an individual's relationship with another friend or family member. In this situation, we often become frustrated and perceive them as being "taken" away from us. **Romantic jealousy** is also the result of a partner's relationship with another person, and is associated with perceived intimacy between two people. Consider the following example:

> Justin noticed that his wife, Nicole, had been spending more and more time at work. One evening, he decided to surprise her by taking dinner to her office. As he approached her office, he noticed that she was engrossed in a quiet conversation with an attractive man. Angry, Justin stormed out of the building without saying a word. For the next several days, Justin was very curt in his conversations with Nicole. Finally she asked him what was bothering him. Justin exploded, "So who is the new guy at work? And why didn't you tell me that you're spending so much time together?" Nicole was dumbfounded and responded, "I don't know what you're talking about." Justin mentioned that he had stopped by to bring her dinner and had seen them talking quietly in her office. Finally, Nicole understood who he was referring to and responded, "That was Marcus, the consultant who was brought in from Seattle to help with this project. He saw the picture of the kids on my desk and wanted to talk about how much he's missing his own kids since he's been away from them for the past two weeks."

In this scenario, romantic jealousy caused Justin to perceive a potential relationship between Nicole and her co-worker. It should come as no surprise that this type of jealousy has received the most attention in literature. Therefore, many of the studies discussed in this section will refer to romantic jealousy.

The last three types of jealousy examined by Bevan and Samter (2004) involve issues experienced by relational partners. **Power jealousy** is often associated with perceptions that a partner's other relationships or obligations are viewed as more important than your relationship with the person. If a friend changes plans and cannot spend time with you, or decides to invite others to go to the game with the two of you, you may question whether outside issues are more important to her than your relationship. **Activity jealousy** emerges when our relational partner dedicates time to various hobbies or interests. Have you ever become frustrated by the amount of attention that a friend dedicates to PlayStation, fraternity or sorority activities, or sports? In these instances, the activities are perceived as a threat to your relationship. Finally, **intimacy jealousy** is the result of the exchange of intimate or private information that a partner may share with a third party, someone not in the relationship. Suppose your significant other reveals to his best friend that he is undergoing a series of medical tests, but says nothing to you. Your discovery of the "concealed" information results in feelings of intimacy jealousy. Later, you may discover that your partner simply did not want you to worry, and decided not to tell you until the results of the test were returned.

Why Does Jealousy Occur?

What causes us to experience feelings of jealousy? Laura Guerrero and Peter Anderson (1998) suggest that there are at least six jealousy-related goals. An extensive body of research on this topic has concluded that individuals evoke or suppress feelings of jealousy to obtain a variety of goals or objectives in their personal relationships. In the next sections we examine the six jealousy-related goals identified by researchers.

An attempt to make yourself appear more "attractive" than the competition may just make you look insecure.

Maintain the Primary Relationship. First, we become jealous in situations where we wish to maintain the primary relationship. Specifically, we are concerned with preserving the relationship. When individuals are interested in maintaining a current relationship, they will often compare themselves to a rival and try to appear more rewarding to their partner by compensating for any perceived shortcomings (Guerrero and Afifi 1999). Making oneself appear more "attractive" than the competition (also referred to as **compensatory restoration**, see table 8.1) may be an effective maintenance strategy—up to a point. Making incessant comparisons to rivals may cause your partner to perceive you as being desperate or insecure.

Preserving One's Self-Esteem.   A second goal associated with jealousy is focused on preserving one's self-esteem. This jealousy goal is concerned with maintaining one's pride, and with feeling good about oneself. Individuals who are concerned about protecting their self-esteem rarely seek out circumstances that may threaten how they view themselves (Kernis 1995). Therefore, it comes as no surprise that the more an individual is focused on preserving his or her self-esteem, the more likely he or she is to avoid or deny jealous situations (Guerrero and Afifi 1999). Since jealousy has a negative connotation in our culture and is related to perceptions of "weakness," it makes sense that these individuals are less likely to question or scrutinize their partners' behavior or to communicate jealous feelings.

Reducing Uncertainty about the Relationship.   Another goal of jealousy is to reduce uncertainty about the relationship. The purpose of this type of jealousy is to help an individual learn where one stands in the relationship, predict the future of the relationship, and understand how the other partner perceives the relationship. This was the only goal found to predict open and non-aggressive communication between partners (Guerrero and Afifi 1999). If the purpose of jealousy is to reduce uncertainty and learn more about the partner, it makes sense that open and direct communication are essential to accomplishing this goal.

Reducing Uncertainty about a Rival Relationship. A fourth goal involves reducing uncertainty about a rival relationship. This jealousy goal determines the threat of the competition, or how serious the rival relationship is. Individuals who focus on this goal often resort to indirect strategies, such as spying, checking up on the partner, or questioning the rival about the situation (Guerrero and Afifi 1999). They may do this to save face with their partners so they are not perceived as "jealous" people.

Re-assess the Relationship. When individuals are questioning the status of a relationship, they may use jealousy in an attempt to re-assess the relationship. This goal is concerned with comparing the cost with the benefits associated with the relationship. When analyzing this goal, Guerero and Afifi (1999) found that individuals typically engage in indirect strategies such as avoidance, distancing, or making the partner feel jealous. When we are evaluating a relationship, we typically step back to reconsider our own perceptions of autonomy (see our discussion of the relationship stages of coming apart in Chapter Ten). Therefore, it may make sense to give the relationship space.

Restoring Equity through Retaliation. Do you know anyone who purposely evoked jealousy to get back at someone or to make his or her partner feel bad? The last goal of jealousy refers to this idea of restoring equity through retaliation. The purpose of evoking this type of jealousy response is to show the partner what it is like to experience negative emotions and to hurt the person as retribution for something the partner has done.

There are clearly a number of different reasons that relationship partners attempt to evoke jealousy responses from their partners. Not surprisingly, experiencing heightened amounts of jealousy in relationships negatively affects relationship satisfaction (Guerrero and Eloy 1992). Thus, it is important for you to understand the reasons why we evoke feelings of jealousy in others and, at the same time, to refrain from using tactics or strategies that cause others to feel jealous.

Characteristics Associated with Jealousy

Researchers have examined many questions associated with jealousy, including: How does someone become jealous? What types of relationships are more likely to evoke jealousy? What are the results of feeling jealous? Studies have revealed that psychological predictors of jealousy are low levels of self-esteem and feelings of insecurity (Mcintosh 1989). Another study found that jealousy is more likely to occur in relationships of shorter duration (for less than one year) than in those of longer duration (more than one year) (Knox, Zusman, Mabon, and Shriver 1999). What conditions are most likely to elicit jealous reactions? A 1999 study (Knox et al.) found that talking to or about a previous partner is the action or topic that is most likely to evoke jealousy.

Gender Differences and Jealousy

Studies have found no significant differences between males and females with regard to one gender being more likely to emerge as a primary source of jealousy (Knox, Zusman, Mabon, and Shriver

1999). Further, no significant sex differences have been found with regard to the frequency, duration, or intensity of jealousy (Pines and Friedman 1998). However, while males and females do not necessarily differ in their amount of expressed jealousy, research has shown that they do experience jealousy for different reasons, or as the result of the specific characteristics associated with the threat. For example, males are more likely to become jealous as a result of sexual infidelity, whereas females become more jealous over emotional infidelity (Buss et al. 1992). Recent studies have found that, regardless of biological sex, the reactions to different types of jealousy are similar for males and females (Dijkstar and Buunk 2004). That is, emotional infidelity typically evoked responses of anxiety, worry, distrust, and suspicion, while responses to sexual infidelity were associated with feelings of sadness, rejection, anger, and betrayal. The physical or social attractiveness of the perceived competition also plays a role in determining the amount of jealousy experienced. Women experience more jealousy in response to a physically attractive threat, while men become more jealous when the threat is perceived as being more socially dominant (Dijkstra and Buunk 1998). Evolutionary psychologists argue the reason for this

The attractiveness of perceived competition plays a role in determining the amount of jealousy experienced.

gender difference is due to the fact that our society typically rates a female's value in a relationship as determined by her physical attractiveness, whereas the relationship value of males is often evaluated by their status or dominance (Townsend and Levy 1990).

Coping with Jealousy

The way people initially express feelings of jealousy to a partner will ultimately influence how the partner responds. Stephen Yoshimura (2004) found that responses such as integrative communication and negative affect expression (e.g., crying) were perceived as evoking positive emotional responses by the partner (see Table 9.1). In other words, expressing your feelings openly and directly with your partner and appearing hurt by the threat produces positive emotional and behavior outcomes. This same study also found that negative emotional outcomes were more likely to produce violent behavior and manipulation attempts by the other partner. See Table 9.1 for a complete list of the ways people respond to feelings of jealousy.

While we have explored some of the reasons for becoming jealous and have proposed some methods for managing situations that cause the green-eyed monster to emerge, let us take a moment to consider the role that perceived influence and power can play in causing us to experience envy.

Table 9.1 – Communicative Responses to Jealousy

Strategy	Definition/Examples
1. Negative affect expression	Nonverbal expressions of jealousy-related affect that the partner can see. *Examples:* acting anxious when with the partner, appearing hurt, wearing "displeasure" on face, crying in front of the partner
2. Integrative communication	Direct, nonaggressive communication about jealousy with the partner. *Examples:* disclosing jealous feelings to the partner, asking the partner probing questions, trying to reach an understanding with the partner, reassuring the partner that we can "work it out"
3. Distributive communication	Direct, aggressive communication about jealousy with the partner. *Examples:* accusing the partner of being unfaithful, being sarcastic or rude toward the partner, arguing with the partner, bringing up the issue over and over again to "bombard" the partner
4. Active distancing	Indirect, aggressive means of communicating jealousy to the partner. *Examples:* giving the partner the "silent treatment," storming out of the room, giving the partner cold or dirty looks, withdrawing affection and sexual favors
5. Avoidance/denial	Indirect, nonagressive communication that focuses on avoiding the jealousy-invoking issue, situation, or partner. *Examples:* denying jealous feelings when confronted by the partner, pretending to be unaffected by the situation, decreasing contact with the partner, avoiding jealousy-evoking situations
6. Violent communication/threats	Threatening or actually engaging in physical violence against the partner. *Examples:* threatening to harm the partner if they continue to see the rival, scaring the partner by acting as if they were about to hit the partner, roughly pulling the partner away from the rival, pushing or slapping the partner
7. Signs of possession	Publicly displaying the relationship to others so they know the partner is "taken." *Examples:* putting an arm around the partner and saying "he or she is taken," constantly introducing the partner as a "girl/boy friend," telling potential rival of plans to be married, kissing the partner in front of potential rival
8. Derogating competitors	Making negative comments about potential rivals to the partner and to others. *Examples:* "bad mouthing" the rival in front of the partner and his or her friends, expressing disbelief that anyone would be attracted to the rival
9. Relationship threats	Threatening to terminate or de-escalate the primary relationship or to be unfaithful. *Examples:* threatening to end the relationship if the partner continues to see the rival, threatening infidelity
10. Surveillance/restriction	Behavioral strategies designed to find out about or interfere with the rival relationship. *Examples:* spying or checking up on the partner, looking through the partner's belongings for evidence of a rival relationship, pressing the redial button to see who the partner called last, restricting the partner's access to rivals at parties
11. Compensatory restoration	Behavior aimed at improving the primary relationship and/or making oneself more desirable. *Examples:* sending the partner gifts or flowers, keeping the house cleaned and nice, trying to present oneself as better than the rival, trying to appear more physically attractive
12. Manipulation attempts	Moves to induce negative feelings in the partner and/or shift responsibility for communicating about the problem to the partner. *Examples:* flirting with others to make the partner jealous, inducing guilt, calling the partner's "bluff" by daring him to break-up and go off with the rival, bring the rival's name up in conversation to check for a reaction, asking a friend to talk to the partner about the situation

Table 9.1 – Communicative Responses to Jealousy, continued...

Strategy	Definition/Examples
13. Rival contacts	Direct communication with the rival about the jealousy situation, rival relationship, or partner. *Examples:* telling the rival to stop seeing the partner, informing the rival that the partner is "already in a relationship," saying something "mean" to the rival, asking the rival about the relationship without revealing one's identity, making negative comments about the partner in order to discourage the rival from pursuing the partner
14. Violent behavior	Directing violence toward objects, either in private or in the presence of others. *Examples:* slamming doors, breaking dishes, throwing the partner's possessions

Source: Adapted from Guerrero and Anderson 1998; Guerrero, Anderson, Jorgensen, Spitzberg, and Eloy 1995.

INTERPERSONAL POWER AND AGGRESSION

A possible factor contributing to our tendency to encounter jealousy in relationships may be explained by the interpersonal power perceived by relational partners. In this section, we will take a closer look at the potential implications of power in relationships and explore power's relationship to verbal aggression and violence. **Power** can be defined as one's ability to influence others to behave in ways they normally might not. Popular television shows such as *Super Nanny* and *Nanny 911* often identify power as the key issue affecting families. What types of power impact our relationships with others?

In the role of a parent, one holds legitimate power in the relationship.

Types of Power

French and Raven (1960) identified five types of power that individuals typically use when they are attempting to influence others. The five classic power bases are explained below.

Reward Power.   **Reward power** is based on a person's perception that the source of power can provide rewards. Example: I'll clean up the apartment and maybe my roommate will invite me to go with him on the ski trip with his family this weekend.

Coercive Power.   **Coercive power** focuses on the perceived ability of the source to punish or to enact negative consequences. Example: I have to finish this report today or I know my boss will make me come in this weekend.

Legitimate Power.   Legitimate power is centered on the perception that the source has authority because of a particular role that she plays in the relationship or a title that she holds. Example: Because I'm the mommy, and I said so.

Referent Power. Referent power is based on a person's respect, identification and attraction to the source. Example: No matter how ridiculous I feel, I will dress up in a costume and go to this Halloween party because I am really attracted to you and want you to like me.

Expert Power. Expert power is grounded in the perception that the source possesses knowledge, expertise, or skills in a particular area. Example: I will listen to what she says about our household budget because she is the financial wizard in the family.

French and Raven propose that it is the perception of the receiver of the message that is the key to analyzing power. Consider our earlier discussions about interpersonal communication in Chapter Two. In that discussion we noted that it is important to consider the receiver's perception of the source to predict future interactions. But do individuals have power if we do not give it to them? Based on the important role that receiver perception plays in the communication process, probably not. Consider the following scenario:

> Alan had very little respect for his mother. At thirteen years old, he was completely out of control. He skipped school, ignored his mother's rules, and even hit his mother on several occasions when she attempted to discipline him. Finally, his mother had reached the breaking point. One night she caught Alan doing drugs with his friends in the basement. She reported Alan to the authorities and hoped that it would help him get back on track. But his misbehavior continued.

In this instance, Alan's mother should have legitimate power over him. However, his behavior is an obvious indicator that he does not perceive her to have any power in the relationship. Even when his mother attempts to utilize coercive power by calling the police, it does nothing to change Alan's perception. His inability to view his mother as having reward, coercive, or legitimate power even results in Alan's occasional use of physical violence. If you do not perceive your relational partner as having the power, then it is unlikely that you would comply with any requests he or she makes.

In Chapter Eight we discussed the role of attraction in interpersonal relationships. Understanding the relationship between attraction and power may help explain why some influence attempts are successful whereas others fail. Depending on the perceived power base, receivers will alter their perceptions of the source's attractiveness and determine the level of acceptance or resis-tance in response to the request. Suppose your best friend uses a threat, or coercive power, in an attempt to influence you. This will typically decrease your level of perceived attraction for your friend, and chances are that you will resist their request. On the other hand, if you perceive that the friend has the power to reward you as a result of the request, it is likely that you would find them more attractive and would have minimal resistance to the request. These same principles can be applied in a variety of relationships. What if your mother told you that if you cleaned your room she would reward you with $5.00 and a trip to the movies? You would be more willing to agree to her request and you would find her to be more interpersonally attractive than if she would have said, "If you don't clean your room, you will have to pay me $5.00 to do it for you, and you'll be grounded from the movies for the next week." Threats and coercive behavior typically breed resentment and result in higher levels of resistance.

Table 9.2 – Power and Impact on Levels of Influence

Types of Power	Levels of Influence		
	Compliance	Identification	Internalization
Reward	X		
Coercive	X		
Legitimate	X		
Referent	X	X	X
Expert	X	X	X

Source: Adapted from Kelman 1961; Richmond, McCroskey, and McCroskey 2005.

Relationship between Power and Interpersonal Influence

To better understand the impact of power in our decisions of whether to comply with requests made in our interpersonal relationships, we look at the three levels of influence that can be achieved. These include compliance, identification, and internalization (Kelman 1961). **Compliance** occurs when an individual agrees to a request because he can see a potential reward or punishment for doing so. This level of influence is likely to persuade someone to do something, but his motivation is typically low and the change in the behavior is usually quite temporary. When you tell your roommate that she can have your car for the weekend if she drives you to the airport and she later complies with your request, you have influenced her at the compliance level. In this example, the only reason the roommate complies with the request is to obtain a reward.

If a person decides to agree to an influence attempt because she recognizes the potential benefits of doing so, or perhaps she wishes to establish a relationship with the source, then **identification** has occurred. A student agrees to his teacher's recommendation that he take honors level courses next semester to help prepare him for college instead of "cruising" in the regular classes with his friends. In this instance, individuals are typically more motivated to comply because they agree with the source's goals, interests and values. The last level of influence, **internalization,** is employed when an individual adopts a behavior because it is internally rewarding. In other words, it feels like the right thing to do. This type of influence is successful because the person sees the requested behavior as fitting within his or her existing value system. The individual agrees to the behavior because he intrinsically believes it should be done, not just because someone told him to do so. An example of this might be a spouse who takes on the responsibility of extra household or childcare duties in order to assist a partner who is experiencing a difficult time at work. In this instance, the person agrees to the request because of the value placed on family and the level of commitment made to the relationship. Table 9.2 summarizes the level of influence that can be achieved as a result of each of the five types of power.

Power versus Dominance in Relationships

What is the difference between power and dominance? Burgoon and Dillman (1995) argue, "Because power is broadly defined as the ability to exercise influence by possessing one or more power bases, dominance is but one means of many for expressing power" (65). In other words, power is the potential to influence another's behavior, whereas **dominance** is a mechanism typically associated with attempts to express power and take control in a relationship. What is the relationship between talking and influence? One study found that the more an individual talks, the more opportunities he has to gain influence over others (Daly, McCroskey, and Richmond 1977). A separate study suggests that managing what individuals talk about and "controlling the floor" are perceived as forms of interpersonal dominance or control (Palmer 1989).

VERBAL AGGRESSION

Perhaps one of the most vivid examples of verbal aggression in action can be witnessed in the movie and book, *The Devil Wears Prada*. As she attempts to navigate her way in the fashion magazine industry, Andrea Sachs learns that dealing with verbal attacks from her boss and co-workers is part of the "game," and something she must endure if she wishes to pursue a career in the field. She encounters both direct and indirect influence attempts. Miranda, her boss, prefers an influence style that attacks Andy's self-esteem. She bluntly tells Andy that she has "no style" and publicly criticizes Andy's work in front of her colleagues. To make matters worse, Emily, a co-worker, refers to Andy as being "hopeless." Nigel, the photographer who befriends Andy, eventually convinces her that she needs to change in order to make it in the business. He provides her with logical facts and arguments containing tips to help her succeed in the industry. It becomes apparent that Nigel's approach of presenting arguments was much more effective in helping Andy comply, and ultimately succeed, than the aggressive approach used by Miranda and Emily.

Attempts to gain influence over others are often made in one of two ways. First, rational arguments can be presented for why compliance should occur. A second strategy is to attack the other person's self-esteem or character. As you can see, one of these strategies is positive, and the other is negative and potentially damaging to relationships. So why do some individuals choose to present rational arguments while others choose to attack? The explanation rests in the distinction between communication traits known as argumentativeness and verbal aggression. **Argumentativeness** refers to the extent to which an individual challenges a position or issue (Infante and Rancer 1982). A person can question or debate whether they should comply with a request without directly addressing the personal characteristics of the person making the request. When a request is addressed with a response that attacks the self-confidence, chararacter, and/or intelligence of another person, **verbal aggressiveness** is being used (Infante and Wigley 1986). Suppose your best friend asks you to let him borrow your car to drive to a concert, but you do not wish to comply with his request. An argumentative person might respond with statements such as, "It's probably not a good idea, since you aren't insured to drive my car. Besides, I don't want to rack up miles on it since it's a lease."

The request is addressed with logical, rational points. An example of a verbally aggressive response might be, "Are you stupid? Why in the world would you be crazy enough to think that I would trust you with my car?" In this instance, the person's intelligence, sanity, and trustworthiness have been attacked. Examples of verbally aggressive messages might include attacks on one's character or competence, teasing or ridiculing, or even making threats or jokes about another's appearance.

Loreen Olson suggests that there are four levels of aggression that are experienced in our interpersonal encounters (2004). **Low aggression** is characterized by yelling, crying, refusing to talk, or stomping out of the room. **Moderate aggression** involves more intense acts of verbal aggression such as verbal insults, swearing at the other, and indirect physical displays of anger such as kicking, hitting, throwing inanimate objects, or threatening to engage in these behaviors. Next, **high aggression** refers to intensive face threatening, and verbal belittling, and direct physical contact with the other person in the form of slapping, shoving, or pushing. The most severe level, **severe aggression,** includes intense verbal abuse and threats and involves physical attacks that include kicking, biting, punching, hitting with an object, raping, and using a weapon. Not only can verbally aggressive acts occur before relational conflicts, they occur as a consequence to partner aggression and also serve to escalate the conflict. In relationships, struggles for power and control are often at the heart of reciprocated and escalating aggression between partners (Olson 2004).

While our first tendency is to assume that aggression and violence are often restricted to close relationships with romantic partners or family members, this is not the case. Researchers have examined their presence and impact in a variety of relational contexts.

Verbal Aggression in the Classroom

Since verbal aggression is perceived as a negative communication behavior, it should come as no surprise that researchers have identified several negative outcomes associated with teachers who use words to attack students in the classroom. Students who perceive their instructors as being verbally aggressive report that they are less motivated in that class (Myers and Rocca 2001). Also, they evaluate the teacher as being less competent and as behaving inappropriately (Martin, Weber, and Burant 1997). In an environment where a student fears becoming the target of verbal abuse, less learning occurs (Myers 2002) and the chances are greater that students will choose to avoid the situation by skipping class (Rocca 2004). When you consider that aggressiveness fosters a negative learning experience, the power of a teacher's communication becomes apparent. The same principles hold true in other instructional contexts. In the movie *Kicking and Screaming*, Phil (Will Farrell) volunteers to coach his son's soccer team. In the beginning of the film, Phil's coaching style and communication are patient and nurturing—he even goes so far as to bring the boys finches as rewards for their hard work. Eventually, Phil's competitive nature emerges, and his interactions with the boys and their parents become verbally aggressive. At one point he taunts a young player who misses a goal by screaming at him in front of the entire team, "You've just been served a plate of humiliation!" While the purpose of these athletic experiences is to provide training, the aggressive communication could have serious negative implications.

Workplace Bullying

Another context that has been the target of research on verbal aggression is the workplace. Because it is likely that all of you either have been employed, or will be at some point in your life, it is important to understand the potential for verbal aggression and emotional abuse to occur in this environment. Approximately ninety percent of adults report that they have been a victim of workplace bullying at some point during their professional career (Hornstein 1996). Workplace bullying, intimidation,

The vast majority of workplace bullies are bosses.

© Jaimie Duplass, 2007, Shutterstock.

employee humiliation and organizational manipulation are all considered to be **Employee Emotional Abuse (EEA).** EEA is defined as repeated, targeted, unwelcome, destructive communication by more powerful individuals toward less empowered individuals in the organization, which results in emotional harm (Lutgen-Sandvik 2003). In February 2006, a Vallejo, California high school teacher agreed to an out-of-court settlement after suing the state administrator and other district officials for alleged harassment and discrimination. The school district agreed to pay the teacher $225,000, to compensate her for the emotional distress she experienced at work.

So who is most likely to engage in bullying at work? The results may surprise you. According to the United States Hostile Workplace Survey in 2000:

- Women comprised fifty percent of the bullies.

- Women bullies target other women an overwhelming eighty-four percent of the time; men bullies target women in sixty-nine percent of the cases; women are the majority (seventy-seven percent) of targets.

- The vast majority of bullies are bosses (eighty-one percent); they have the power to terminate their targets at will.

- Approximately forty-one percent of targets were diagnosed with depression.

- More than eighty percent of targets reported effects that prevented them from being productive at work (severe anxiety, lost concentration, sleeplessness, etc.).

- Post-Traumatic Stress Disorder (PTSD) symptoms afflicted thirty-one percent of the women who experienced workplace bullying; twenty-one percent of the men who had been bullied reported PTSD symptoms.

OBSESSIVE RELATIONAL INTRUSION

In some cases, verbal aggression and violence have been linked to instances of obsessive relational intrusion (ORI). William Cupach and Brian Spitzberg (1998) developed the concept of ORI to address the interpersonal aspect of stalking. All of us have heard stories in the news of celebrities who have been stalked: prior to his death in 1980, John Lennon was stalked by Mark Chapman; tennis champion Monica Seles was stabbed by a stalker who was a fan of her opponent, Steffi Graf. Cupach and Spitzberg (1998) distinguish ORI from stalking in the sense that ORI occurs out of a desire to initiate a relationship, whereas stalking often has a purpose of harming, and possibly even destroying, another person. The communication that takes place in ORI is typical of most relationships, the exchange of messages via phone calls, letters, or gifts. Many of these communicative behaviors are an attempt to either initiate or escalate a relationship; however, one person often becomes jealous and sometimes even possessive.

Obsessive relational intrusion is defined as the "repeated and unwanted pursuit and invasion of one's sense of physical or symbolic privacy by another person, either stranger or acquaintance, who desires and/or presumes an intimate relationship" (Cupach and Spitzberg 1998, 235). In a study of 341 college students, nineteen percent of the men and ten percent of the women indicated that they had obsessively pursued another person using various methods and strategies. As far as gender differences in the types of tactics used to communicate an interest in another, there were no significant differences found. Examples of the most frequently reported tactics by both men and women include the following:

As more relationships are initiated via the Internet, it is important to understand the potential dangers.

- Sending/communicating unwanted messages
- Expressing exaggerated affection
- Giving or sending unwanted gifts
- Monitoring the other person's actions
- Intruding in the interactions of the other person
- Intruding on the other person's friends and/or family
- Covertly obtaining information about the person

Perhaps as you read this description of ORI, you may discover that you or someone you know has experienced this dark aspect of interpersonal relationships. To understand how victims of ORI manage these unwanted advances, Spitzberg and Cupach (2001) conducted an analysis of the coping strategies identified across a variety of studies. A summary of these coping strategies is presented in Table 9.3.

Table 9.3 – Summary of Obsessive Relational Intrusion Coping Strategies

Coping Strategy	Examples
Moving inward	Ignore or deny the problem and hope it goes away Blame yourself Engage in self-destructive means to escape (e.g., alcohol, drugs, suicide)
Moving outward	Seek sympathy from others Seek social support from friends and/or family Seek legal assistance (e.g., police, attorney)
Moving away	Control interactions with the person (e.g., maintain a closed body position, avoid eye contact) Use verbal avoidance or escape tactics (e.g., make excuses) Restrict accessibility (e.g., change schedule, switch work shifts, obtain caller ID, change email address, use pseudonyms online)
Moving toward	Diminish seriousness of the situation (e.g., joke or tease the pursuer) Employ problem-solving tactics or negotiation Mutually negotiate relationship definition (e.g., discuss your preferences for the type of relationship you would like with the other)
Moving against	Issue verbal warnings/threats Build a legal case (e.g., save emails, letters, keep a record of calls) Use protective responses (e.g., email blocker, restraining order)

Source: Reprinted from *Aggression and Violent Behavior, Volume 8*, B.H. Spitzberg and W.R. Cupach, "What Mad Pursuit? Obsessive Relational Intrusion and Stalking Related Phenomena", 345–375, Copyright 2003 with permission from Elsevier.

Unfortunately, relational obsession and stalking are not restricted to face-to-face interactions. As more and more people use the Internet as a forum for initiating and building relationships, it is important to understand the potential dangers associated with these types of relationships. Cyberstalking refers to harassment, or obsessive communication, via the Internet. Several television news shows have recently conducted in-depth investigations regarding this phenomenon, focusing on the use of online communication by pedophiles to form relationships with children and minors. It is important to note that cyberstalkers often obtain personal information about their targets that is disclosed on the Internet and may use this information to harm others.

While you may be thinking that obsessive relationships are the result of posting personal information to online dating sites, consider the information that is posted on a variety of social networking websites that are gaining in popularity. More than 100 million people engage in interactions via online social communities where personal information is exchanged. Two of the most popular sites among college students and teenagers are MySpace and Facebook. Why have these online sites gained so much popularity in recent years? A study conducted at Carnegie Mellon University by students revealed that individuals join Facebook for several reasons: (1) as a result of peer pressure by friends encouraging them to create an online profile, (2) to maintain relationships at a distance, (3) to form new relationships, or (4) to get assistance with classes (Govani and Pashley 2005). While students report that they turn to these sites to assist in initiating and maintaining relationships, the harsh reality is that online behaviors have actually damaged many relationships. Incidences of students posting pictures depicting themselves in sexually provocative ways, or while engaging in illegal or excessive drinking have prompted university officials

Table 9.4 – Facebook in the News

April 2005	University of Mississippi students were threatened with a civil lawsuit for leading a Facebook group that devoted their desire to sleep with a certain female professor. They made a public apology. (*www.dukechronicle.com* 03/08/2006)
May 2005	LSU swimmers were kicked off the team after athletics officials discovered they belonged to a Facebook group that posts disparaging comments about swim coaches (usa.com-athletes sound over athletes Facebook time, 03/08/2006)
September 2005	Northern Kentucky men's basketball coach found Facebook photos of his underage athletes with alcohol. They were let off with a warning. (usa.com-athletes sound over athletes Facebook time, 03/08/2006)
October 2005	North Carolina State University resident advisor reported nine of her students for underage drinking when she found evidence in one resident's Facebook photo album (*www.dukechronicle.com* 03/08/2006)
	Penn State University police used Facebook as a tool to identify students who rushed the football field after the Ohio University game. (*http://www.thepost.ohiou.edu*)
December 2005	Florida State athletes were given ten days to cleanse their profiles. (usa.com-athletes sound over athletes facebook time, 03/08/2006)
	Loyola University of Chicago athletic director forbids his athletes to join to protect them from gamblers or sexual predators who can learn more about them (usa.com-athletes sound over athletes facebook time, 03/08/2006)
	Colorado athletes were accused of sending a racially threatening Facebook message to a fellow athlete. Campus police issued tickets for harassment. (usa.com-athletes sound over athletes facebook time, 03/08/2006)
January 2006	Kentucky athletic director told athletes to scrub their profiles of anything that could shed a bad light on the school. (www.usatoday.com-athletes sound over athletes Facebook time, 03/08/2006)
February 2006	Students at the University of Kansas living in the scholarship hall were written up for pictures uploaded to Facebook.com that indicated a party violating the alcohol policy. (Kansan.com)

to use sites such as Facebook to identify improper and illegal behavior. Table 9.4 highlights some of the ways in which colleges and universities have used the Facebook site to monitor and discipline students.

While it is important to be aware of the potential dangers and risks of exchanging and revealing personal information online, the more critical issue involves learning how to manage and use these new communication mediums appropriately. In Chapter Thirteen we present a detailed overview of computer-mediated communication (CMC) research and provide suggestions for using CMC effectively and appropriately as a means of social networking. It is important to be selective in the information that you choose to share via CMC. Also, realize that people can and do lie about themselves in both face to face and computer mediated contexts.

SUMMARY

While the topics discussed in this chapter may not be particularly pleasant, it is important to address their role in our communication with others. Not all relationships are enjoyable. To use the analogy of a roller coaster, virtually all relationships experience ups and downs. In this chapter we have discussed the concept of interpersonal deception and explored the potential impact of telling lies on the future of our relationships. In addition, we discussed the potential embarrassment that pops up from time to time and causes us to become "red-faced" in our interactions. In keeping with color analogies, relationships often encounter the "green-eyed monster" when jealousy emerges and causes us to respond in ways that we might not otherwise. We identified power and influence as a potential source of jealousy and as something that can affect our interactions with others. The distinction between argumentativeness and aggressiveness was made, as we offered a glimpse into the ugly side of power, when it results in verbal attack against others. Finally, we discussed the concept of obsession in relationships and presented the concept of obsessive relational intrusion. We concluded this discussion by addressing the dark side of relationships and computer mediated communication. While at first glance social networking sites like Facebook and Myspace may seem beneficial, there is a dark side to these as well.

Oftentimes we hear the phrase, "Communication is the key to success." The purpose of this chapter was to introduce a few communication situations in which communication was not part of the solution, but was, in fact, part of the problem. It is important to remember that communication is a tool that can be used for good or evil purposes. It is up to us to understand how to effectively use communication to accomplish our goals and to become more competent in our interactions with others. By offering you a glimpse into the "dark side" of communication, it is our hope that your relationships will encounter more "ups" than "downs."

APPLICATIONS

Discussion Questions

A. Most people would agree that there are times when it is okay to deceive a friend, family member, or romantic partner. Have you ever been in a particular situation where you felt it was okay to deceive someone? Describe the situation and your reasons.

B. What are some ways to make sure that your partner does not feel jealous in regard to your romantic relationship? What are some suggestions for dealing with someone that often reports jealous feelings?

C. What is the best way to influence a friend or family member to change a problematic behavior? What type of persuasion and social influence tactics could you employ to get the friend or family member to change? Describe the tactics that you would use and those that you would avoid.

D. Provide three examples of types of information that should not be disclosed on social networking sites such as Facebook and Myspace."

ACTIVITY 9.3 Reactions to Chapter 9

1. List three examples of relationships in your life where your communication has been influenced by the stage each relationship is in. Describe how communication is used in these relationships.
2. What kinds of barriers do you encounter that make it difficult to maintain important relationships?
3. How does self-disclosure influence your relationships?
4. How does understanding the role of communication in relationships help you establish and maintain meaningful relationships in your life?

"ACTIVITY 9.4³

PURPOSE

The purpose of the assignments will help students and others in the class understand the "dark side." The assignments will involve ways where students can identify, compare, understand, and show how the dark side relates to various relationship types.

1. Ask each student to make a collage of the type of person (friend, family members, co-workers, etc.) that relates to jealousy. They can use newspapers, magazines, books, etc. Have the student to bring their collage to class and show the class and state why they included the items as being a jealous relationship. Allow 3 -5 minutes long as their presentation time in class.
2. Research a dark side relationship case or issue of your choice. Write a one – two page paper giving a brief overview of the case or issue, explaining the main points, giving the results, and your feedback regarding the issue/case and the results (what would you do different). Include your references in APA or MLA format.

TERMINATING AND DE-ESCULATING RELATIONSHIPS

From the old "Greensleeves" (Alas, my love, you do me wrong to cast me off discourteously . . .) to gleeful songs like "Already Gone," from most of Garth Brooks' repertoire to rock songs like Hoobastank's "The Reason," we are as concerned with the end as with the beginning. Romantic relationships are hardly exclusive; throughout life, relationships of different forms will be left as closed books. How?

We have discussed how our interpersonal relationships are initiated and, in some instances, how they turn dark. In this chapter, we turn to the process of relationship disengagement for all types of relationships. Not surprisingly, the research, like Neal Sedaka's song, notes that "Breaking up is hard to do," and usually results in pain for one or both partners. Throughout this chapter, we examine the most common reasons for ending both platonic and romantic relationships. We also take an in-depth look at research involving both potentially aggravating and mitigating strategies used by individuals in relationship termination. We then face the aftermath of relationship disengagement, exploring suggestions for surviving relationship disengagement and ultimately moving on.

TERMINATING FRIENDSHIPS

Friendships are some of the most enduring relationships we have. There are friendships that we have had since youth with a shelf life of "forever." There are other friends who tend to drift in and out of our lives like last season's shoes. Why do some friendships tend to outlast others? Often, friendships are forged from commonalities in our life. For example, we meet certain people in a class who live in the same dorm, have the same major, work at the same job, share the same religion or social group, or share the same enemy or mutual friend. Friendships

Why do some friendships tend to outlast others?

may terminate because the very thing that brought them together no longer exists. People move away, change jobs, or move on to a different life stage (i.e., marriage, children, etc.) and no longer share the proximity and closeness that once protected the relationship. The *Friends* are all singles in New York; the *Desperate Housewives* share Wisteria Lane; the Dundler Mifflin employees on *The Office* work together, as do the *Grey's Anatomy* interns. Remove the binding element and friendships

may fade. Consider how, when not killed off, characters are removed from shows, particularly the cast-rotating *ER*. Whether for career, love, or family, a resident leaves the hospital and Chicago and, as a result, is detached from the life of the colleagues previously seen daily. While employed as a plot device to remove a character, such occasions illustrate an aspect of reality.

There are a number of reasons individuals end friendships. The most common reasons reported for terminating a friendship were less affection (22.8 percent), friend or self changed (21 percent), no longer participate

When they graduate and go their separate ways, will this friendship end?

in activities or spend time together (15.4 percent), and increase in distance (13 percent). (Johnson, Wittenberg, Haigh, Wigley, Becker, Brown and Craig 2004). Additional findings suggest that male same-sex friendships tend to dissolve for different reasons than female same-sex friendships. Females were more likely to terminate friendships due to a conflict situation, whereas males were more likely to terminate friendships as a result of fewer common interests.

The way that someone ends a friendship depends on the intimacy, or closeness, experienced in the relationship. Another study compared the differences in dissolution between casual and best friends (Rose and Serafica 1986). Researchers found that proximity was a stronger predictor of dissolution in casual friends, while decreased affection was more important in best friends. One reason reported for best and close friendships dissolving was the interface from other relationships, such as romantic relationships. This plays a particularly detrimental role in female friendships. When one individual begins to spend more time interacting with her romantic partners' male friends than with her own friends, the neglected female friends are likely to become frustrated with her behavior.

As a friendship grows apart, we can neglect the responsibilities of the relationship by choosing to provide less of our time, energy, trust, understanding, and support. When an individual is neglecting the responsibilities of the friendship, individuals may start weighing the costs and rewards of the relationship. **Social Exchange Theory** refers to an assessment of costs and rewards in determining the value of pursuing or continuing a relationship (Thibaut and Kelley 1959). Rewards consist of behaviors or aspects of the relationship that are desirable, and that the recipient perceives as enjoyable or fulfilling. In friendships,

A friendship reward is having fun when you're together.

© Jason Stitt, 2007, Shutterstock.

rewards are how much fun you have with the person, and the extent to which he or she is trustworthy, honest, sincere, helpful, and supportive. By contrast, costs are perceived as undesirable behaviors or outcomes. Costs in friendships may be characterized as "toxic" behaviors: the extent to which a friend may be controlling, demanding, depressing, self-absorbed, deceitful, and unfair. Also, friendships take time and energy, which may be perceived as costs when we have less time and energy to devote to them. According to Social Exchange Theory, when the costs of the relationship outweigh the rewards, we contemplate ending the friendship. We may use indirect or direct methods to end a friendship.

Using Indirect Methods to End a Friendship

Indirect methods work best if your goal is to decrease the intensity of the friendship by increasing the emotional and physical distance between you and your friend. Indirect methods reflect your intentions of gradually letting go of the relationship. Examples of indirect methods include calling the friend less, sending fewer emails, blocking the friend from your Buddy List or switching your screen name, and spending less time with the friend.

There are drawbacks to using indirect methods to gradually weaken relationship bonds. For example, giving excuses for not hanging out may backfire. Florence Isaacs, author of *Toxic Friends/True Friends: How Your Friends Can Make or Break Your Health, Happiness, Family, and Career* (1999), suggests that giving excuses allows the other person an opportunity to overcome your refusal; he or she may answer your "Oh, I can't afford the gas to get out there," with "That's okay, I can pick you up."

In addition, because indirect methods are not the most honest approach, the friend is often left confused about your true feelings. Often he or she will keep trying and will not understand your indirect attempts to slow down, or even end, the friendship. If this is the case, it may be time to move to more direct approaches of ending the relationship.

Using Direct Methods to End a Friendship

Direct methods work best if your friend does not recognize the intent of your indirect attempts or if you are interested in terminating the friendship abruptly (due to some hurtful circumstance). As you can imagine, direct approaches are specifically telling the friend how you honestly feel. Sometimes this is not an easy task, but there are some tools you can use to ease this uncomfortable situation. First, use "I" statements. For example, "I'm very busy with my new girlfriend and with work so I cannot hang out with you every weekend," or "I was really hurt by your comment at dinner the other night and I'm not interested in being friends with someone who doesn't respect me." Direct methods leave little room for misinterpretation. While they are effective, they can be hurtful and sometimes shocking to hear from the perspective of the receiver. If you choose to engage in this approach, be prepared to be assertive and provide a valid reason for why you are ending the friendship.

TERMINATING ROMANTIC RELATIONSHIPS

"There must be fifty ways to leave your lover," and though Paul Simon suggests mainly variations on "slipping out the back," some individuals prove highly creative in their personal spins on "it's not you, it's me." The common causes of relationship disengagement, however, are more limited. There are several significant reasons individuals have provided for terminating romantic relationships. Typically, the decision to leave a romantic partner is a difficult and arduous task. In this section, we examine four common reasons individuals leave romantic relationships (adapted from Cupach and Metts 1986). These include: (1) infidelity, (2) lack of commitment, (3) dissimilarity, and (4) outside pressures.

Infidelity

Infidelity can be defined as behaving in a way that crosses the perceived boundary and expectation of an exclusive relationship. Infidelity can take many forms, including physical (holding hands), sexual (kissing and other activities), and emotional (sharing intimate conversation) (Spitzberg and Tafoya 2005). Research suggests that men are more likely to be upset with a partner's sexual infidelity, while women tend to be more upset with a partners' emotional infidelity (Glass and Wright 1985). Studies have also shown that infidelity is more likely to exist inside marriages with marital instability, dishonesty, arguments about trust, narcissism, and time spent apart (Atkins, Yi, Baucom and Christensen 2005). While approximately ninety-nine percent of married persons expect sexual fidelity from their spouse (Treas and Giesen 2000), not many couples are meeting those expectations.

Although infidelity statistics are difficult to measure, we report some interesting findings that describe the pervasiveness of infidelity. Atwood and Schwartz (2002) estimate that fifty to sixty percent of married men and forty-five to fifty-five percent of married women engage in some form of extramarital affair at some point in their marriage. The *Washington Post* reported that, according to counselor Janis Abrahms Spring, author of *After the Affair*, affairs affect one of every 2.7 couples. Other interesting findings suggest that ten percent of extramarital affairs last one day. Of those that last more than one day:

- Ten percent last less than a month
- Fifty percent last more than a month but less than a year
- Forty percent last two or more years

According to Spring's statistics, few extramarital affairs last longer than four years.

Additionally, a longitudinal study found that infidelity is the most frequently cited cause of divorce (Amato and Rogers 1997). Another study found that forty percent of divorced individuals reported at least one extramarital sexual contact during their marriage (Janus and Janus 1993). These alarming statistics imply that although not many condone infidelity, there is a significant proportion of people engaging in these types of behaviors.

Our culture has both romanticized and rebuked infidelity. The archetypical story of Tristan and Isolde, wherein a young queen cheats on her kind husband with the knight she truly loves, was turned into a hit 2006 film of the same title by Ridley Scott. Guinevere and Lancelot's doomed love that betrays the noble King Arthur, whom they both care deeply for, is continually retold in musical form. *Walk the Line* was another recent movie dealing with the relationship between Johnny Cash and June Carter, which caused the dissolution of Cash's previous marriage. Movies like *Fatal Attraction* and *What Lies Beneath*, however, offer deadly punishment for adultery. According to research, relationships in which one or both individuals have potential alternative partners with highly attractive qualities are "particularly vulnerable" to dissolution (Simpson 1987), and when a relationship's rewards fall below the expected rewards of an alternative relationship, it is most likely to end (Thibaut and Kelley 1959). Hollywood, California, where attractive individuals live in extremely close proximity, seems to be a natural hub for infidelity in all three of its forms.

Lack of Commitment

Another reason individuals provide for terminating romantic relationships is a lack of commitment. Although infidelity is one way to demonstrate an individuals' lack of commitment, other ways include: not spending enough time together, not prioritizing the relationship, not valuing the other's opinion, experiencing power struggles, and not nurturing the maintenance and development of the relationship. Lack of **commitment** in a relationship can foster feelings of abandonment and loneliness. Some relationship experts argue

High commitment to a relationship is a strong predictor of its stability.

that partners' commitment to the relationship is a stronger predictor of relationship stability than feelings of love (Lund 1985). Researcher Mary Lund studied heterosexual dating relationships in an attempt to determine whether love or commitment served as a stronger predictor of relationship stability. She found that couples with higher levels of commitment were more likely to continue the relationship than those with high levels of love and low levels of commitment. In this study, couples' expectations of staying together proved to be more important to relationship stability than their feelings of love for one another.

Lack of commitment to the relationship may be a catalyst for more damaging outcomes, such as infidelity; couples often attempt therapy to resolve these issues. One study found two characteristics that identified unsuccessful couples in therapy. They are "inability or unwillingness to change" and "lack of commitment" (Whisman, Dixon, and Johnson 1997). Another report found that the most significant problems for couples who attended therapy are a lack of loving feelings and lack of communication, power struggles, extramarital affairs, and unrealistic expectations (Whisman, Dixon, and Johnson 1997).

Can previous relationship experiences affect an individual's willingness to commit to future relationships? Communication researchers explored how past relationship solidarity was related to current relationship commitment, satisfaction, and investment among college students in dating relationships. They found that an individual's past relationship experiences may be to blame for a current relationships' lack of commitment with, specifically, a negative relationship between participants' past relationship solidarity and current relationship commitment and satisfaction. It is important to note that these relationships were only significant for the female participants in the study. Researchers argue that these findings may be based on the different ways in which "men and women cope with break-ups and how these differences might have affected their retrospective reports of their past relationships" (Merolla Weber, Myers, and Booth-Butterfield 2004, 261). Women may be more in tune with their physical and emotional closeness in past relationships than males. Males, on the other hand, may be more inclined to employ emotional distraction techniques after break-ups to avoid dealing with their feelings (Merolla et al. 2004).

Dissimilarity

Scholars have identified similarity as one of two components that relationship dyads consider when deciding whether to stay together or to break up (Hill, Rubin, and Peplau 1976). A longitudinal study suggested that couples who were most similar in educational plans, intelligence, and attractiveness were most likely to remain together, whereas couples that were different in the levels of these aspects were more likely to break up. Some may say, "opposites attract," but the truth is, **dissimilarity** creates more problems than solutions. Having differences in backgrounds (religion, family values), intelligence (educational goals, IQ), attitudes concerning family roles, ethics, and communicating about conflicts, and temperament (argumentativeness, assertiveness) can contribute to conflict situations and misinterpretations of behavior.

Couples who share similar beliefs and interests are more likely to stay together.

A communication concept that is strongly linked to similarity is interpersonal solidarity. Lawrence Wheeless defined interpersonal solidarity as feelings of closeness between people that develop as a result of shared sentiments, similarities and intimate behaviors (1978). With that in mind, it makes sense that solidarity increases as relationships become more intimate, and it decreases as relationships turn toward termination (Wheeless, Wheeless, and Baus 1984). As solidarity increases in romantic relationships, so do individuals' levels of trust, reciprocity, and self-disclosures (Wheeless 1976). Also, the closer we feel to our partner, the more likely we are to provide emotional support (Weber and Patterson 1996). It makes sense to say that if individuals in romantic relationships perceive differences between themselves, there will be less trust, reciprocity, and emotional support, and fewer self-disclosures will be shared.

Writers often use a lack of interpersonal solidarity as the basis to break up fictional couples, particularly in cases when infidelity would be seen as out of character. On *Gilmore Girls*, for instance, Rory Gilmore ultimately breaks up with her devoted boyfriend when his lack of interest in books and of drive to strive beyond the community college in their town runs contrary to her love for literature and dream to attend Harvard. The contrast is made acute by a boy friend of hers who shares her interests in intellectual debate and matches her fast-paced banter. This sense of a widening gap between two individuals will commonly terminate a relationship.

Outside Pressures

External or **outside pressure** from friends, family, or occupations may negatively impact relationship satisfaction. Family members may put pressure on romantic relationships when they ask questions like "When are you two getting married?" or make comments such as, "You should save your money for a house!" and "I want to be a grandparent!" Friends also may exert pressure on romantic relationships by hinting that not enough time is spent with them, pressuring you to do things without your significant other. For couples in the public eye, the paparazzi acts as the external pressure peering over the hedge, demanding details and pushing theories of engagement, pregnancy, etc., on the pair.

According to **self determination theory,** people have an innate psychological need to feel autonomous, or self-governing, in one's behavior (Deci and Ryan 1985, 2000, 2002). In other words, we want to feel free to choose our own path in relationships, rather than be coerced or pressured into certain behaviors. Ultimately, this self-initiated behavior will lead to better

Stressful career demands can impact the satisfaction in relationships.

personal and social adjustment. Trait autonomy, or the extent to which we are self-determined, is related to feelings of well-being and security in relationships (La Guardia et al. 2000). Hence, those who report feeling responsible for, and in control of, their own decisions are also more secure and positive about their relationships with others.

Work relationships or job stressors can impact the satisfaction in our romantic relationship. An increase in job demands, hours, and travel requirements are examples of significant occupational pressures that may affect relationship stability. The time-consuming career of a doctor, for instance, can be seen in the media as being a challenge to relationships lasting, particularly on shows like *ER*, wherein constant relationship disengagement occurs.

HOMOSEXUAL VERSUS HETEROSEXUAL RELATIONSHIP DISSOLUTION

Although scant research has addressed gay and lesbian relationship termination, Lawrence Kurdek has found that cohabitating gay or lesbian partners are more similar than different when compared to married heterosexual partners (Kurdek 1992; 1998). In his 1998 longitudinal study, he examined relationship satisfaction among partners from gay, lesbian, and heterosexual married couples over five annual assessments. He found that neither gay nor lesbian partners differed from heterosexual partners in both the trajectory of change and the level of relationship satisfaction over time and that all three groups showed a similar decrease in satisfaction over the five years. However, some differences were detected. Both gay and lesbian partners reported more frequent relationship dissolution compared to married spouses. Additionally, gay and lesbian partners reported more autonomy than married people. Furthermore, lesbian partners reported significantly more intimacy and equality than married individuals (Kurdek 1998).

ASSESSING RELATIONSHIP PROBLEMS

When considering whether to stay in a relationship or not, we often assess the trouble occurring in the relationship and the explanations for these problems. For example, we ask ourselves questions such as, Why does he act that way? Why did she say that to me? or Why would he or she hurt me? To address these questions, it is necessary to recall our discussion of attribution theory and the Fundamental Attribution Error from Chapter Four. These theories provide a framework for understanding how we explain our own and others' behaviors. Recall our discussion of the **fundamental attribution error** which holds that people tend to attribute others' behaviors to internal, rather than external, causes. Rather than consider external or situational causes for others' behavior, which are also not always readily available, we often tend to take the "easy" way out and attribute others' behaviors to internal, or stable, factors, such as personality traits.

Not surprisingly, appraisals of our relationship partner's intentions relate to how satisfied we are in the relationship. Researchers have identified a consistent link between the attributions, or explanations, about relationship partners' intentions and reported relationship satisfaction (Fincham 1994; Waldinger and Schulz 2006). Much of the research on attributions in romantic relationships has examined how an assessment of a partner's accountability for a relationship transgression affects relationship satisfaction (Waldinger et al. 2006). It is natural to want to understand why our partner is acting a certain way, and eventually, these judgments influence our evaluation of our partner.

When relationship partners offer consistently negative attributions or explanations for a partner's behavior, they are more likely to report lower relationship satisfaction (Fincham and Bradbury 1993; Miller and Bradbury 1995). Thus, when a relationship partner forgets to buy a birthday present or forgets to recognize an important date, the offended partner may offer negative explanations for the behavior, especially if the negative behavior has been repeated over time. The offended partner may say, "He didn't get me a present because he is lazy," or "She didn't remember our anniversary because she is so self-absorbed." When individuals view a partner's behavior as selfishly motivated and intentional, they are more likely to view their partner in a negative way and to report decreased relationship satisfaction (Fincham, Harold, and Gano-Phillips 2000). Recent research indicates that relationship satisfaction can also affect the types of attributions partners make about each other's behavior, with less satisfied partners being more inclined to provide negative attributions for a partner's behaviors. Thus, the relationship between attribution processes and relationship satisfaction is described as a bidirectional one, which makes this somewhat challenging for researchers to study (Fincham et al. 2000).

Anita Vangelisti (1992) interviewed dating couples to determine the association between relationship problems and relational dissatisfaction. In her study, she recognized a problem as significant for relationship partners when it meets at least two of the following criteria: (1) the behavior must be negatively valenced on the relationship, (2) it must occur with some degree of frequency, and (3) it must be salient enough for one or both partners to remember it and recall it as a continuing source of dissatisfaction within the relationship. This makes sense, because if it is an annoying habit (such as not looking at your partner while listening) and it is consistent over time, it may reach the point where it becomes a relational problem. However, a salient behavior (such as kissing a colleague at happy hour) may only have to happen once, but is prominent enough to continually cause displeasure in the relationship, even though the behavior was never repeated. This study found that the most frequently reported communicative problem was withholding expression of negative feelings; the feelings of anger, fear, distress, disgust and shame.

Once we assess the relational problems, we may conclude that there is some form of inequity. **Equity theory** suggests that couples are happiest in relationships when there is a balance of inputs and outputs. If you perceive you are receiving too little from the relationship compared to what you are contributing, this will impact your satisfaction. Alternatively, if you are receiving more outputs from the relationship than you are contributing, you will feel a sense of guilt from the imbalance. However, this is highly subjective in terms of one's personal view of inputs, outputs, and fairness.

DECISION MAKING DURING RELATIONSHIP TERMINATION

Now we turn our attention to Duck's (1982) four-phase model of decision-making during relationship termination to understand how individuals determine whether or not to end a relationship.

Intrapsychic Phase

When one partner recognizes that something is wrong in a relationship and that he or she is no longer happy, feelings of frustration set in. The individual begins to consider the costs and rewards of the relationship and to explore the possibilities of alternative relationships. The "leaver" finds fault and places blame on the partner until finally, enough justification to withdraw from the relationship has accumulated. This initial phase in the relationship termination process is the **intrapsychic phase.** During this phase, the leaver spends considerable time contemplating whether the relationship is worth saving.

Dyadic Phase

When the leaver officially announces to the partner that he or she is leaving or thinking of leaving, the **dyadic phase** begins. This phase opens the flood gates for discussion and justifications. This often emotionally exhaustive phase is characterized by long talks and rationalizations of how the partnership "got to this place." During this phase, the other partner may make attempts to reconcile the relationship and to illustrate the costs of withdrawing. This phase typically continues until someone admits, "I have had enough."

Social Phase

If the relationship cannot be salvaged, the relationship termination then goes public. When the relationship termination is focused less on the relationship and more on the relationship partners' friends and family, it is a sign that we have moved to the **social phase.** For example, the question, What are we going to tell people? is often negotiated in this phase. Stories, blaming, and accounts of situations are articulated to friends and family. At this time, friends will often choose sides. In terms of the relationship partners, the rules and roles of their post break-up status are discussed. In other words, questions like, Can we still be friends? or Can I still call you? are negotiated.

Grave Dressing

The last phase is **grave dressing.** This phase is called grave dressing because partners typically "dress up" the dead relationship (or grave) by promoting a positive image of their role in their particular version of the relationship. Grave dressing also refers to "officially burying" the relationship. Partners are able to articulate the explanation of the termination and create their own versions of the relationship, whether truthful or not. Some people in this stage will have a ceremonial burying phase by burning pictures and returning, giving away, or selling items given to them by their "ex."

FIVE STAGES OF RELATIONSHIP DISSOLUTION

Knapp's model of relationship dissolution is both similar to and different from the model presented by Steve Duck (1982). Mark Knapp's model of relationship dissolution focuses more on what happens between the relationship partners and less on how the partners interact with their social circles (Vangelisti 2002). You may recall our discussion of Knapp's (1978) stages of coming together in Chapter Eight; he also developed a five-stage model that depicts how relationships typically come apart, or dissolve. The five stages of dissolution are labeled: differentiating, circumscribing, stagnating, avoiding, and terminating. Remember our earlier discussion of stage models; it is possible that (1) partners are not in the same stage together, (2) some stages last longer than others do, and (3) partners often skip stages. It is important to note that this model seems to depict what actually happens when relationships deteriorate, not what should happen (Knapp 1978).

Differentiating

While in the stages of coming together, couples tend to emphasize hobbies, interests, and values that they have in common; in the **differentiating** stage, partners highlight their differences. Individuals accentuate their unique attributes and use more "I" and "me" statements. During this phase of relationship dissolution partners may engage in a great deal of conflict that often emphasizes all of the ways they differ from one another. For example, if someone says she likes eating out, the partner expresses a preference for cooking at home. If an individual tells his partner that he likes action movies, the partner immediately states her affinity for romantic comedies. One's independence from the relationship is the central focus of this stage, which has both positive and negative implications. On one hand, when individuals reassert their individual needs, they may choose to do things on their own, spend more time with friends, and reestablish their identity. This process can be healthy for a relationship. For example, let us say before two individuals entered into a relationship, he enjoyed playing hockey and she enjoyed participating in a yoga class. But as the relationship developed, there was less time for each person to enjoy his or her personal activity due to favoring more collaborative activities with the partner. In due course, these interests were neglected. In the differentiating stage, those roots may be returned to, with hockey or yoga classes being taken up again. This may provide a "spark" needed in the relationship and provide alternative topics for the partners to discuss. On the other hand, if the individual taking part in the activity excludes the significant other from his or her feelings and experiences, this independence may ultimately create more emotional distance in the relationship. If the partner is kept involved in emotional travels, this stage may have beneficial outcomes.

Circumscribing

When there is not a conscious decision to keep the partner involved, the relationship may drift apart. The next stage of relationship dissolution is labeled the **circumscribing** stage. During this stage, the communication between the relationship partners is often described as restricted, controlled, or constrained. Akin to the "don't talk about politics or religion" standard, relationship partners choose to talk about safe topics that will not lead to some type of argument (Vangelisti 2002). Both the quality and quantity of information exchanged between the relationship partners deteriorates as partners attempt to avoid sensitive subject matter. Relationship partners discuss "safe" topics such as plans for the day, current events, and the weather, which are barely deeper or warmer than material used in conversation with an acquaintance.

Stagnating

The third stage of relationship dissolution is the **stagnating** stage. This stage is often described as two people who are merely "going through the motions" in their relationship because their communication has come to a virtual standstill. There is very little interaction within the relationship and partners continue to do things separately. When they think of bringing up any issues regarding the relationship they tell themselves, "It will just turn into an argument," so they resort to holding things inside to avoid a conflict. They conserve

When couples resort to holding things inside to avoid conflict, communication is stagnant.

© iofoto, 2007, Shutterstock.

their energy for their daily activities and do not exert any energy on preserving the relationship. Roommates, friends, and even family members may feel stagnant in their relationships with one another. Extended time in this stage can be particularly problematic as individuals may lose their motivation to fix the relationship. Over time, the thought of having to face the partner may become arduous. Therefore, it is often easier to just avoid the partner.

Avoiding

The fourth stage of coming apart is accurately labeled the **avoiding** stage. During this stage, relationship partners will actively fill their schedules to avoid seeing their partners. Vangelisti

(2002) describes this stage as particularly difficult, noting that when the partners do talk to one another, "they make it clear that they are not interested in each other or in the relationship" (666). Relationship partners will arrive early to work and come home late in an effort to avoid one another. The idea of seeing the relationship partner is exhausting and any dialogue with this person is short, to the point, and often superficial. On the inside, individuals are exhausted from creating activities to avoid their partner and have increased disdain for him or her.

Termination

As we grow increasingly disappointed in a relationship and in our partner, we reach a threshold and we want to move on. This is when we reach the final stage of coming apart, the **termination** stage, which marks the end of the relationship. Relationship partners may choose to divorce the partner, move out, or call an end to any type of formal or contractual commitment with the partner. When relationship partners do communicate during this stage, they make attempts to put physical and/or psychological distance between themselves and their relationship partner. Relationship partners will also make attempts to disassociate themselves from their relationship partner. Some married individuals will disassociate themselves from their partners by using their maiden names or explicitly stating to friends, co-workers, and family members, "We are not a couple anymore." See Table 9.5 for examples of typical communication that occur during the stages of coming apart.

Table 9.5 – Typical Communications in Knapp's Stages of Coming Apart

Stage	Communication Example
Differentiating	"You always stare at my sister!"
	"You are just so different from me!"
	"I hate when you don't wash the dishes!"
Circumscribing	"It's going to rain tomorrow."
	"Did you let the dog out yet?"
	"I am not going to answer that because it will just lead to a fight!"
Stagnating	"Oh, you're home."
	"What is the point of discussing this anymore?"
	"I know, I know. The usual."
Avoiding	"I have to work nights all this week."
	"I will not be home for dinner."
	"What time are you going?"
Terminating	"I don't want to be in this relationship."
	"Sorry, but we can't date anymore."
	"I'm moving out."

STRATEGIES USED TO TERMINATE RELATIONSHIPS

Determining how one should end a relationship can be quite stressful. Whether you are terminating a relationship with a romantic partner, a roommate, or a neighbor it can create much anxiety. When we are stressed we often turn to easily accessible solutions that are not always effective. However, we recommend that you do not employ any of the romantic relationship break-up lines provided in Table 9.6 below.

Once the leaver decides to verbalize his or her intentions, he or she typically relies on relational disengagement tactics. During the relational disengagement period, there is obviously a great deal of conflict. Leavers will use different strategies, depending on the type of the relationship and the timing of the disengagement. For example, more polite and face-saving tactics are typically used in the beginning of the relationship termination phase. However, if the rejected partner does not respond to these tactics, or if the leaver is in a dangerous relationship and immediate action is needed, more forceful and direct tactics may be necessary. Researchers have studied what people specifically recall saying during a break-up (Baxter 1982; Cody 1982) and they have identified five tactics used during relational disengagement.

Positive Tone Messages

First, **positive tone messages** are created to ease the pain for the rejected partner. These messages have a strong emotional tone and usually imply that the leaver would like to see less of the other person, but not entirely end the relationship. When individuals employ this strategy they usually want to try to end the relationship in a positive and pleasant way. An example of a positive tone message would be, "I really like you as a person, but I do not feel as strongly about you, as you do me." In other words, the classic "It's not you, it's me." Here the leaver tries to ease the pain of the break-up by suggesting that he or she still likes the rejected partner and is interested in a friendship.

De-escalation Messages

The second tactic also involves reducing the amount of time spent with the partner. **De-escalation messages** are less emotional than positive tone messages and typically provide a rationale for

Table 9.6 – Worst Break-Up Lines

1. I think we both know this is not working out.
2. I think one of us knows this is not really working out.
3. I am trouble, baby, with a capital T.
4. My wife is having a bigger problem with us dating than I thought she would.
5. It is not you, it is me.
6. It is not me, it is you.
7. Buh-bye.

Source: Adapted from www.esquire.com/features/articles. Ted Allen and Scott Omelianuk

wanting to see less of the rejected partner. For example, "I think we need a break," or "My feelings for you have changed since the start of this relationship," would both be de-escalation messages. This strategy may be problematic because it is only perceived as a partial or temporary type of relationship termination strategy. Individuals who want to end the relationship for good may want to follow up with a more direct strategy for ending the relationship.

When the relationship is not working, you may feel justification to end it.

Withdrawal or Avoidance

A third tactic, **withdrawal** or **avoidance,** refers to actively spending less time with the person. This includes dodging phone calls, blocking IMs, and rerouting daily activities in order to avoid the individual. When you do run into the person, conversations are kept brief and shallow. This strategy is very indirect and can affect the individuals' ability to maintain a friendship in the future.

Justification Tactic

A fourth way to disengage from a relationship involves the **justification tactic.** This tactic has three important elements. First, the relationship partner states that he or she needs to stop seeing the other person. Next, the relationship partner provides a reason for ending the relationship with the other person. Finally, the relationship partner recognizes that the relationship is not salvageable and may even become worse if the relationship continues. An example of this tactic is, "This relationship is not giving me what I need so we need to stop seeing each other." A person might say to his roommate, "I cannot live with you anymore because all we do is fight and argue and I do not see things getting any better. I am worried that if we stay roommates, things will get even worse than they are now!"

The last tactic is typically used as a last resort to terminate a relationship or when relationship partners are in need of immediate disengagement.

Negative Identity Management Tactic

A strategy which is used to hurry the disengagement process and has little consideration for the rejected partner is called the **negative identity management** tactic. Manipulation is often part of this tactic. For example, the leaver may spark a disagreement with the partner to create an unpleasant situation and then suggest, "See, this isn't working . . . we should see other people."

REDEFINING THE RELATIONSHIP AFTER THE BREAK-UP: REMAINING "JUST FRIENDS"

After a break-up, we often want to remain friends with our "ex." This makes sense because we have self-disclosed personal information to each other, relied on this person for emotional support and guidance, and have a number of things in common. Think about everything that drew you two together in the first place. But what are the chances that this new definition of your relationship will be successful? Some research suggests that a couple is much more likely to stay friends when the man has been the one who precipitated the break-up (or when the break-up was mutual) than when the woman initiated the break-up (Hill, Rubin, Peplau 1976).

Other research studies suggest that if the romantic couple were friends prior to the romantic involvement, their chances of returning to a friendship is significantly higher than those who never maintained a friendship (Metts, Cupach, and Bejlovec 1989). Additionally, if the partners were still receiving rewards or resources from the relationship, these could influence the impact of a partner's satisfaction with the post break-up friendship (Busboom, Collins, and Givertz 2002).

Certain relationship disengagement strategies are more effective in creating a positive post break-up relationship. When we ask our students how they would prefer to end a romantic relationship, most agree that they would desire an honest and direct strategy. Negative disengagement strategies, such as withdrawal, neglecting, or avoidance have been identified as inhibiting post-dating relationship quality (Metts et. al. 1989; Banks et al. 1987; Busboom, Collins, and Givertz 2002). If relationship partners would like to remain friends, it is a good idea to use positive tone messages, direct strategies or other tactics that protect the other person's feelings.

Although it is certainly possible to remain friends after a break-up, it is important that both parties agree with the new relational "rules." Discuss the boundaries of the relationship and be open about what is appropriate and inappropriate behavior. It is not unusual for post break-up friendships to cross the friendship boundaries in times of distress due to the familiarity, comfortableness, and security of the relationship (think Ross and Rachel from the television show *Friends*). It is important to remember you broke up for a reason!

After a break-up, keep yourself busy with family or friends you may have neglected during the relationships.

© digitalskillet, 2007, Shutterstock.

METHODS OF COPING WITH RELATIONSHIP DISSOLUTION

Scholars also note that the dissolution of a romantic relationship can be one of the most painful and stressful experiences people endure in their personal lives (Feeney and Noller 1992; Simpson 1987). This section will discuss methods of coping with relationship dissolution and creating closure.

Because ending a relationship can be one of the most emotionally charged events we experience, often there is no easy or painless way. No two relationships are identical in nature and there are no scripts to terminate relationships. We are flooded with different emotions including sadness, anger, fear, denial, guilt, and confusion. Sometimes we are relieved that the relationship is over and we are anticipating more rewarding relationships. Here are some methods of coping with relationship dissolution:

1. Recognize that relationship dissolution is a process. Allow yourself time to feel a range of emotions. This is normal and healthy. Do not reject your feelings or hide them behind negative coping strategies such as binge eating (or refusing to eat), binge drinking, or drug use. Also, do not rush into another romantic relationship without properly healing from the past.

2. Rely on your support network. Discuss your feelings with friends and family. Engage in activities that were neglected during your romantic relationship. Stay busy and redirect your attention. For example, find a new hobby or go on vacation with some of your friends.

3. If you feel you are burdening your friends and family, or you continue to feel depressed or angry, talking with a professional can help. Often, counseling is covered by health insurance. Most university counseling services are provided free of charge to students; take advantage of resources that are included in your tuition. Discussing issues with a third party that has no personal involvement in your existing relationships can provide a fresh perspective.

CLOSURE AND FORGIVENESS

Closure refers to a level of understanding, or emotional conclusion, to a difficult life event, such as terminating a romantic relationship. In this situation, closure often includes the rationale for the break-up. Some research suggests that individuals need a certain level of closure of their break-up before they can effectively move on (Weber 1998). The purpose of closure is to discuss things that "worked" in the relationship as well as to discuss the challenges of the relationship in order to learn from them. Remember, the purpose of this discussion is to make future relationships more effective, and not to resurrect the terminated relationship. Therefore, blaming, accusations, and name-calling are anti-productive. If properly executed, closure is helpful in understanding what went wrong in the relationship, providing some direction for future relationships.

Granting forgiveness is one strategy used during closure. Forgiveness does not mean you forget, accept, understand, or excuse the behavior; it simply implies that you will not hold your partner in debt for his or her wrong-doing. Granting forgiveness is a powerful tool. When you forgive someone that you are terminating a relationship with, you set yourself and your partner free from harboring negative feelings toward each other and perceptions of the relationship.

Self-forgiveness refers to you giving yourself permission to heal and move forward. You give yourself permission to shed yourself of the burden, guilt, pain, and anger that is held inside of you. Once you grant yourself forgiveness you can focus on how to become a better person and make healthier choices in the future.

Creating closure optimally involves getting together with your "ex" face-to-face to discuss the good times and the bad. In most situations, this option is impossible because either it is too difficult to sit in the same room or a partner has physically moved away. Therefore, closure is often difficult and not easily attainable. One way to create an emotional conclusion to a relationship is to reframe the event. Frequently, this is a way individuals can create a sense of closure without relying on the ex-partner. **Reframing** is a psychological process in which you change the way you look at the romantic termination in order to foster a more productive resolution. For example, if you are angry and hurt that your partner cheated on you, you may reframe the event by thinking about how dishonest the partner was. Instead of focusing on your hurt and anger, you psychologically emphasize that untruthfulness is not a characteristic of a person you want to share a romantic relationship with. You focus on recognizing signs of the cheating behavior and predictors of his or her behavior so you can be more aware in future relationships. By reframing the event, you are looking at the event in a different light, which enables you to move forward.

SUMMARY

In Hoobastank's hit song "The Reason," the singer apologizes for the choices he made in their relationship. "I've found a reason for me/ To change who I used to be. . . . and the reason is you," he claims, suggesting he has learned from the mistakes made in the relationship and has grown as an individual. Although there are countless break-up songs, we deliberately chose this one because it demonstrates that relationship dissolution can be a learning experience. This chapter reviewed the indirect and direct ways individuals dissolve relationships. We reviewed the four-phase process of decision-making during relationship termination: intrapsychic phase, dyadic phase, social phase, and grave dressing phase, and also explored the five stages of relationship deterioration: differentiating, circumscribing, stagnating, avoiding, and terminating. Furthermore, we identified the five tactics used to terminate romantic relationships: positive tone messages, de-escalation messages, withdrawal tactics, justification tactics, and negative identity management tactics. Finally, we discussed consequences of relationship dissolution, including closure, forgiveness, and reframing the event."

ENDNOTES

1 From *Communicate! A Workbook for Interpersonal Communication*, 7th Edition, by Communication Research Associates. Copyright © 2004 by Kendall Hunt Publishing Company. Reprinted by permission.
2 & 3 From *Interpersonal Communication: Building Rewarding Relationships*, by Kristen Campbell Eichhorn, Candice Thomas-Maddox, and Melissa Bekelja Wanzer. Copyright © 2008 by Kendall Hunt Publishing Company. Reprinted by permission.

CHAPTER 10

Friendship and Romance

STUDENT LEARNING OUTCOMES

Critical Thinking			Communication			Team Work		Social Responsibility	Personal Responsibility	Activity Measured
Creative Thinking/ Innovative	Analysis & Evaluation	Synthesis of Information	Writing	Visual	Oral	Differing Viewpoints	Work with Others	Intercultural Competence	Ethical Decision Making	Activity
X		X			X					10.1
X	X		X	X	X		X	X		10.2

FRIENDSHIP AND ROMANCE

Being Friends and the Stages of Life

Have you ever heard of the saying "BFF" (Best Friends Forever)? You hear that a lot with many people today but are they really "BFF"? After reading this section called Friendship and Romance, you will understand being friends and the stages of life, romance and qualities, types of love, and relationship strategies. The hope is that once you better understand friendship and romance, would you still want to say "BFF"?

Throughout your life you have meet many people who you may have called your friend but how many people today can you really say they have a friend or a best friend from their earlier years? Let's begin with a definition of friendship. An interpersonal relationship between two people that is unconditionally, includes trust, and you enjoy being around is defined as friendship. Let's explore friendship further.

Friendship is an interpersonal relationship: meaning that communication interactions takes place between people and reacts to each other as a complete person. This could consist of something that is unique, genuine, and being with a person that you do not want to replace. *Friendship must be unconditionally*: this relationship is developed based on conditions among the involved parties. *Friendships are characterized by mutual positive regards*: You and your friend likes each other because you are able to trust each other, have emotional support, and share common or non-common interest.

Even though we are friends unconditionally, all friendships are not the same. According to Reisman (1979, 1981), friendships consist of three types: friendships of reciprocity, receptivity, and association.

- Friendship of reciprocity is and ideally type of friendship. Loyalty, self-sacrifice, mutual affection and generosity are positive characteristics that are involved and based on equality. Giving and receiving benefits and rewards in relationships are also individually shared.

The quote below by Stieg Larsson, The Girl with the Dragon Tattoo relates to friendship of reciprocity and it states that:

> *"Friendship- my definition- is built on two things. Respect and trust. Both elements*
> *have to be there. And it has to be mutual. You can have respect for someone, but if*
> *you don't have trust, the friendship will crumble."*
> —Stieg Larsson, *The Girl with the Dragon Tattoo*

- Friendship of receptivity is when one person may give or receive more than the other person as friends. Each of the people involved may gain something from the relationship which could result as satisfaction. An example of this type of relationship may involve friendship between teacher and a student or between a doctor and a patient.
- Friendship of association may be a friendly relationship rather than a true friendship. This type of relationship could be one with classmates, neighbors, or coworkers which may be a cordial one. No loyalty, trust, or giving or receiving is involved in this type relationship.

When having friends and our needs change, what we look for in our friends also changes. Our old friends may no longer be our friends and we begin to form a new circle of friends who will meet the new needs such as different talents and skills that may help in achieving our goals and/or leadership abilities. Friendship develops in stages; from strangers (just meeting) to intimate (love and romance). Three stages of friendship will be discussed: (1) initial contact and acquaintanceship, (2) casual friendship, and (3) close and intimate friendship.

The first stage called *Initial Contact and Acquaintanceship* is what happens when you meet first meet someone. Usually many people are cautious and are guarded at the initial stage because you do not know each other. Meeting at this stage, you are not seen as a unit and the confidence of that person is represented by their personality rather than their relationship because you do not know each other well. Stage two, *Casual Friendship* is more of togetherness because you tend to participate in activities as two rather than as individuals. At this stage you normally will go to the mall, movies, sit in class with, or get a ride to and from places with that person. Good eye contact, posture, and gestures are no longer uncomfortable to each other. Responding openly and being honest to one another is no longer an issue of being discomfort. Lastly, stage three, *Close and Intimate Friendship* is seen as a more exclusive unit and greater benefits of emotional support. You are now familiar with each other's values, attitudes, and predict each other's behaviors. You begin to understand your friend's nonverbal behaviors which can be used to avoid certain things when needed. This type of friendship is important in your life and the different disagreements are easier to work out as well as compromise different problems.

Romance and Qualities

Many of us have experienced some type of love, have loved someone, or have been in love by someone. This love may have been with parents, siblings, friends, toy, or a pet. As we understand love we also have romantic love which is different from loving parents, siblings, friends, and more. Romantic love is a feeling unlike the feelings you experienced when in love with someone. When we experience romantic love the feelings are exciting and we tend to feel happier and more secure. Usually, this type of love (romantic love) should develop during adolescence. When one experience romantic love, three qualities are discovered: (1) attraction, (2) closeness, and (3) commitment.

Attraction is when "chemistry" about a person is involved. This "chemistry" leads to physical and sexual interest among two people. With attraction we feel the desire to kiss, be nervous but excited once we are near the other person. Closeness is a bond that we develop with the other person and no one else. This is normally with your boyfriend and girlfriend. You tend to feel cared for, accepted for who you are, and supported. Commitment is the decision to stick by each other through good times and bad times of the relationship. As well as being able to communicate and listen effectively to each other.

When a person has attraction without closeness, it is a crush or infatuation. Attraction and closeness combined is romantic love. Friends can move from being friends and being intimate friends to being together forever.

Types of Love

As we fall in love, our love may consist of one or more of the six different types of love. Those loves are as follows:

> Eros Love: focuses on beauty and physical attractiveness. This type of love can be erotic and sometimes unfulfilled.

> Ludus Love: is when fun and game playing is involved. The better the lover can play the game, the greater the enjoyment. Ludus lovers have self-control and are always aware of the need to mange love rather than allow it to be in control. This type of love is for entertainment and excitement. It is an uncommitted type of love.

> Storge Love: lacks passion and intensity. This type of love is for companionship. It is a peaceful type of love and it is slow. Sharing interest and activities with this type of love is done gradually. When sex is involved in storge love, it comes later on with no great importance in the relationship.

> Pragma Love: needs a practical relationship that works. This type of love wants compatibility and a relationship in which their needs and desires are satisfied. Family and background are important in this type of love since feelings are not relied much on. The pragma lover chooses their mates carefully and on similarities as well as realistic romantic expectations. This love can be unromantic and sex can be seen as a need to have children.

> Mania Love: can be a love that is obsessive, possessive, and jealousy involved. One in this type of love may stalk their mate because love is so important to them. An example of this type of love is shown in the movie Fatal Attraction.

> Agape Love: is a love that is caring, brotherly, giving, or gentle. This type of love can be spiritual; can be love without concern for personal reward or gain. Mother Theresa is an example of this type of love.

The different types of love can be combined with one another for different patterns since different people want different things and all people are not alike. Also, love changes and develops in positive or negative ways.

ACTIVITY 10.1

Ask the students if they believe in love at first sight. Based on their answer ask them if they ever been in love at first sight or do they know of anyone who has been in love at first sight? Discuss the type of loves and the type(s) of love you experienced. Did you enjoy it, why or why not?

ACTIVITY 10.2

Discuss your viewpoint on Interactional Relationships. Discuss the type of relationship and the ethnic group involved. Discuss how the relationship may or may not affect the culture and traditions? If you were involved in an interactional relationship discuss how you are able to relate to each other and their culture. Give two examples.

CHAPTER 11

Family and Workplace

STUDENT LEARNING OUTCOMES

Critical Thinking			Communication			Team Work		Social Responsibility	Personal Responsibility	Activity Measured
Creative Thinking/ Innovative	Analysis & Evaluation	Synthesis of Information	Writing	Visual	Oral	Differing Viewpoints	Work with Others	Intercultural Competence	Ethical Decision Making	Activity
X		X		X	X	X	X	X		11.1, 11.3, 11.5
X		X			X					11.2, 11.6
X	X				X	X	X			11.4
X		X		X	X				X	11.7, 11.8
X	X		X							11.9, 11.10
X	X		X						X	11.11
X		X		X	X				X	11.12

FAMILY AND WORKPLACE

I begin this chapter by advancing an important question about family communication: What makes family relationships unique from the other types of interpersonal relationships we experience in a lifetime? Vanglisti (2004) describes the significance of the family by labeling it "the crucible of society" (p. ix). Family relationships are unique from other types of interpersonal relationships because they are described as both voluntary and involuntary and play a significant role in shaping self-perceptions. Our family relationships usually offer our first glimpse of what is means to form an intimate connection with another person.

"Erma Bombeck wrote for three decades, chronicling absurdities encountered in life, such as families.[1] Families contain unique communicative features. Each of us has a frame of reference for understanding communication in families since these are the first and often the longest-lasting relationships formed in our lives. Perhaps the best way to understand family relationships is to take a look at the role of interpersonal communication in the family and how it shapes our sense of identity and serves as a model for communication choices. Even in situations where relationships with family members have become strained, the bonds have likely shaped an individual's sense of self, served as a model for desirable or undesirable communication, and shaped expectations for future relationships. In this chapter we examine some of the classic and contemporary family communication research, theories and concepts. We will also address interpersonal communication concepts as they apply across the family life span, focusing on both the positive and challenging aspects of these interactions.

Definition of Family

If you were asked to list the number of people you consider to be part of your family, would you include in-laws, close family friends, close personal friends, neighbors, siblings' spouses, stepfamilies, co-workers? Would you include only those relatives related by blood or marriage? When students are asked this question, they often include a wide range of individuals in their list of family members. Most family relationships are described as involuntary types because we do not get to choose our parents, siblings, cousins, aunts, uncles, grandparents, and so on. Some family relationships may be formed of voluntary members. For example, the television series Friends shows how non-biological relationships can fulfill family roles. As we grow older, our choices of who we include in our "family" expand. Voluntary families are created as a result of conscious decisions made to include others in the familial relationship. For example, we select our spouse or life partner. We all have experience with family relationships, but have you considered the unique nature of these bonds? A scene from the 2005 film The Family Stone illustrates this obligation. Sarah Jessica Parker portrays a young woman struggling to be accepted by her fiancé's close-knit family. At one point she becomes frustrated and asks her future mother-in-law, "What's so great about you guys?" Diane Keaton replies, "Uh, nothing . . . it's just that we're all that we've got." Each family member recognizes other family members' idiosyncrasies, but also realizes that the strength of the family bond surpasses all other relationships."

ACTIVITY 11.1

DISCUSSION QUESTIONS

1. Talk about the definition of the term family with several other students. Who would you include in your family? Explain why these individuals are included. What individual differences affect how you define this term (e.g., sex, culture, age, your family of origin, relationship experiences) and who you include in your family?

2. Identify a family from one of your favorite television shows. Use systems theory to analyze the characters' communication patterns and relationships with one another (e.g., interdependence, wholeness, etc). Would you describe the family members' communication and relationships as healthy or unhealthy? Defend your response to this question and be sure to use specific examples to support your arguments.

"TYPES OF FAMILY RELATIONSHIPS[2]

It is difficult to describe a "typical" family in the twenty-first century. Over the years, the structure of the typical American family has changed. The *Handbook of Family Communication* explores several different family forms, such as intact families, divorced or single parent families, stepfamilies, and the families of lesbian women or gay men. But while the forms may have changed, core relationships continue to exist and have provided scholars with opportunities to take a glimpse into how communication develops in these relationships. While we do not have the space to discuss all family forms, three specific interpersonal relationships that exist in the family structure will be discussed: marital relationships, parent-child relationships, and sibling relationships.

Marital Relationships

In a recent issue of *Psychology Today* anthropologist Helen Fisher wrote "I have long been captivated by one of the most striking characteristics of our species: We form enduring pair bonds. The vast majority of other mammals—some 97 percent—do not" (Fisher, 2007, 78). These enduring pair bonds, or marriages, often provide individuals with a great deal of social support, happiness, personal fulfillment and satisfaction. According to family communication researchers Turner and West (2002), "marriage is often seen as the most important intimate relationship two people can share" (232). Some research indicates that individuals in healthy marriages tend to be both healthier and happier than unmarried individuals or those in unhealthy relationships. The longstanding question posed by researchers from a variety of academic and professional fields has always been how to obtain and maintain an enduring marital relationship.

Individuals in healthy marriages tend to be healthier and happier than others.

© sonya etchison, 2007, Shutterstock.

Each life partner brings his or her own set of expectations to the marital relationship. If you have ever tuned into a television talk show, you have probably seen a couple asking the host to solve their marital problems. It is not unusual for the host to identify differing expectations as the root of the problem. Earlier in this text, we mentioned that messages have both content and relational dimensions. The same is true of our expectations for relationships—couples hold content expectations and relational expectations for their partnership.

Content Expectations.   **Content expectations** focus on how the relationship is defined by the role each partner plays. Roles are defined by the expectations held for a position in family. The popular ABC television show *Wife Swap* focuses on the role expectations established for wives in two different types of families. In each episode, the wives switch families for two weeks. Clashes ensue over differing content expectations for husbands' and wives' roles in housekeeping and child-rearing. It is important to note that one of the difficult tasks involved in the marital relationship is ensuring that the two sets of expectations are congruent.

Relational Expectations.   **Relational expectations** refer to the similarity, or correspondence, of the emotional, or affective, expectations each partner has for defining the relationship. In one episode of *Wife Swap*, the Kraut and Hardin wives exchange households. One wife spends considerable time shopping and focusing on the current fashion trends, while her husband tends to the household duties. The other wife expects all family members to participate in household chores, and the couple has formed the expectation that the role of the wife will include being responsible for home schooling the children. When the two families swap wives for the two-week period, they discover that their relational expectations are incongruent in the new environment. This often causes the sparks to fly! When the wives are in their own homes, communication is more satisfying because their spouses and children have congruent expectations for the relationship. They understand what their family roles are, and they have become comfortable with the communication expectations associated with these roles. Marital satisfaction is greater in relationships where couples discuss their expectations for the relationship—failure to talk about expectancies is often equated to playing "guess what's inside my mind."

Traditional couples adopt conventional sex roles in their marriages.

© Losevsky Pavel, 2007, Shutterstock.

To explain the various expectations that couples have for communication and for the relationship, Fitzpatrick (1987) developed a model to distinguish each couple type and how they view role conventionality, interdependence, and approach to conflict. Three couple types were identified: traditionals, separates, and independents (see also Table 11.1).

Table 11.1 – Description of Marital Types

Marital Type of Couples	Characteristics
Traditionals	Demonstrate a high amount of interdependence and sharing; adopt traditional or conventional sex roles
Separates	Emphasize each other's individual identity over relational maintenance; typically avoid conflict
Independents	Respect the need for autonomy; negotiate a high level of communication and sharing; adopt nonconventional sex roles (husband stays home and wife works outside of home)

Traditionals. Those who exhibit a high level of interdependence and sharing are considered traditional couples. Conventional sex roles are adopted in traditional couples, with males performing tasks such as lawn care, automobile maintenance, and taking out the garbage. Women fulfill the role of nurturing caregiver and are responsible for housekeeping and childcare duties. In her research, Fitzpatrick (1987) found that traditionals tend to be the most satisfied of the three couple types.

Separates. Separate couples tend to emphasize each individual's identity and independence over maintaining the relationship. In addition to maintaining conventional sex roles in the relationship, this couple is characterized by their avoidance of conflict. As is evident, this couple type typically reports a low level of marital satisfaction.

Independents. Independent couples simultaneously respect the need for autonomy and engage in a high level communication and sharing with one another. Sex roles in the independent relationship are nonconventional or nonexistent. While it may appear that independents enjoy a happily married relationship, research shows that many independent couples report low levels of satisfaction. By applying this model to our examination of marital communication, we see that one of the characteristics that distinguish the various couple types from one another is their expectations for sex roles and their approach to conflict situations.

Parent-Child Relationships

The first family relationship formed is between a parent and a child. As well as having a legal responsibility to care for and protect their children, parents are responsible for the moral and character development of their children—not an easy task. In his book, *Family First,* Dr. Phil McGraw (2004) discusses the role that parents play in preparing children for life's challenges, and points out that parents need to realize the influence they have as a result of the messages they communicate to their children. A parent's role is complicated; biological and emotional attachments create a special bond that makes communication both rewarding and frustrating at times. Television shows such as *Nanny 911* and *Super Nanny* provide parents with advice for managing interactions with their children. They also provide a glimpse into the parenting challenges experienced by others, offering support to parents who can see that others are enduring the same, or worse, situations.

Over the course of the family life cycle, communication between parents and children evolves as new events occur. It is during this time that the dialectical tensions between autonomy and connection are perhaps the strongest. In the beginning of their lives children are totally dependent on the parents to provide for them and look out for their best interests. In the United States, many parents begin teaching children at a young age to become independent. Children are encouraged to learn to eat by themselves, pick out their own clothes, and to explore their individual interests in sports and other extracurricular activities.

Young children assert their independence as they "do it all by myself."

But even while encouraging independence, many parents simultaneously reinforce the message that they are still connected to their children. Providing children with cellular telephones is one strategy currently used by parents to stay connected as their children explore autonomy.

In her article *"Putting Parents in Their Place: Outside Class,"* Valerie Strauss (2006) illustrates how "too much parent involvement can hinder students' independence" as she explains parent involvement with the "millennial generation."

Putting Parents in Their Place: Outside Class

They are needy, overanxious and sometimes plain pesky—and schools at every level are trying to find ways to deal with them.

No, not students. Parents—specifically parents of today's "millennial genera- tion" who, many educators are discovering, can't let their kids go.

They text message their children in middle school, use the cellphone like an umbilical cord to Harvard Yard and have no compunction about marching into kindergarten class and screaming at a teacher about a grade.

To handle the modern breed of micromanaging parent, educators are devising programs to help them separate from their kids—and they are taking a harder line on especially intrusive parents.

At seminars, such as one in Phoenix last year titled "Managing Millennial Par- ents," they swap strategies on how to handle the "hovercrafts" or "helicopter parents," so dubbed because of a propensity to swoop in at the slightest crisis.

Educators worry not only about how their school climates are affected by intrusive parents trying to set their own agendas but also about the ability of young people to become independent.

"As a child gets older, it is a real problem for a parent to work against their child's independent thought and action, and it is happening more often," said Ron Goldblatt, executive director of the Association of Independent Maryland Schools.

"Many young adults entering college have the academic skills they will need to succeed but are somewhat lacking in life skills like self-reliance, sharing, and conflict resolution," said Linda Walter, an administrator at Seton Hall University in New Jersey and co-chairman of the family portion of new-stu- dent orientation.

Educators say the shift in parental engagement coincides with the rise of the millennial generation, kids born after 1982.

"They have been the most protected and programmed children ever—car seats and safety helmets, play groups and soccer leagues, cellphones and e-mail," said Mark McCarthy, assistant vice president and dean of student development at Marquette University in Milwaukee. "The parents of this generation are used to close and constant contact with their children and vice versa."

Strauss, Valerie. 2006. Putting Parents in Their Place: Outside Class; Too Much Involvement Can Hinder Students' Independence, Experts Say. *Washington Post*, March 21.

DISCUSSION QUESTION

How is the "millennial generation" parent different in terms of parent-child communication than the parents of past generations?

As children progress through adolescence, a new set of communication issues needs to be considered. Up to this point, children have been encouraged to become independent, but eventually the dialectical tension between autonomy and connection kicks in and parents may begin to feel that children are becoming too independent. Adolescence is often a difficult transition period for both children and parents alike, and it is not uncommon for conflicts to occur during this time in the family life cycle. A common communication issue during this period involves the negotiation of rules, with new guidelines for behavior being added on a regular basis as parents and children clash over preferences for clothes, manners, curfews, and activities. As the occurrence of parent-child conflict increases during adolescence, issues that once seemed unimportant now take on new relevance. Consider the issues you and your parents disagreed on during your adolescence. Why do you think communication surrounding these issues was so problematic?

As children grow up, identify their aspirations, and pursue their goals, families may find that their time is divided, and this provides yet another source of tension in the household. One recent study found that parents and their teenage children spend less than one hour per day talking to one another *(http://www.familycommunication.org/)* and the number of families who report that they share meals at the dinner table each day has dwindled over the years.

While many adult privileges are granted to children when they reach the age of eighteen, parents and children view and negotiate the transition to adulthood in different ways. The period when children begin the separation process from their parents is often referred to as the **"launching" stage.** However, this term is often misleading because many families continue to experience a sense of interdependence in their lives for a period of time after the child reaches legal age. For example, after returning to college after Christmas break, one student was overheard saying, "It was kind of nice being back home and knowing that my mom would stay up and wait for me to come in at night. I guess I have to admit that I missed that during my first semester at college." While some may find comfort in the old routines, others may find that new rules need to be negotiated during the launching stage. Adult children who live in their parent's home while getting started in their careers may find that while they are independent in terms of their professional life, they are still dependent on their parents for need fulfillment in their personal life. Daily chores, financial contributions, and respect for household rules often emerge as topics requiring negotiation.

Divorce and remarriage create additional issues to consider in parent-child interactions. Stepfamilies face unique challenges that revolve around issues relating to discipline, resources, and ties to the biological family unit. An estimated one-third of Americans are likely to experience life in a stepfamily (Bumpass et al. 1995). Should stepfamilies and stepchildren expect communication and relationships to be similar to those between biological parents and children? Family communication scholars describe the experience of entering a stepfamily as similar to starting a novel halfway through the book (Coleman, Ganong, and Fine 2004). One student recently described the experience of joining a stepfamily as similar to reading the description of a movie on the back of a DVD and then making a decision about whether or not you will like the movie. Based on the brief description, the movie seems like a good choice. However, once you begin watching the movie, you learn that it

During adolescence, issues that once were insignificant can create conflict.

is not at all what you expected. Similarly, individuals enter stepfamily situations and often expect them to function like intact families when often this is not the case (Coleman et al. 2004).

Images of stepfamilies portrayed in stories and the media often depict these relationships as filled with challenges and negative communication. In the 1998 film *Stepmom*, a conversation between the biological mother (Jackie) and her daughter (Anna) about her stepmother (Isabel) illustrates one of many potential communication issues associated with stepfamily relationships.

Anna: I think Isabel's pretty.

Jackie: Yeah, I think she's pretty too . . . if you like big teeth.

Anna: Mom?

Jackie: Yes sweetie?

Anna: If you want me to hate her, I will. (*Stepmom* directed by Chris Columbus, 2hr. 4 min., 1492 Pictures, 1998.)

Anger or guilt can impact communication about the relationship, and both children and parents may find it difficult to be open about their true feelings. Another communication hurdle faced in the stepparent-stepchild relationship is the use of names to refer to the relationship. In a 2003 interview on Moviehole.net, Jada Pinkett Smith revealed that she refers to her stepson as her "bonus child," and Demi Moore's daughters refer to stepdad, Ashton Kutcher, as "MOD" which stands for "My Other Dad." (*http://people.aol.com/people/articles/0,19736,1090617,00.html*).

Maintenance in Parent-Child Relationships.   Parents and children often find the need to increase efforts in maintaining their relationship as children grow older and gain more autonomy. Activities, new friends, and, eventually, the process of starting a new family can detract from the time and energy available for relationships with parents. In some instances, the onset of these maintenance challenges begins much earlier when parents decide to divorce. Non-custodial parents are faced with identifying new strategies to maintain the relationship with their children in the absence of the close physical proximity they once shared. While many strategies used to maintain the relationship are similar to those found in other types of relationships, in a 1999 study Thomas-Maddox identified several strategies unique to this context. Non-custodial parents indicated that they depend on mediated communication (sending letters, emails, phone calls) and material/monetary offerings (sending gifts, taking children on "exciting" trips) to maintain their relationship. Responses from children revealed that there are additional strategies they initiate to maintain a relationship with

their non-custodial parents. Strategies listed most frequently by children include mediated communication, proximity (living with non-custodial parent during summer vacations and breaks by choice), and suggesting joint activities (proposing ideas such as going to the movies). While being physically separated as a result of this difficult decision may not be easy for parents and children, there are communication strategies that are used to continue the relationship from a distance.

During younger years, siblings often spend more time together than with their parents.

Sibling Relationships

Relationships with siblings generally last the longest, given that our brothers and sisters are often still with us long after our parents are gone. Approximately eighty percent of individuals have siblings and, with the exception of first-born children, sibling relationships are simultaneously formed with parent relationships. In their younger years, siblings often spend more time playing and interacting with one another than they do with their parents. But that does not necessarily mean these relationships are always positive. One minute siblings may be collaborating to "team up" against their parents, and the next minute they may be fighting like cats and dogs.

Communication in the sibling relationship often reflects both negative and positive aspects. As family resources such as time, parent's attention, or physical objects are perceived to be scarce, siblings may engage in conflict or competition.

Studies have shown that same-sex siblings tend to be more competitive than opposite-sex siblings. In some instances, siblings may be expected to fulfill the role of teacher or "co-parent." If you have siblings, chances are you have probably been instructed to "Watch out for your brother (or sister)" at some point in time. Often this occurs in single-parent families or in families where both parents are employed outside the home.

As siblings approach adolescence, their relationship experiences new transformations. Perhaps the competition for resources may become more intense, or siblings experience frustration when they are compared to one another. In these instances, a sibling may seek deidentification from other siblings. **Deidentification** is defined as an individual's attempt to create a distinct identity that is separate from that of their siblings. Have you ever had a teacher compare you to an older sibling? Or perhaps you have had friends at school who point out how similar or different you are compared to your brother or sister. When siblings are constantly evaluated against one another, they may experience a desire to create a unique identity and sense of self. Perhaps your ability to play soccer was often compared to one of your siblings that also played soccer. In an effort to distinguish yourself from your sibling, you quit playing soccer and started wrestling instead.

Maintenance in Sibling Relationships

Relational maintenance is of particular importance in the sibling relationship as the relationship between brothers and sisters typically lasts longer than any other family relationship. In a study designed to investigate unique maintenance strategies employed by siblings, six behaviors were identified (Myers and Weber 2004). These include confirmation, humor, social support, family visits, escape, and verbal aggression.

Confirmation.   Confirmation strategies consist of messages used to communicate the importance or value of siblings in one's life. Statements such as, "I'm lucky to have you as my brother" or "I really appreciate having you here to support me" are often viewed as validating the relationship.

Humor.   Often siblings use humor as a way to bring amusement or enjoyment to their relationship. Sharing private jokes about family members or making fun of their behaviors are ways siblings use humor to strengthen their bond.

Social Support.   Siblings provide social support to one another by using verbal and nonverbal comforting strategies to assist one another through difficult times. Asking a sibling for advice or sharing information about difficulties in other relationships illustrates the trust that is present in the relationship.

Family Events. Siblings often maintain and strengthen their relationships with each other and other family members through participation in family events. They may agree to visit their parents at the same time during the summer or holidays to spend time together.

Escape. Sometimes we view our relationships with our siblings as an escape during difficult situations. Have you ever agreed to attend a family wedding or reunion only because your sibling agreed to attend? Doing so solidifies the bond by communicating the dependence that you have on one another to provide an outlet during difficult times.

Verbal Aggression. While the final strategy, verbal aggression, may seem counterintuitive to maintaining a relationship, this maintenance mechanism allows siblings to vent their frustrations with one another. Over the years, they may have discovered that yelling at one another is the most effective method for having their concerns heard."

© Galina Barskaya, 2007, Shutterstock.

Siblings often maintain their connections through participation in family events.

ACTIVITY 11.3

Based on the type of families discussed in this section, identify a family from one of your favorite television shows. State the type of family and explain how the family relates to the type that you mentioned.

ACTIVITY 11.4

Ask students to talk to their friends or peers about their family types.

- What is the family structure?
- Does the millennial generation differ from the person interviewed?
- What were the outcomes?
- What were some of the challenges if any were faced in the family?

ACTIVITY 11.5

If you had to choose a family type from a movie which movie would you choose and why? Name two things about the movie that you feel are important to you and families.

"FAMILY COMMUNICATION THEORIES[4]

Several theories can be applied to the study of communication in family relationships. Recall the definition of interpersonal communication: a process which occurs in a specific context and involves an exchange of verbal or nonverbal messages between two connected individuals with the intent to achieve shared meaning. The family is one context of connected individuals in which these interactions occur. Scholars of family communication have applied a variety of interpersonal theories to explain these interactions. In essence, virtually any theory of interpersonal communication could be applied to the study of families. Three theories which have implications for the family relationship in particular are systems theory, family communication patterns theory, and symbolic interactionism.

Systems Theory

Systems theory has been employed by family scholars to explore a variety of interactions, including children's attitudes about their single parent dating (Marrow-Ferguson and Dickson 1995), family involvement in addressing children's problems at school (Walsh and Williams 1997), and adolescent abuse of their parents (Eckstein 2004). **Family systems theory** is one of the most frequently used theories in family communication scholarship (Stamp 2004). The basic premise behind this theory is that family relationships can be treated as systems and can include the study of systemic qualities such as wholeness, interdependence, hierarchy, boundaries, calibration, and equifinality (Stamp 2004). Each of the elements of systems theory is particularly relevant in explaining how and why family members relate to one another.

Wholeness. **Wholeness** implies that a family creates its own personality or culture, and that this personality is unique from that of each family member. Many studies that have applied systems theory recognize that in order to understand the dynamics of families, the role of individual family members must be considered as well.

Interdependence. **Interdependence** proposes that the family system is comprised of interrelated parts, or members. A change experienced by one family member is likely to result in changes that impact all other family members. Suppose a child catches the flu and cannot attend school for several days. If both parents work outside the home, one will have to make adjustments to his work schedule to stay at home with the child. To protect other family members from being exposed to the illness, family routines such as sharing dinner or watching television together may be altered.

Hierarchy. All systems have levels, or a **hierarchy,** present. Typically, parents take on the powerful roles in the family and are responsible for seeing that children's needs are fulfilled and that discipline and control are maintained in the system. Perhaps the system element that has gained the most attention in family studies is boundaries.

Typically the parents are responsible for taking care of children and maintaining the powerful roles in the family.

Boundaries. Families create **boundaries** to communicate to members who are to be considered part of the system. These boundaries are often flexible as the family expands to include friends and pets. **Ambiguous boundaries** often create confusion about who family members perceive as being part of the system. In the movie *While You Were Sleeping,* Lucy (Sandra Bullock) discovers that the man the family refers to as Uncle Saul (Jack Warden) is included in the family's boundaries due to their strong friendship. Uncle Saul says, "Lucy, the Callaghans, well, they took me in as part of their family. I'd never let anyone hurt them." Even though the family bonds are not biological, he communicates that he is dedicated to protecting the family and views them as an important part of his life.

Calibration. The system element of **calibration** is the mechanism that allows the family to review their relationships and communication and decide if any adjustments need to be made to the system. Television shows such as *Nanny 911* provide examples of families that can be used as a basis for comparison. Feedback communicated through messages received from others can also be taken into consideration. While waiting in line at the grocery store, a mother might be complimented on how well-behaved her children are. This provides her with feedback to gauge her performance as a mother.

Equifinality. The final systems element, **equifinality,** refers to families' abilities to achieve the same goal by following different paths or employing different communication behaviors. For example, one family may teach the children independence by communicating the expectation that the children are responsible for getting themselves up and getting ready for school in the morning. In another family, the mother might enter the bedroom and gently sing "Good Morning" to the children, lay out their school clothes, and have breakfast ready for them. Both families accomplish the same goal: working through the morning routine of getting to school on time. However, each family has a different method for accomplishing the goal.

Family Communication Patterns Theory

Perhaps one of the most complicated phenomena to factor into the family communication equation is the role that intrapersonal communication plays in the process. **Family communication patterns theory** is a comprehensive theory that focuses on the cognitive processes used to shape and guide our interpersonal interactions. Originally developed by McLeod and Chaffee (1972, 1973) as a way for explaining family members' interactions associated with television viewing, the goal of the theory was to explain how parents help children to understand messages received from multiple sources through mediated channels. But consider for a moment all of the different messages received from outside the family that are processed on a daily basis. Ritchie and Fitzpatrick (1990) expanded the focus of this theory beyond mediated messages to focus on how a variety of messages are processed and discussed within the family to create shared meaning. This revised theory identified two primary orientations used by families: conversation and conformity.

Conversation.   **Conversation orientation** refers to the level of openness and the frequency with which a variety of topics are discussed. Families who adopt a high conversation orientation encourage members to openly and frequently share their thoughts and feelings with one another on a wide variety of topics. It is rare that a topic is "off limits" for discussion in families who have a high conversation orientation. On the other hand, families with low conversation orientation experience less frequent or less open interactions, and sometimes there are limits with regard to what topics can be discussed.

Conformity.   The second dimension of the communication pattern analysis focuses on the family's conformity orientation. **Conformity** refers to the degree to which a family encourages autonomy in individual beliefs, values, and attitudes. Families who emphasize a high level of conformity in interactions encourage family members to adopt similar ways of thinking about topics, often with the goal of avoiding conflict and promoting harmony in the family. At the other end of the conformity continuum, family members are encouraged to form independent beliefs and attitudes, and these differing opinions are often perceived as having equal value in discussions and decision-making. To explain the interrelationship between conversation orientation and conformity orientation, Koerner and Fitzpatrick identified four different family types (2002). These include pluralistic, consensual, laissez-faire, and protective families. See Table 11.2 for an integration of the family types into the two family orientations.

Table 11.2 – Family Types as Identified by Family Communications Patterns Theory

	High Conformity	Low Conformity
HIGH CONVERSATION	CONSENSUAL Strong pressure toward agreement encouragement to take interest in ideas without disturbing power in family hierarchy independence of ideas	PLURALISTIC Open communication and discussion of ideas is encouraged but with little emphasis on social constraint; fosters communication competence as well as
LOW CONVERSATION	LAISSEZ-FAIRE Little parent-child interaction; child relatively more influenced by external social settings (e.g., peer groups)	PROTECTIVE Obedience is prized; little concern for conceptual matters; child is not well-prepared for dealing with outside influences and is easily persuaded

Parents who encourage their children to form relationships outside the home and couples who believe that each partner should pursue his own network of friends typically do so in an effort to broaden the perspectives of individuals within the family. Use the scale in Table 11.3 to find out what you perceive your family orientation to be.

Pluralistic. **Pluralistic families** adopt a high conversation orientation and a low conformity orientation. Almost anything goes in this family! A wide range of topics are discussed, and family members are encouraged to have their own opinions without feeling the pressure to agree with one another. Children in pluralistic families are often encouraged to participate in decision-making on topics ranging from where the family should go for vacation to the establishment of family rules.

Consensual. **Consensual families** adopt both a high conversation and a high conformity orientation. These families often encourage members to be open in their interactions with one another, but they expect that family members will adopt similar opinions and values. Parents in consensual families promote open conversations, but they still believe that they are the authority when it comes to decisions in the family.

Laissez-Faire. **Laissez-faire families** adopt both a low conversation and low conformity orientation. Rarely will family members talk with one another, and when conversations do occur, they are focused on a limited number of topics. Children are encouraged to make their own decisions, often with little or no guidance or feedback from their parents in the laissez-faire family.

Protective. **Protective families** score low on conversation orientation and high on conformity. The phrase "Children should be seen but not heard" is characteristic of this family type. Parents are considered to be the authority, and children are expected to obey the family rules without questioning them.

Identifying and understanding the approaches used to communicate and to promote autonomy and independence is beneficial to understanding how these interactions shape both individual and family identities.

Symbolic Interaction Theory

Symbolic interactionism is perhaps one of the most widely applied theories in the study of family life. In Chapter Five we discussed the role that symbols and messages play in assigning meaning to our experiences, others, and ourselves. Mead's (1934) five concepts of symbolic interactionism (mind, self, I, me, and roles) are particularly useful in understanding the impact that family interactions have on shaping one's identity. In his discussion of the concept of "mind," Mead explains the role that symbols play in creating shared meaning. Children interact with family members and learn language and social meanings associated with words. Similarly, Mead points out that one's sense of "self" is developed through interactions with others. Families are influential in shaping this view of self through the messages and reactions to one another. Family members gain a sense of how they are viewed by others from messages that are exchanged. Statements such as "You're such a good husband!" or "He's such a rotten kid" shape how individuals see themselves.

Table 11.3 – The Revised Family Communication Pattern Instrument

Respond to the following statements as they apply to your communication with your parents while you were growing up. Place a number on the line that best describes your agreement with the statements below, using the following scale:

5 = Strongly Agree, 4 = Agree, 3 = Neither Agree nor Disagree, 2 = Disagree, 1 = Strongly Disagree

_____ 1. My parents often said things like, "You'll know better when you grow up."

_____ 2. My parents often asked my opinion when the family was talking about something.

_____ 3. My parents often said things like, "My ideas are right and you should not question them."

_____ 4. My parents encouraged me to challenge their ideas and beliefs.

_____ 5. My parents often said things like, "A child should not argue with adults."

_____ 6. I usually told my parents what I was thinking about things.

_____ 7. My parents often said things like, "There are some things that are just not to be talked about."

_____ 8. I can tell my parents almost anything.

_____ 9. When anything really important was involved, my parents expected me to obey without question.

_____ 10. In our family we often talk about our feelings and emotions.

_____ 11. In our home, my parents usually had the last word.

_____ 12. My parents and I often had long, relaxed conversation about nothing in particular.

_____ 13. My parents felt that it was important to be the boss.

_____ 14. I really enjoyed talking with my parents, even when we disagreed.

_____ 15. My parents sometimes became irritated with my views if they were different from theirs.

_____ 16. My parents often say something like "you should always look at both sides of an issue."

_____ 17. If my parents don't approve of it, they don't want to know about it.

_____ 18. My parents like to hear my opinions, even when they don't agree with me.

_____ 19. When I am at home, I am expected to obey my parents' rules.

_____ 20. My parents encourage me to express my feelings.

_____ 21. My parents tended to be very open about their emotions.

_____ 22. We often talk as a family about things we have done during the day.

_____ 23. In our family we often talk about our plans and hopes for the future.

_____ 24. In our family we talk about topics like politics and religion where some persons disagree with others.

_____ 25. My parents often say something like "Every member of the family should have some say in family decisions."

_____ 26. My parents often say something like "You should give in on arguments rather than risk making people mad."

SCORING DIRECTIONS:

Items 1, 3, 5, 7, 9, 11, 13, 15, 17, 19, 26 represent the Conformity items.
Add these items and divide by 11 to determine your Conformity score.
Items 2, 4, 6, 8, 10, 12, 14, 16, 18, 20, 21, 22, 23, 24, 25 represent the Conversation items.
Add these items and divide by 15 to determine your Conversation score.

Scoring—Your scores will range from 1–5 and the higher score is more likely to be the perceived communication pattern in your family.

Source: "Revised Family Communication Pattern Instrument" by L.D. Ritchie from "Family Communication Patterns: Measuring Interpersonal Perceptions of Interpersonal Relationships" by Michael E. Roloff, 1990, Communication Research, 17 (4), 523–544. Reprinted by Permission of Sage Publications Inc.

It is important to note that individual differences, such as personality traits or communication predispositions, may cause family members to view the same situation in very different ways. Consider the following scenario.

> Kaija was quiet as Jay drove up the driveway. Jay smiled at her and said, "Trust me, they'll love you!" Kaija was meeting Jay's family for the first time since he had proposed. As they entered the front door, she was bombarded with hugs and kisses from various aunts, uncles, grandparents, and cousins. During dinner the talking never stopped! Kaija felt so left out—and nobody even seemed to care enough to ask her questions about herself. At one point, she slipped out on the back patio just to have a few moments of peace and quiet. As they drove back to campus, Jay commented, "Wasn't it a great evening! Everyone thought you were awesome!" Kaija couldn't believe what she had just heard. How could Jay have come to the conclusion that his family liked her? After all, they didn't take the time to find out anything about her. And the hugs and kisses were so intimidating. Kaija's family would have never shown such open displays of affection the first time they met Jay. She was confused—how could Jay have thought the evening went so great when she thought it had been horrible?

Who was correct in his or her assessment of the evening's events? Symbolic interactionism would indicate that both Jay and Kaija formed accurate perceptions. Each of them had formed his own meaning of the event based on his interpretation of the messages and behaviors. We learn in the scenario that Kaija's family would not have displayed affection so openly, while Jay's family background shaped his acceptance of effusive greetings. Our experiences in our family of origin shape our meanings of events, messages, and behaviors. The fact that Jay's family did not ask Kaija about herself caused her to perceive them as being uninterested. But suppose Jay had shared with his family that Kaija was an only child and tended to be shy around large groups. He may have asked them to refrain from bombarding her with questions that might cause her to feel uncomfortable. To better understand how symbolic interactionism applies to this scenario, it might be useful to examine the three underlying assumptions of the theory (LaRossa and Reitzes 1993).

First, *our interactions with family members influence the meanings we assign to behaviors and messages.* Children determine if they should evaluate experiences as being positive or negative by watching the reactions of family members to various events and messages. A child whose parents avoid conflict may believe that conflict is a negative behavior that should be avoided at all costs. Coming from a family that shows caring through conversation, Kaija assigned a negative meaning to Jay's family's failure to ask her questions about herself.

Next, *individuals create a sense of self which serves as a guide for selecting future behaviors.* We assess situations and take into consideration whether others will perceive behaviors and messages in a positive or negative way. This assumption goes beyond our own evaluation of events to include the perceptions of others. A child whose father has told him "You're a rotten kid" and "You'll never amount to anything" has learned to misbehave. As the negative messages are repeated, he comes to believe that others expect him to misbehave.

Finally, symbolic interactionism posits that the *behavior of family members is influenced by culture and society.* Perhaps this assumption sheds light on the reasons families are reluctant to admit that they experience conflict from time to time. Based on media portrayals of family life and from listening to the happy stories of other families, an expectation has been established that "normal" families do not fight.

CREATING A FAMILY IDENTITY

While individual family members form their own identities, the family as a unit also creates a collective identity. Communication is the primary mechanism for creating, this family identity, with various messages and behaviors providing insight as to how the family view itself as a group. Four ways that families create and sustain an identity as a unit are through stories, myths, themes, and metaphors. As we discuss each of these elements, reflect on your own family of origin and how these communicative acts shaped your sense of what it means to be a part of your family.

Family Stories

Family stories are narratives recounting significant events that have been shared by members. In essence, family life is comprised of a series of stories. Because they are about shared experiences, these stories are often personal and emotional; they may evoke positive or negative feelings in family members. Individuals often use these stories to shape their own sense of identity. One of the authors of your text had a difficult time gaining confidence in her driving ability. Do you think it might be due in part to the fact that her family members enjoyed telling and retelling the story of how she was responsible for wrecking the family car when she was four years old?

Three types of family stories that have been studied by family scholars in an attempt to explain how families define their experiences are birth stories, courtship stories, and stories of survival. **Birth stories** describe how each person entered the family and can define how members "fit" into the system. One woman shared a story of enduring a forty-two hour labor prior to the birth of her son. She stated, "I guess I should have known then that he would always be challenging me because he gave me such a difficult time from the beginning!" **Courtship stories** provide a timeline for tracing romance in the family. They are often used to describe how parents and grandparents met and how they decided that they were right for one another. A young woman who was engaged to be married asked her grandfather how he met her grandmother. He explained that she was working in the fields on her family farm and that it was love at first sight. He joked, "I knew she was a hard worker, so I asked her

Families share special stories of a child's birth to connect the child within the family.

to marry me!" But he went on to explain that he knew she was devoted to helping her family and knew that she would be dedicated to her own family. **Stories of survival** are narratives used to explain how family members have overcome difficult times, and they are often told to help family members cope with challenges they face. Three sisters who, at a young age, were physically abused by their father, discussed sharing their stories with one another as well as with other young girls to assist them in coping with similar experiences. While some might perceive the retelling of these stories as being too painful, the sisters viewed the stories as therapeutic and reinforced the notion that if they could survive the abuse of their father, they were strong enough to face any situation.

Family Myths

Family **myths** are created to communicate the beliefs, values, and attitudes held by members to represent characteristics that are considered important to the family. These myths are often fictional as they are based on an ideal image the family wishes to convey to others. Consider the following example:

> "I couldn't believe what I was hearing! At my grandfather's funeral, my dad's family members were all talking about what a great man my grandfather was and how much they would miss him. My grandmother sobbed as she whispered, 'He was such a loving and caring man. I don't know what I'll do without him.' After the service, I asked my father why they were all referring to my grandfather that way. For years I had heard stories of the physical abuse that had taken place in the family during my dad's childhood, and I had heard my grandfather yell at my grandmother on numerous occasions. My dad responded, 'It's just easier on your grandmother if we all remember him in a positive way.' "

In this scenario, the family creates a myth that portrays the grandfather as a loving, caring man. Doing so enables them to protect the grandmother and to perpetuate the belief that he was a good father and husband. In the movie, *Doing Time on Maple Drive*, a family goes to great lengths to portray the image of the "perfect family" to their friends and neighbors. At one point, the son reveals to his parents that he attempted to commit suicide because he would rather be dead than admit to them that he is gay. This scene illustrates the power of family myths and the tremendous amount of pressure placed on family members to live up to the expectations communicated in these myths.

Metaphors

Sometimes families create **metaphors** to assist in communicating how family life as a system is experienced by members. Family metaphors make reference to specific objects, events, or images to represent the family experience and a collective identity. The metaphor of a "three-ring circus" may be used to describe the chaos and disorganization that exists within one family, while the "well-oiled machine" can depict the emphasis on control and organization that is the norm for another family. Metaphors can provide those within the family and outside of the family with an understanding of what behaviors are valued as well as how family members are expected to behave. A person from a "well-oiled machine" family can use the metaphor to understand the expectations associated with being a member of the family.

Themes

Family **themes** represent important concerns regarding the expected relationship between family members and can assist family members in understanding how to direct their energy as a family unit. These themes often emerge from two primary sources—the background or experience of parents, and the dialectical pulls experienced by the family. Suppose Joe and Marnie are having a difficult time managing the tensions of autonomy and connection as their children grow older, begin dating, and spend more time with friends than with family members. In an attempt to communicate their concern for the growing independence of family members, they remind the children that "Blood is thicker than water" and "Friends may come and go, but family is forever." These themes are intended to remind the children that while they may form many relationships outside the unit, the strongest ties should be reserved for those in their family."

ACTIVITY 11.6

DISCUSSION QUESTIONS

1. Talk about the definition of the term **family** with several other students. Who would you include in your family? Explain why these individuals are included. What individual differences affect how you define this term (e.g., sex, culture, age, your family of origin, relationship experiences) and who you include in your family?

2. Identify a family from one of your favorite television shows. Use systems theory to analyze the characters' communication patterns and relationships with one another (e.g., interdependence, wholeness, etc). Would you describe the family members' communication and relationships as healthy or unhealthy? Defend your response to this question and be sure to use specific examples to support your arguments.

ACTIVITY 11.7

When you were young, what type of family stories did your family have (birth stories, courtship stories, or survival stories). State what you liked or disliked about the story.

"CONSEQUENCES OF FAMILY RELATIONSHIPS[5]

Throughout out this text, various communication variables have been identified as being both beneficial and harmful to our interpersonal relationships. Because families play such a vital role in the development of our self-identity, understanding how specific communication behaviors can enhance and damage our relationships and our senses of self is important.

Families can serve as the primary source of understanding and support for individuals. As we grow older, we receive messages that let us know that we are cared for and accepted. These perceptions are often shaped by the types of verbal and nonverbal cues we receive from others and are often linked to the formation of our sense of self. Three types of messages are often used to indicate whether family members view us in the same way we see ourselves.

Confirmation

Confirmation occurs when we treat and communicate with family members in a way that is consistent with how they see themselves. A child who perceives himself to be independent is confirmed when a parent gives him responsibility and allows him to make his own decisions.

Rejection

Rejection occurs when family members treat others in a manner that is inconsistent with how they see themselves. Can you recall a time when you felt like you were "grown up" but your parents treated you as though you were still a child? Perhaps you felt you were responsible enough to be left alone while your parents went out for the evening, but they hired a babysitter to stay with you. At times, family members communicate with one another in a way that is disconfirming.

Disconfirmation

Disconfirmation occurs when family members fail to offer any type of response. This behavior can be viewed as lack of acknowledgement for how they view other family members. We often get caught up in our busy schedules and fail to communicate with family members. Even though our response is neither positive nor negative, it can cause others to feel dissatisfied with the relationship. A parent who fails to comment on a child's report card, or a wife who fails to acknowledge the efforts of her husband's attempts at cooking dinner are

Offering encouragement fosters development of a more intimate relationship.

examples of disconfirming responses. Understanding and supportive communication are related to family satisfaction. If we perceive family members as being there for us, we are more willing to exert energy toward developing a more intimate relationship.

COMMUNICATING INTIMACY

Earlier in this text we discussed the concept of intimacy in romantic and marital relationships. Our first experience in developing intimacy in relationships is often a result of our interactions with parents, siblings, and other family members. **Intimacy** refers to close relationships in which two or more people share personal and private information with one another. Young children are often more willing to disclose their fears and goals with family members than with others, and this is often the result of the perceived trust and affection associated with these relationships. How do you show affection for your family members? Chances are that the most basic way this is demonstrated is through our willingness to share disclosures. While we know that intimacy is fostered through our self-disclosures, these revelations are not necessarily exchanged equally between family members. Studies of disclosure in families have found that wives engage in disclosures more often than husbands, and both male and female children report disclosing more information to their mothers than to their fathers. As children grow older, their disclosure patterns often change. College students often disclose more to friends than to their parents. Consider the changes in your own disclosure patterns with your parents. As you get older, you may discover that you are more willing to share negative and honest information about yourself with your friends than you are with parents.

DIFFICULT COMMUNICATION

We have addressed the positive and supportive aspects of interpersonal communication in family relationships, but it is important to note that families are not immune to difficult communication. Just as romantic partners and friends experience highs and lows in relationships, so do families. Because families evolve as members grow and encounter new life experiences, additional communication challenges emerge. The key to effectively managing these issues and maintaining a positive relationship is to understand the role of communication in guiding us through the muddy waters.

Family Stress

Reuben Hill developed the **ABCX model** to study the stress experienced by families during war (1958). Each component of this model provides a glimpse into how different families cope with stress. To begin, "A" represents the stressor event and resulting hardship. "B" refers to the resources a family has available to manage the stress. Given that different families define stress in unique ways, "C" is used to explain how the family defines the stress. Depending on how a family defines "A" "B" and "C," the perception of an event as a crisis is represented by "X." The model is useful for understanding how and why families label situations as stressful and cope with stressors.

"A" represents the stressor event of a young mother stationed with the U.S. military in Iraq. In this story, extended family members serve as resources to assist with the care of a three-year old child in the absence of his mother, in this case representing the "B." The confusion experienced by the grandmother as she tries to help her grandson cope with the separation causes her to define the stressor as emotionally draining (C). While the family knows that the daughter will return home eventually, they also understand that she chose to serve her country and realize the danger associated with this responsibility. This may keep the family from evaluating the stress as crisis (X). Take a look at Table 11.4 to review each step of the ABCX model.

Stressor events can take many forms; Boss (1988) developed a typology of stressors that families face. These include stressors that are internal versus external, normative versus non-normative, voluntary versus involuntary, and chronic versus acute. **Internal stressors** are those that evolve from a family member. Examples might include a daughter's upcoming wedding or a teen who has tried to run away from home. **External stressors,** on the other hand, are often the result of an event that occurs outside the family, such as a hurricane destroying a family's home or even just an increase in the price of gasoline.

Normative stressors are those that are expected to occur at some point during the course of the family life cycle. The birth of a child or the death of an elderly parent is are events that families anticipate dealing with at some point in time. **Non-normative stressors** are unpredictable and often catch families "off guard." While most people think that winning the lottery would be a great stressor to experience, families do not typically anticipate coming into such a large sum of money and have difficulty dealing with new challenges posed by their good fortune.

Voluntary stressors are those events that family members seek out, such as changing careers and moving to a new city or deciding to run for political office. **Involuntary stressors** are events that simply occur—a family member being injured in a car accident or the announcement of an unplanned teen pregnancy.

Illnesses such as cancer or alcoholism are examples of **chronic stressor** events that require families to cope with the situation for an extended period of time. **Acute stressors** are relatively short-lived and include events such as a student getting suspended for misbehaving or losing the only set of keys to the family car.

Table 11.4 – The ABCX Model of Family Stress

A	Event producing the stress	Parent of a small child stationed overseas in the military
B	Resources a family has available	Extended family members (grandparents) assist with child care back home in the U.S.
C	Meaning family assigns to the stress	Grandmother finds the child's questions to be emotionally draining, to cause sadness
X	Perception of ability to manage stress (crisis or manageable)	Knowledge that parent chose to go overseas to serve in military; knowledge that this situation will eventually end keeps family from perceiving this as a "crisis"

Violence and Abuse in Families

Some of us learn at a young age that family is a source of caring and support and will be throughout our lives, but this is not always the case. Often family members encounter stress in their lives and turn to alcohol, drug abuse, or domestic violence as a means to escape from their problems. In these situations, the sad reality is that family members often hurt the ones they love the most. In 1998, nearly one million incidents of violence against a former spouses, boyfriends, or girlfriends were reported (U.S. Dept. of Justice 1998). Unfortunately, abusive behavior often follows a pattern in families, with fifty percent of men who admitted to assaulting their wives reporting that they also frequently abused their children (Strauss, Gellas, and Smith 1990). Abuse may come in the form of physical violence, or verbal and psychological mistreatment. While spousal or child abuse are the forms most often discussed, it is important to note that there are numerous occurrences of elder abuse as well as incidents of abuse in same-sex couples. Disclosures may serve as a mechanism through which family reports reveal abuse, but often the abuse goes unreported.

As children gain more power in the family, incidents of parental abuse by adolescent children have increased (Eckstein 2004). The parent-child relationship is not meant to be equal. Parents need to have control and authority in this dependent relationship. However, in some instances, the reverse is true, with children assuming power in the relationship. Three forms of parental abuse have been identified: physical, psychological, and financial. Physical abuse involves hitting, slapping, and pushing parents. In a 1989 study, nearly fourteen percent of parents reported being physically abused by their adolescent children at least once (Agnew and Huguley). Children may also engage in psychological forms of abuse. Examples of this type of abuse would be creating a sense of fear and include making threats to run away or hurt themselves, or name-calling. A final form of mistreatment is financial abuse. Children who steal from their parents, make demands for things beyond the family's budget, or damage the family's home or possessions are guilty of this type of abuse.

So what mechanisms are available to help family members through these damaging and harmful situations? Before any other step, family members need to admit abuse occurs and to seek assistance in dealing with the situation. Family members often feel ashamed or perceive that the family is a failure by admitting that there is physical or psychological abuse in the home. Seeking professional assistance is a crucial first step in resolving these potentially harmful issues."

ACTIVITY 11.8

Invite an attorney who specializes in family law or a violence counselor to the class. Have the guest to discuss violence against children, sexual violence, or marital violence.

"WORKPLACE RELATIONSHIPS[6]

From popular television shows such as The Office and The Apprentice, to films such as Office Space, work relationships are depicted as everyday circumstances in our lives. Throughout this text, we have discussed the theoretical foundations and concepts central to understanding the role communication plays in interpersonal relationships. As we continue to examine how and why our relationships are impacted by contextual issues, it is important to take a closer look at one context where many adults spend the majority of their time interacting with others—workplace. Many Americans spend more than the average forty hours per week at their jobs. Consider the fact that many employees take work home with them, and the amount of time dedicated to work relationships increases. For some individuals, this many mean that they could potentially spend more time engaged in communication in their work relationships than in any other context.

This chapter addresses the unique aspects of interpersonal communication in relationships associated with one's professional career. In this chapter, we discuss how and why work relationships differ from other types of interpersonal bonds, and explore different types of work relationships, as well as diversity in the workplace. We explain how technology impacts our work relationships, and address the issues faced when exploring the link between work and family.

THE UNIQUE NATURE OF WORK RELATIONSHIPS

Each of our interpersonal relationships is characterized by unique features, and the bonds formed with others at work are no exception. As we begin our discussion of interactions at work, we first need to consider the characteristics of these relationships. How are work relationships different from relationships we form with friends, family, and at school? Work relationships can be described as voluntary, involuntary, and temporary, and are often impacted by the presence of a hierarchy or status differential.

Voluntary

Very few employees remain at their first job for their entire lives. A study conducted by the U.S. Bureau of Labor Statistics found that employees report an average of 9.6 different jobs from age eighteen to age thirty-six. Consider the fact that the majority of our work relationships are voluntary. Organizational relationships are voluntary in the sense that individuals have the choice to interview with the organization and, if offered a job, they have the choice to accept the position and to become a member or not. Deciding to become a member of an organization indicates that a person is interested in pursuing the relationships associated with being an employee. While the initial decision to join an organization is voluntary, some tasks assigned to an employee may result in the formation of involuntary relationships. Involuntary relationships exist between members who did not have any initial desire to initiate a relationship. If you have ever been appointed by your supervisor to work on a project or a team, the relationship between you and the new team members was likely involuntary.

Temporary

Work relationships are also often temporary in nature. While family bonds are long-lasting, employees have the option to continue the relationships with those at work or to seek employment and, therefore, new co-workers, elsewhere. Further, some of the relationships formed in the workplace may be temporary in nature due to the task associated with them. For example, if Martha is assigned to work on a project that is scheduled to be completed six months from now, chances are that the relationships formed during the term of this project are temporary in nature.

The relationships you form when working on projects may be temporary ones.

Hierarchy/Status Differential

A final characteristic of work relationships is that the interactions are often regulated by a hierarchy or status differential. Our relationships with others in the workplace are impacted by a hierarchy that implies status differentials between members in the organization. Some organizations are "tall" structures with many levels of supervisors, administrators, and employees, while others have relatively "flat" structures with few hierarchical levels separating supervisors from employees. Within the workplace, both implicit and explicit rules and norms for communicating with those of different status exist. For example, persons of lower status understand that they are expected to wait for those of higher level status. Have you ever waited for your academic advisor or professor to show up for his office hours to discuss an assignment that is due? Chances are you are willing to wait ten or fifteen minutes if he is late. It is not likely that the professor would be willing to wait that amount of time for a student to show up for an appointment. Organizational hierarchies form the backbone and/or foundation for a company. Managers and their employees must form relationships in order to meet mutually agreed-upon goals, co-workers are required to interact with one another in order to accomplish tasks and fulfill the goals, and numerous relationships are formed with individuals and other organizations that the company depends upon for its success.

Consider the following example. Clear Mountain Bank is a small community bank with branch offices located in several surrounding communities. By examining this small organization, we can see a vast number of relationships. The bank's officers and branch managers must interact with one another to ensure that they fulfill the organization's goals. If the bank is to succeed, its tellers must establish satisfactory relationships with its customers. But let us take a look beyond the confines of the bank buildings. In order to attract new customers, the bank is required to form relationships with the local media. To ensure that the bank is complying with federal regulations, interactions must be held with those responsible for insuring that regulations are met. Given its presence in the community, Clear Mountain may also form relationships through sponsorship of the local elementary school, as well as several youth athletic teams. This is but a small glimpse of the vast number of relationships formed within a single small organization. Let us take a closer look at the types of relationships formed in organizations.

Have you ever stopped to consider the number of organizations that influence your life each and every day? Given that you are a student, you are obviously influenced by your school. To ensure your physical care, relationships have been formed with those in your doctor's and dentist's offices. If you work while going to school, chock up one more organization you may interact with on a daily basis. In essence, we all exist in an organizational world. As you reflect on the relationships that you have formed in organizations, chances are that many of the communication variables we have discussed in this text have been influential. Whether the task involves building trust, listening to colleagues, providing feedback to your manager or clients, or initiating and maintaining relationships, communication plays a pivotal role.

TYPES OF RELATIONSHIPS AT WORK

As you can see from the Clear Mountain example, there are a variety of relationships that can be formed within a single organization. Research that has focused on communication in organizations has primarily focused on two types of work relationships: superior-subordinate relationships and co-worker relationships. **Superior-subordinate** interactions are characterized by a status differential between individuals, and focus on the interactions that take place between supervisors or managers and their employees or subordinates. **Co-worker,** or peer, relationships evolve as a result of interactions between members of an organization at the same status level. Regardless of the type of relationship, communication factors play a vital role in achieving interpersonal effectiveness. Factors such as trust, listening, and feedback are critical.

Superior-Subordinate Relationships

Superior-subordinate relationships differ from other types of interpersonal bonds because of the explicit status differential that is present. Factors impacting relationships between organizational leaders and members include channels of communication, emphasis on task versus relational needs, and communication flow. As we take a closer look at the relationships between supervisors and subordinates, it is important to trace the theoretical foundations that have guided managers in developing various styles of communication.

Early theories of organizational communication focused on information being communicated downward from supervisor to subordinate. **Classical theories** viewed communication as being primarily one-way. Managers sent information down the channels to employees, and messages were typically formal and focused exclusively on task issues. The notion of hierarchy in organizational relationships is demonstrated by Taylor's principles of scientific management. Taylor's theory (1911) asserts that there are distinct differences between managers and employees. The manager's role

Co-worker relationships are those among people on the same status level.

is to plan and direct the workers as they perform physical labor. Over time, researchers realized that something was missing from this communication model. Meeting the interpersonal needs of workers emerged as an essential element in achieving high productivity and worker satisfaction.

Abraham Maslow's (1943) Hierarchy of Needs was one of the first theories used to specifically acknowledge the higher level needs of organizational employees. While previous theories had acknowledged the presence of worker's physiological and safety needs, Maslow's theory addressed needs for affiliation, esteem, and self actualization. Affiliation needs are placed at the third level of Maslow's hierarchy. These needs are often fulfilled through interpersonal relationships with managers and co-workers. Maslow's theory paved the way for scholars to examine the relationship between work factors, employees' higher-order needs, job satisfaction, and productivity. While many of the **human relations** theories of management provided valuable insight into the value of social relationships at work, one weakness was the overemphasis on informal communication and the assumption that face-to-face interactions were most effective.

As organizational theories evolved, the importance of the superior-subordinate relationship became more evident. In the 1960s, researchers began to explore the impact that interactions between supervisors and subordinates had on organizational efficiency, effectiveness, and satisfaction. Many of the theories developed during this time period are classified as **human resources** approaches. What distinguishes these theories from their earlier counterparts in the Classical and Human Relations approaches is the attention focused on multi-directional communication and the appreciation for both formal and informal communication styles. Human Resources managers recognize that while relationships are an essential part of organizational success, in order to effectively operate as a team, task messages should be regarded as crucial to accomplishing goals. A unique feature of the Human Resources approach is its focus on teams in organizations. Communication is no longer viewed as being strictly upward or downward. After all, employees need to interact not only with their supervisors, but may rely on communication with leaders and members of other teams in the organization, or even their peers within their own teams. Multi-directional communication paved the way for contemporary theories of communication in organizations. See Table 11.5 for a summary of the three approaches to superior-subordinate relationships.

Leader-member exchange theory, or LMX, explains the process of relationship development between superiors and subordinates (Graen 1976; Graen and Cashman 1975; Graen and Uhl-Bien 1995). In essence, this theory states that leaders in organizations develop relationships with all members and that there are qualitative differences in these bonds. These relationships exist on a continuum ranging from perceptions of "in-group" to "out-group" status. According to LMX, high quality, or "in-group," relationships are the result of subordinates receiving support from supervisors, having influence on decisions that are made in the organization, and being given greater responsibility. Communication in interactions in high LMX relationships is often characterized by trust, liking, and support by both members (Dansereau, Graen, and Haga 1975). The obvious outcome of these positive factors is greater amounts of interaction, and ultimately, higher levels of satisfaction. Low quality, or "out-group," relationships are characterized by little supervisory support and limited influence in decision-making. In this low LMX context, communication can be compared to that of a secret club—one in which information is only shared by those in control or power. Interactions are characterized by the roles and rules to be followed within the hierarchy and, as a result, members of the organization often report being less satisfied and the organization often experiences higher levels of employee turnover. It is quite possible that you have experienced high- or low-quality LMX relationships within educational organizations. Recall a teacher with whom

Table 11.5 – Approaches to Communication and Relationships

Approaches to Management	Direction of Communication	Focus of Messages	Manager's Style of Communication
Classical	Downward	Task	Formal
Human relations	Upward and downward	Relational	Informal
Human resources	Upward, downward, across, and diagonal	Task relational	Informal, with formal as needed

you developed a high quality LMX relationship. If you demonstrated a high level of interest in the subject matter being taught by the teacher, chances are that the instructor engaged in several interactions with you on topics of common interest. You may have even been asked to take on additional responsibilities, such as tutoring peers. But suppose a teacher disagrees with a student's opinions, or views the student as being disinterested in the subject. Fewer attempts may be made to engage in interactions, and a low-quality LMX relationship may evolve.

So what factors contribute to the development of high-quality exchanges among superiors and subordinates? You might be surprised to discover that concepts we have been discussing throughout this text play an influential role in forming these relationships. The concepts include similarity, attraction, and trust. First, the more similar supervisors and subordinates perceive themselves to be, the more likely they are to communicate with one another and to develop a high-quality relationship (Turban and Jones 1988). The more similar two people

If you are particularly interested in a certain subject, you may develop a high quality LMX relationship with that instructor.

© Lorraine Swanson, 2007, Shutterstock.

perceive themselves to be, the more attractive they are to one another. Task attraction, which is based on factors that have the potential to help accomplish a goal, is influential in the development of quality LMX. Similarity and task attraction result in increased interaction among leaders and members, thus contributing to the level of trust. Supervisors trust in-group subordinates and allow them to contribute to decision-making by delegating responsibility. On NBC's *The Office*, ambitious subordinates attempt to encourage in-group relationships with branch manager Michael Scott. For example, Andy, the transfer from the Stamford branch who hopes to rise in power, uses "personality mirroring" by imitating Michael. Also, Dwight Schrute is delegated the extra responsibility of assistant regional manager/assistant-to-the-regional-manager because he is in Michael's in-group and is trusted.

As organizations become increasingly diverse, cultural competence is critical for the development of high-quality LMX relationships. Both superiors and subordinates must engage in the process of perspective taking. To avoid falling into the trap of stereotyping one another, each party must be open-minded and committed to learning from the other's perspective. Doing so potentially increases the chances for high-quality LMX relationships to emerge. Suppose a manager from a U.S.-based organization was working with employees in Japan. It would be important for the manager to keep in mind that her Japanese employees are uncomfortable being "singled-out" from the group and prefer to adopt a collectivistic approach to problem-solving. By allowing the employees the opportunity to collaborate in the problem-solving process and by acknowledging the contributions of the group rather than of specific individuals, the manager will likely enhance the LMX relationship. The television show *The Office* has repeatedly lampooned political correctness in the office, particularly since manager Michael Scott is incredibly offensive, unintentionally but continuously stereotyping both the women and minorities in his office. In one episode, manager Michael Scott's version of "Diversity Day" had his employees wearing cards with the name of a race stuck to their foreheads. Employees were then told to treat each other according to the corresponding stereotype of each race and, as expected, managed to offend just about everyone. Not surprisingly, Michael has developed an exceptionally low-quality LMX relationship with a majority of his employees, continually getting even lower as he singles out individuals from the group and communicates inappropriately.

Peer Relationships at Work

Managers and scholars have recognized that perhaps the most influential relationships in the workplace are those that form among co-workers, or peers. Several types of peer relationships have been examined by communication scholars. These include friendships, mentoring relationships, and romantic relationships. Stop for a moment and consider the number of times you interact with peers in your workplace in a given day. These relationships are often a central focus for understanding organizational life because, in many cases, we interact with peers in the workplace more frequently than we do with supervisors.

Do you find you develop closer relationships with people whose work area is located near you?

To understand the evolution of peer interactions in organizations, it is important to consider the factors which cause these relationships to form and strengthen. As we take a closer look at various types of peer relationships, the impact of factors such as physical proximity, communication climate, task/goal dependence, and dual meanings on relationship development will become evident.

Physical Proximity.   First, physical proximity affects relationship development among co-workers. Several studies have found that proximity increases opportunities for interaction (Fine 1986, Monge and Kirste 1980). The more opportunities that exist for interactions, the greater the chance that peer relationships are formed. Colleagues whose cubicles are located next to each other are more likely to form relationships and interact with one another than with those who are located across the building. One employee who describes his office as a "rat maze" of cubicles illustrates the role of proximity by stating, "Sometimes I just roll my office chair into the next cubicle and blow off steam after a meeting. It's like having a neighbor you can vent to when things get rough." Remember that most employees report spending an average of forty hours per week at work. More time together provides greater opportunities to share.

Communication Climate. A second factor influencing the development of peer relationships is the communication climate between superiors and subordinates. An inherent hierarchical structure often contributes to the development of an "us versus them" mentality. Studies have found that co-workers come together to provide social support in situations where managers are perceived to be unfair or untrustworthy (Odden and Sias 1997; Sias and Jablin 1995). High levels of employee cohesiveness often result from these negative communication climates.

When you're frustrated at work, it's easier to commiserate with those who are in the same environment and understand it.

Consider a time when you have been frustrated by something that happened at work or at school. You probably chose to communicate your frustrations to a co-worker or classmate who could relate to the situation you were experiencing because he was familiar with the environment. While family members or friends outside the workplace could certainly listen and offer support, they may not be able to understand the climate as well as a colleague who has experienced the same things that you have. In December 2005, New York City transit workers organized a strike a few days before Christmas that shut down subway and bus service to thousands of workers and tourists. Employee strikes are just one example of the "us versus them" phenomenon that often leads to employees joining forces against the supervisors. This collaborative force is unavoidable, as employees spend more time interacting with one another than they do communicating with their supervisors.

Task/Goal Dependence. Task or goal dependence is a third factor influencing the development of peer relationships. By their very definition, organizations exist for the purpose of accomplishing a specific task or goal. Its members must work together to carry out its mission. Peer influence is an essential factor in fulfilling these goals. As we discuss team relationships in organizations later in this chapter, you will learn how shared tasks bring organizational members together. Team members depend on one another to meet the goals. If one team member "drops the ball," other members may communicate pressure in an attempt to encourage compliance. In some instances, co-workers may even have more influence over peer behaviors than supervisors do. In essence, peer influence in organizations is not that different from peer influence witnessed among teens in today's society. Have you ever been a part of a student organization that was sponsoring an event on campus? Students at a small midwestern university were organizing a blood drive as a service project on their campus. One committee was responsible for promotion and publicity, another was responsible for signing up donors, and a third committee was responsible for assisting the American Red Cross workers on the day of the event. Strong interpersonal relationships between members of the student organization resulted in a successful event. Each of the colleagues understood their common goal and engaged in communication to accomplish the task.

Dual Meanings. A final factor that plays a key role in understanding the formation of relationships in organizations is the dual meanings communicated in messages. Messages exchanged between peers often contain "clues" to help define the nature of the relationship in addition to communicating specific information. Recall the example of the blood drive. If the chairperson of the committee to sign up donors states to a member that, "We're going to have to put it in high gear if we hope to meet our goal for this project," she is sending a message that they perceive themselves as being in a position to evaluate the performance of the group. The content dimension is clear—the number of donors needs to increase in order to meet the group's goal, and an implied relational message is present as well. By referencing the group through the use of pronouns such as "we," the chairperson communicates to the members that there is a bond that links them together.

As stated earlier, there are three types of co-worker relationships that have gained the interest of communication scholars: friendships, mentoring relationships, and romantic relationships. Let us take a closer look at the communication dynamics in each of these relationships in organizations.

FRIENDSHIPS IN ORGANIZATIONS

Reflecting on the proximity principle of peer relationships, it should come as no surprise that many friendships are formed as a result of organizational affiliations. As we explore the prevalence of these relationships, consider the friendships you have formed as a result of your membership in work, education, volunteer, or social organizations. Some individuals even create labels to describe these relationships by identifying a person as "a friend from work" or "a friend from my church." Our decision to form friendships at work is voluntary. While you may not have any choice regarding those you form relationships with at work, you do have options when it comes to forming friendships.

Tensions can arise when a friend doesn't accomplish work expectations.

Friendships provide organizational members with social support and assistance throughout the socialization process. Communication scholars have realized the prevalence of these types of relationships and have applied theories to explain the dynamics of friendships at work. Bridge and Baxter (1992) identified five tensions experienced by friends in organizations, three of which are new to the study of struggles experienced in relationships. They point out that friendships in the workplace are unique, due to the blending of "personal" and "role" expectations. Tensions emerge because of the struggle between the behaviors we expect of someone as a friend and behaviors expected of that same person in his or her role as co-worker. Have you ever been frustrated with a friend at work who failed to pull her weight to accomplish a task? Determining which expectations to use as a guide for behaviors can be difficult when friends work together. The familiar tensions of autonomy/connection and openness/closedness that are typically experienced in intimate relationships also occur as a result of friendships formed at work. New tensions identified in the study include struggles between equality/inequality, impartiality/favoritism, and judgment/acceptance (Bridge and Baxter 1992).

Autonomy/Connection

Tension between **autonomy** and **connection** is fueled by the fact that friends at work are together several hours each day. Working together in close proximity enables friends to form close bonds. Stories about things that happen in the organization are shared, and trust between friends develops as they may depend on one another for the successful completion of tasks. But this same closeness may sometimes cause persons to feel "too" close. In the social world outside the organization, friends may find that discussions revert back to events at work. Extreme connection can lead to the feeling of being "smothered." An employee at a major retail store described the tension she experienced. "My friends at work and I are so much alike! In fact, I would describe Jo as my best friend. But sometimes it gets rough because I want to be considered for promotions, but I don't want to compete against Jo and end up jeopardizing our friendship."

Openness/Closedness

Tensions that are also experienced between friends at work are **openness** and **closedness.** Disclosures are common between friends—sharing stories about events that happen inside the office and at home strengthens the friendship bond. However, organizations often have confidentiality guidelines that could potentially restrict topics of discussion among friends. Consider the following situation. Lisa and Alonzo had been friends ever since they met at their new employee orientation session. As a human resources associate, Lisa was privy to information regarding cuts in the sales force over the next three weeks. Unfortunately, Alonzo was a member of the sales department that was targeted for these cuts. Because of their friendship, Lisa struggled with the desire to share this information with Alonzo, and the obligation to keep this information private until management decided to announce the cutbacks.

Equality/Inequality

Another tension experienced by friends at work focuses on the contradictory struggle between **equality** versus **inequality.** Earlier, we discussed the fact that organizational relationships are characterized by status differentials created by the presence of a hierarchical structure. As friends, two employees may view themselves as being equal in their relationship status. However, when role status as an organizational member is factored into the equation, inherent inequalities may emerge. One person may be placed in the position of reviewing the performance of the friend, and the inequities in the relationship become evident.

Impartiality/Favoritism

Friends at work may struggle between being **impartial,** treating all members the same, and showing **favoritism** to friends. Furthermore, friends trust that each one will look out for the other's best interests. While an inherent characteristic of friendship is to provide support, ethical or moral codes may prescribe the equal treatment of all employees. Abbey's story of the employee review process at work illustrates this type of tension that can emerge among friends. As manager of the restaurant, she was responsible for providing feedback on the performance of servers. One of the servers, Janelle, had become friends with Abbey over the past several months. Janelle, a single-mother of two young children, had been a source of support when Abbey found herself in the midst of a divorce, wondering how she could juggle work and raise her children alone. Recently, Janelle's daughter had been having some problems at school. Janelle was often called to meet with teachers during the day, requiring her to call off from work at the last minute. Abbey knew that she had to assess Janelle's absences in the report, but she felt horrible about giving her a low evaluation because she knew all of the issues Janelle had been struggling with. In this instance, we see the struggle between treating all employees fairly and wanting to make accommodations for a friend.

Judgment/Acceptance

A final tension encountered at work is the struggle between **judgment** and **acceptance.** Friends are expected to provide support and understanding to one another without judgment. However, depending on the role expectations associated with one's position in an organization, colleagues may be required to assess one another's work or performance. Consider Abbey and Janelle's situation. As a manager, Abbey knows that she needs to address the attendance issues with Janelle. But as Janelle's friend, she is reluctant to say anything because she is sympathetic to her situation. Part of Abbey's position is to provide feedback and sometimes that feedback is negative. Providing and taking criticism from a performance review from a friend may form a tension that otherwise may not exist in the workplace.

In an attempt to understand how friendships evolve in the workplace, Sias and Cahill (1998) interviewed nineteen pairs of friends in organizations. Individuals were asked to indicate the changes that occurred in their friendships between the initial meeting and the present time. Results of the study support the notion that there are three distinct phases of friendship development at work. Phase one involves the transition from acquaintances to friends, and is often experienced as the result of two employees working in close proximity for a period of time. Employees in the study stated that their decision to transition to the friendship stage during this time was the result of similarities that were discovered through interactions with one another. The second phase, friend to close friend, is often the result of supportive messages exchanged as a result of either personal or professional experiences. During this phase, friends socialize more outside the workplace than before, and the increase in interactions provides opportunities for more personal information to be shared. A final phase involves the transition from close friends to "almost best" friend (Sias and Cahill 1998). As the level of intimacy in the relationship increases and as more personal information is disclosed, friends experience an intense level of trust and support.

MENTOR RELATIONSHIPS

Friendship is only one type of interpersonal relationship that provides organizational members with support. **Mentor relationships** are characterized by a more experienced member serving as a role model, teacher, or guide for a colleague who is less experienced. Establishing a relationship with a mentor has repeatedly been linked to an individual's career progress, organizational influence, and upward mobility within an organization (Ragins and Cotton 1991). Examples of mentoring in today's workplace would be an experienced employee providing guidance

Those who establish a relationship with a mentor often achieve greater career success.

for a new colleague and a successful woman being called upon to offer guidance and advice to female colleagues who aspire to leadership positions. Dr. Phil McGraw has credited Oprah Winfrey for mentoring him through the early stages of his career. In the film *Up Close and Personal*, Robert Redford's character served as a mentor to news anchor Tally Atwater, portrayed by Michelle Pfeiffer.

Mentoring partnerships may be formed on a voluntarily or involuntarily basis. When organizational members seek out mentors who possess qualities or characteristics they admire, they form a voluntary or informal mentoring relationship. Similarity in personality, goals, attitudes, or background is often a force that guides the decision to pursue voluntary mentor relationships. Other members may establish these relationships through formal or involuntary mentor programs available in their organization. These involuntary, or assigned, mentoring partnerships may involve formal, written agreements that address the expectations for each person. Regardless of the method for initiating the relationship, several communication characteristics are common. Just as other types of relationships involve highs and lows, so does the mentor relationship. Mentors and protégés may have different goals which need to be negotiated, and the differences have the potential to result in jealousy or conflict. Trust is an essential part of the relationship, as both parties expect the other to be honest and open in their assessment and advice. Due to the time invested in this relationship, the concept of social exchange may become an issue to be resolved.

In their study of organizational mentoring, DeWine, Casbolt and Bentley (1983) identified various types of mentors. While the relationship is generally perceived as being supportive and nurturing, organizational members should be aware of the fact that some mentors approach their responsibility in less sensitive ways. **Supportive mentors** help employees achieve their goals and include types labeled as the "parent," the "cheerleader," and the "groom." **Parent mentors** are those who are considered to be "older and wiser" as a result of their tenure in the organization. Protégés often describe the parent mentor as having significant influence on their career. The **cheerleader mentor** is one who provides encouragement, and the mentor often describes the pride resulting from the protégé's success. **Groom mentors** are those who hold positions of power in an organization and are viewed as "grooming" a protégé for specific responsibilities or roles. However, not all mentor relationships result in positive experiences for the protégé. **"Self-promoter" mentors** are described as those who want to work with the best new members in order to surround themselves with high quality colleagues. The **"guilt-trip producer"** is a mentor who motivates a protégé by communicating messages of disappointment when performance fails to meet expectations. Phrases such as "I expected more from you" or "You know you can do better than that" are often associated with this type of mentor.

The outcomes of mentoring relationships can be beneficial for the individuals involved as well as for the organization. Mentors report a sense of satisfaction in seeing protégés achieve their goals, and protégés often credit their career success to the advice provided by mentors. Studies have found that employees who are mentored report more desirable occupational outcomes and advance more quickly in their professions (Ragins and Cotton 1991). An obvious benefit for organizations is the job satisfaction that results from mentoring relationships. While many mentoring relationships evolve as a result of friendships at work, it is important to remember their purpose and refrain from confusing the roles of friend and mentor."

ACTIVITY 11.9

Interview a manager in either a large or mid-sized organization and ask some of the following questions: 1) how much of your day is devoted to dealing with relationship or communication problems or issues? 2) can you give an example of a typical relationship-type of issue that you had to manage and how you addressed this situation? 3) how important are peer relationships to your employees? 4) what does your organization do to help foster healthy peer relationships?

"ROMANTIC RELATIONSHIPS AT WORK⁷"

With more women in the workplace and employees working longer hours, it should come as no surprise that romantic relationships have captured the attention of communication scholars in recent years. In a 2002 report, the U.S. Department of Labor found that women spend an average of 1,584 hours in the office each year. A female employee in a large corporate banking center provided this explanation for her decision to pursue romantic relationships at work, "How can I not help being attracted to men at my office? They're dressed for success and I know they're career-driven. It's just easier to date someone at work than to spend time hanging out at bars where everything is so uncertain." A 2005 survey by vault.com stated that fifty-eight percent of employees reported that they have been involved in an office romance. In his book *The Office Romance*, Dennis Powers (1998) states that eight million co-workers will discover romance at the office, with nearly half of these relationships resulting in marriage. However, for every "happily ever after" that is found at work, there is a horror story for employees whose organizations frown upon workplace romance.

The communication strategy often used to initiate romantic relationships is flirting. While some flirting behaviors may be innocently used to explore interest in pursuing a romantic relationship, these behaviors have also been used for more manipulative purposes in organizations. Employees may flirt with a co-worker for self-serving purposes such as seeking assistance on a project or even advancing one's career.

Co-workers may flirt for romantic reasons or in an effort to advance their career.

Of the fifty-eight percent of employees who reported that they have been involved in an office romance, only nineteen percent indicated that they had been open and honest about the relationship. While nearly half of the employees surveyed indicated that they were unaware of the company's policies regarding workplace romances, those who said that policies did exist in the workplace stated that the guidelines typically involved relationships between superiors and subordinates (vault.com). Policies restricting romance between superiors and subordinates are often designed to protect both parties—issues of perceived credibility and sexual harassment may result from status and power differentials. Supervisors engaged in romantic relationships with subordinates may run the risk of being accused of showing favoritism. The relationship between Michael Scott and his supervisor Jan is comedy fodder on *The Office*. In one episode of *The Office* the characters attempt to keep their relationship a secret from Human Resources but accidentally release compromising photos of their vacation in Jamaica in an email to all employees.

The Civil Rights Act of 1964 made sexual harassment illegal in the workplace. While the main goal of the act was to prevent organizations from discriminating against minorities and women, it also addressed the legalities associated with making sexual relationships a condition for employment. Berryman-Fink (1997) cites the Equal Employment Opportunity Commission's definition of **sexual harassment** as "any unwelcome sexual advances, requests for sexual favors, and other verbal or physical conduct of a sexual nature" (272). In 1986, the definition of sexual harassment was further refined to address behaviors that contributed to an unpleasant or uncomfortable work environment. Today, organizations recognize two types of sexual harassment which they typically label quid pro quo and hostile work environment. **Quid pro quo** is a Latin term that translates as "something for something." An example of this type of harassment might include a boss telling his subordinate that she will not receive a promotion, raise, or opportunity at work unless she engages in a sexual act with him. The second form of sexual harassment, **hostile work environment,** is less clearly defined and might include employees exchanging sexual jokes, stories, or materials in front of other employees, or ongoing unwanted sexual behavior from a co-worker. Sexual harassment is distinguished from flirting and other types of physical, verbal or sexual behavior because it is perceived as unwelcome by the recipient and is reoccurring (Berryman-Fink 1997). There is some data that indicates that sexual harassment appears to be on the decline. A 1995 Department of Defense survey of its employees found that the number of female employees who reported unwanted sexual advances dropped from sixty-four percent in 1988 to fifty-five percent in 1995. Reports from male employees experiencing sexual harassment at work decreased from seventeen percent to fourteen percent.

As scholars, practitioners, and employees debate over whether romance should be allowed in the workplace, several outcomes of these relationships should be taken into consideration. While workers may report higher levels of motivation and involvement in organizations where romance has bloomed, a study by love.com found that online interactions between employees trying to keep their relationship secret resulted in up to forty-two minutes of lost productivity per day. There is additional evidence that organizational romance can lead to favoritism and jealousy in the workplace, loss of colleagues' respect, damage to one's professional image, and loss of productivity (Quinn and Lees 1984; Lowndes 1993). For those employees watching the romance from the sidelines, the relationship may become a distraction, and time and energy is spent focusing on the relationship rather than on issues relevant to work. Consider the climate when relationships between co-workers are terminated. The emotional aftermath has the potential to impact not only those formerly involved in the romance, but also co-workers who are inclined to "take sides." *The Office*, particularly, deals with romantic relationships in an office in all of their forms; from the clandestine relationship of oddball couple Dwight and Angela and the stilted attraction between Michael Scott and Jan, to the captivating relationship of Jim and Pam, who teeter between the flirtation of "almost best" friends, unrequited love, and the awkwardness resulting from the disclosure of feelings. As an example of the potential pitfalls of office romances, Jim ends up transferring to a different branch. Very little work appears to get done at Dunder-Mifflin: time is spent in favor of more amusing activities and relationship woes. The close proximity of work relationships and the difficulty of both terminating them and moving on, though usually not as thoroughly dramatic as their television enactments, do demand having second thoughts when initiating romantic relationships in the workplace."

ACTIVITY 11.10

Conduct research on some of the ways that organizations are addressing the issues addressed in this chapter (e.g., sexual harassment, dating in the workplace, impact of technology on communication, diversity in the workplace and work life balance). What are the organization's policies, procedures and opinions on these issues? Do the organizations that are recognized as some of "**The Best Places to Work in the US**" (e.g., Wegmans) make attempts to address these issues?

ACTIVITY 11.11

Ask the students to find out if they have a sexual harassment policy or process in place at work or at school. If they do, have the student to list six things about the policy or process. Discuss the findings.

"INTERPERSONAL EFFECTIVENESS: COMMUNICATION IN WORK RELATIONSHIPS[8]

Throughout our discussion of superior subordinate and peer relationships in organizations, you might have noticed that many of the communication concepts and theories discussed throughout this text could be applied. The study of relationships across communication contexts often requires scholars to apply fundamental concepts in new ways. Concepts such as similarity and attraction can be used to explain the initiation process between friends, colleagues, or romantic partners. Trust and disclosure are fundamental to strengthening relationships regardless of whether the relationships are between co-workers, family members, or friends. Persuasion, listening, and feedback are essential communication tools for organizational effectiveness. While an entire text could be dedicated to discussing the role of interpersonal relationships in organizations, we examine three of the communication variables that have attracted the attention of organizational communication scholars.

Superiors are always seeking ways to enhance organizational relationships. While several studies have shown that cognitive ability is a strong predictor of job performance, communication scholars have realized the impact of addressing individual differences in achieving effectiveness. Organizational orientation theory identifies three approaches used by members to enact their work roles (McCroskey, Richmond, Johnson, and Smith 2004). Upward mobiles refer to those members who demonstrate a high level of dedication toward accomplishing the organization's goals. They are easily identified by their demonstrated respect for roles and rules they are often described as giving "110 percent" to tasks and the organization. Indifferents, on the other hand, view work as a means to earn a living. They are motivated to work simply to obtain a paycheck, and dedication to the organization is low on their list of personal goals. You will recognize the indifferents in your organization by their reluctance to participate in organizational activities not directly related to their job, and topics of discussion typically revolve around their personal lives rather than work. It should come as no surprise that indifferents make up the majority of organizational orientations at work, and indeed a majority of the characters on *The Office*. Ryan, the temp, who is determined not to be drawn into the world of the Scranton branch and form bonds, is a classic indifferent. The third orientation, **ambivalents,** is often the most difficult to communicate with at work. It is fairly easy to identify this orientation type at work—simply listen for those who point out the "issues" that need to be changed. Often these individuals become frustrated with their jobs, suggest changes that need to be made, and if things fail to turn around, they often decide to seek employment elsewhere. In essence, the ambivalent can be described as the employee who is always looking for a better opportunity. The best advice for communicating with ambivalents is to focus on neutral topics to keep the conversation from turning into a gripe session about the organization's weaknesses.

ORGANIZATIONAL CULTURE

Culture refers to the shared beliefs, values, and attitudes of a geographically similar group of people. Organizations can be considered cultures as well; after all, organizations aspire for supervisors and subordinates to share a common vision which is guided by similarities in beliefs and values for the company. Scholars have begun exploring organizational cultures to understand how members construct their organizational realities. **Organizational culture** is defined as the shared systems of symbols and meanings created by members through their interactions with one another (Trethewey 1997). To better understand how this meaning is exchanged, researchers have focused their attention on how elements such as stories, language, and rituals are used to help members of organizations understand their role in the culture.

Stories

Organizational members exchange stories about events that have shaped the history of the organization and help provide a rationale for the beliefs and values shared by supervisors and subordinates. An administrative assistant at Wendy's corporate headquarters in Ohio told the following story shared by one of her colleagues to describe how the company's founder, Dave Thomas, interacted with his employees during office visits:

> "One day Mr. Thomas came into the office and I was swamped! As the phone was ringing off the hook I greeted him and asked if I could get him a cup of coffee. He smiled and stated that I was the one who was busy and he went to get me a cup of coffee."

The story was used to communicate the value that Dave Thomas had for employees, and how he viewed the organization as a team effort.

Language

Organizational culture is also shaped by the specialized language, or vocabulary, used by members. This shared language serves to strengthen the bonds between colleagues, sometimes creating a means for distinguishing between members and non-members. Students and faculty at Ohio University share a common language to refer to transcripts and the system used to register for classes. TRIPS (touch-tone registration and information processing system) is used to refer to the system students use to register for their classes, and when a faculty member asks a student to bring his DARS (degree audit reporting system) to an advisory meeting, the student knows that he should bring a copy of the transcript. This specialized language helps students, faculty, and staff communicate more efficiently.

What kind of a daily ritual could be implemented to break up the monotony of assembly work?

© PhotoCreate, 2007, Shutterstock.

Rituals

Rituals and routines are mechanisms used by organizational members to make sense of their membership. Daily coffee breaks, annual Christmas parties, quarterly employee recognition ceremonies, or even simple greetings used to acknowledge colleagues each morning provide insight as to how members of an organization define their place in the organization. Powerful messages are exchanged through these routine behaviors, and they serve the function of promoting relationships among organizational members. In a 1960s article, Donald Roy describes the strategic use of everyday rituals such as Coke breaks, banana breaks, and opening the window at a particular time to break up the monotony of assembly work. Because employees spend so much of their time at work, collective attempts are often made by managers or groups of employees to improve employee morale and job satisfaction. Incorporating humor into the workplace through shared humorous stories, language, and rituals is one way of improving organizational culture.

SOCIALIZATION

Just as new members of cultures must assimilate to the new environment, newcomers to an organization experience a similar introductory process to learn information about the expectations for organizational behavior. A story by an employee in a large consulting firm describes the value of socialization to her success in the organization. "I accepted the job offer two weeks before I graduated from college. Boy, was I in for a surprise! There was no syllabus to tell me what was expected and when things were due. I quickly learned that I better open my eyes and ears and start asking questions." Jablin (1984) describes the process of organizational assimilation as the means by which individuals learn role expectations and what it means to be a member of an organization. Employees may be formally or informally socialized on the expectations of membership. An organization that conducts formal orientation programs or assigns mentors to new employees applies more formal methods for ensuring that employees learn the ropes. Informal socialization may result from an employee joining colleagues for lunch and learning that the supervisor sets strict deadlines and gets angry with those who do not meet goals.

Socialization typically evolves through three stages: anticipatory socialization, organizational encounter, and metamorphosis (Jablin 2001). In the **anticipatory socialization phase** new members form expectations regarding their role in the organization. These expectations can be formed as early as childhood, as when a young girl creates beliefs about what it is like to be a lawyer by watching her mother, or they can evolve through research about organizations or through stories portrayed in the media. Once a newcomer enters the organization, the **encounter phase** begins. While technically an employee, the newcomer may find that she may not yet be considered part of the group. Organizations use a variety of methods to socialize members during this phase. Methods may be formal or informal in nature and can include orientation or training programs, mentoring, and opportunities for employees to seek information. In a study of first-year medical students, friendships with older students were identified as a means for assimilating into and navigating the medical school culture (Zorn and Gregory 2005). The final stage of socialization, **metamorphosis,** involves changes in the new employee's behavior to adapt to the role expectations in the new environment. At this point, the employee begins to be viewed as an "insider." Unspoken expectations are often discovered during this phase. While a manager may say that attendance at weekly update meetings is optional, an employee may soon learn that important information is shared during these sessions and that managers actually expect employees to be present. In essence, socialization can be the key to a successful organizational experience or a negative one.

CONTEMPORARY ISSUES IN WORKPLACE RELATIONSHIPS

As we reflect on the changes that have evolved in the ways supervisors, subordinates, and peers communicate with one another in the workplace, several trends become apparent. Managers have come to value the contributions of employees in decision-making and solicit their opinions and advice in these situations. As the number of males and females in organizations become more equal and more time is spent at the office, romance at work has gained the attention of scholars. Interpersonal relationships are the key to organizational success in industries. As the demographics of our work population continue to change, so does our need to address issues which will demand the attention of communication scholars in the twenty-first century. Three areas for focus are: diversity in the workplace, balancing work and family, and the impact of technology on interactions at work.

DIVERSITY IN ORGANIZATIONS

Many organizations have found themselves faced with the task of conducting business with partners from around the world. Globalization has increased the potential for interactions with clients and colleagues from other countries and cultures. Effective communication requires an understanding of cultural differences, and those who understand these differences can avoid embarrassing or insulting others.

As we consider cultural differences, it is important to note the role of organizational culture that was discussed earlier. As larger corporations buy out smaller organizations, employees from diverse organizational cultures are often expected to not only adapt to one another, but also to be satisfied and productive. In January 2004, J. P. Morgan Chase announced its acquisition of and merger with Bank One, making it the second largest bank in the nation and drawing on each organization's strengths in consumer and corporate business. But the "blending" of these two large organizations would take time. Countless hours of negotiation occurred before the deal was signed; eventually it was decided that the board membership would have equal representation from Bank One and J. P. Morgan. Careful communication was designed to communicate the organizational changes to employees and the public. In January 2006, two years after the new organizational structure was announced to the public, many banks still retained the name "Bank One," and will do so until the process of forming the new culture is complete.

Age diversity has created a new set of issues for organizations. Current trends have found that older employees are making the decision to postpone retirement, and many more have decided to return from retirement. The result is a wider age range among employees, often with older workers being supervised by those who are younger. This role reversal may produce an uncomfortable situation for employees, with younger managers experiencing reluctance to give orders to their elders.

Effective organizations will realize the value of addressing the contributions that diversity can offer. Those of diverse cultural backgrounds can be used as resources to assist in training others to do business in their native cultures. Managers should recognize the value of diverse backgrounds and viewpoints in brainstorming and decision-making, and encourage openness and respect. However, it is important to note that diverse opinions could potentially result in conflict, requiring organizations to explore new approaches to conflict management. As our opportunities for interacting with those around the world increases with the emergence of new technologies and globalization, an organization's success depends on its ability to manage diverse interpersonal relationships.

Communication scholars argue that "training could be the key to unlocking the potential of diversity in the organization" (Gonzalez, Willis, and Young 1997, 290). During the last few years, diversity training has become a buzz word in many organizational circles. For this training to be truly effective at building effective interpersonal relationships in the workplace, three steps are required. First, members of organizations should be encouraged to explore the differences that do exist in the workplace. Rather than assume that everyone is similar based on the fact that they chose to become members of the same group, organizations could benefit from encouraging the exploration of differences among co-workers. For example, what are the specific diversity issues that this particular organization is facing? Next, diversity training should address the presence of differences in communication styles and address how these unique approaches impact the organization's goals. Finally, training should encourage individuals to identify ways in which cultural differences in communication can be integrated to create a work team that is both cohesive and satisfying.

Increasingly there is a wider age range among employees working together in organizations.

© Yuri Arcurs, 2007, Shutterstock.

BALANCING WORK AND FAMILY RELATIONSHIPS

We all strive to achieve balance in our work and family relationships. After all, achieving balance in our personal and professional lives contributes to our self-esteem and relational satisfaction. In Chapter Three, we explored the relationship between roles and one's identity. One's self-esteem is often linked to having well-established roles. When our resources for fulfilling personal roles are limited, stress results and we start to question our identity as a good parent or a productive employee. The struggle appears to be more prevalent among female employees. Studies examining role conflict experienced by employees have found that

© Bartosz Ostrowski, 2007, Shutterstock.

Women use routinizing and improvising to manage daily home and work responsibilities.

women report dividing their time between various household and work-related tasks, while men report that the majority of their time is focused on tasks relating to work. So what can organizations do? Employees who perceive their supervisors as being supportive of their efforts to balance work and family often report higher levels of job satisfaction. Some organizations are addressing these issues and providing resources to help employees achieve balance in their personal and professional lives. Child and elder care opportunities are provided at some work sites, and options are being made for flexible work schedules through job sharing, compressed work weeks, and telecommuting.

Communication scholars have realized the value of peer, or co-worker, relationships and are addressing strategies to assist organizational members in achieving balance in different areas of their lives. Farley-Lucas (2000) discovered that valuable social support can be offered to working mothers through conversations with co-workers about child rearing, and employers who encouraged these dialogues were perceived as being more supportive of working mothers. To understand the strategies used to manage the stress of balancing work and family, Medved (2004) interviewed thirty-four mothers and asked them to describe their "typical" day balancing work and family life. Medved discovered that two types of actions, routinizing and improvising, are used to balance work and family responsibilities and illustrate the role that interpersonal communication plays in managing multiple demands.

Routinizing actions incorporate recurring patterns or interactions to accomplish daily routines. One communicative strategy used on a regular basis was **connecting.** Daily calls to coordinate schedules with a spouse, or contacting the child care facility to check in on the child are examples of this management strategy. **Alternating** involves interactions between spouses to negotiate "trade-offs" or exchange tasks in the daily routine. Occasionally, a mother is asked to stay late at work to complete a task or to travel out of town on business. In these instances, she may call her spouse and ask him to pick up the children at daycare since her routine

Parents may set up a schedule so Dad gets the baby ready for bed part of the week, while Mom takes over the other days.

has been disrupted. Or perhaps parents have developed a schedule: one parent is responsible for giving the children baths and getting them to bed on designated nights of the week, and the other parent assumes the responsibility for the remaining nights. **Prepping** is a nightly strategy used to maintain order in the routine. Children may be asked what homework needs to be accomplished each evening, school lunches may be packed in the evening, and coats and shoes may be lined up next to the door in anticipation of the morning rush to catch the bus. In some instances, working mothers may need to call on family members or friends to assist with childcare issues. **Reciprocating** strategies often involve conversations to coordinate the exchange of child care issues on a regular basis. Coordinating carpools to sports practice so that a working mother only has to leave work early one evening each week is an example of this strategy. While the answers to the family-work juggling act may seem easy, women still devote the majority of their time to childcare, housework, and shopping. Table 11.6 highlights the discrepancies between the time devoted to these tasks by fathers and by mothers. Regardless of their employment status, women contribute more time to these tasks than do fathers. Consider the fact that mothers who work 40+ hours per week report dedicating an additional 25 hours per week to the household tasks compared to the 14.5 hours spent by fathers.

As much as we like predictability in our lives, there are times when events occur that are beyond our control. During these times, working mothers may use **improvising** action messages to help coordinate the demands of work and family. **Requesting assistance** involves asking others for work accommodations or childcare assistance as a result of last-minute circumstances. A single mother

Table 11.6 – Ratio of Time Dedicated to Household Chores

	Males	Females
Time devoted to childcare, housework, or shopping by working parent	14.5 hours	25 hours
Time devoted to childcare, housework, or shopping by non-working parent	20 hours	39 hours

Source: Robinson, J. P., and G. Godbey. 1997. *Time for life: The surprising way Americans use their time.* State College, PA: Pennsylvania State University Press.

taking college classes may approach an instructor and ask for an extension on an assignment due to the illness of her children, or a neighbor may be asked to watch the children when mom is delayed by a traffic jam. **Trading off,** or alternating, is a strategy that involves negotiating responsibilities between spouses when unique situations arise. One spouse may agree to pick up a sick child from school one day with the agreement that the other parent assumes the responsibility the next time the situation arises. A final improvising strategy, **evading,** involves withholding information, or intentionally deceiving others, as a means for managing multiple demands. A mother may decide that it is easier just to call in sick to work rather than risk explaining to her supervisor that she needs to stay home to care for an ill child. As more women enter the workplace, there will be a greater need for communication scholars to explore how both men and women use communication to balance their relationships at work and at home.

THE IMPACT OF TECHNOLOGY ON WORK RELATIONSHIPS

There is no escaping the impact of technology on how we interact with others at work. Some organizations have replaced live humans at the switchboard with automated voice systems that answer and direct calls, and studies have shown that as many as seventy-five percent of business calls do not reach a person—instead, the game of "phone tag" ensues. Electronic mail (email) has alleviated some of the frustrations of calling on the phone by providing colleagues with the convenience of asking and answering questions at times that are convenient for them. Some organizations have limited the ability of applicants to interact with a human resources representative by requiring them to submit applications online. Our work lives have become so busy that many of us depend on electronic calendars to organize our schedules. Blackberry and the Palm Treo provide employees with the opportunity to engage in work-related tasks away from the office. Look around the next time you are having dinner at a busy restaurant: you will probably see someone using one of these technologies to send messages, and there is a good chance that he is communicating with a supervisor or co-worker.

While these technologies have enabled us to organize our work lives and to enhance our task efficiency, some may question their impact on interpersonal relationships. Indeed, technology has provided employees with the opportunity to telecommute, or to work from home. Individuals

report that technology has caused a "blurring of the lines" between their work and personal lives, and this has made the task of balancing these relationships more difficult. Employees report a struggle to establish boundaries between work time and personal time. A study of employees in an organization that implemented home-based telecommuting found that only fifteen percent of respondents reported having regular social contact with their co-workers (Harris 2003). Decreases in face-to-face contact pose new issues for researchers in understanding the role that technology plays in our interpersonal communication at wo

...can keep people connected to their ...ver they go.

© Darren Green, 2007, Shutterstock.

DATE DUE	RETURNED
SEP 2 0 2016	SEP 1 0 2016 EU

ACTIVITY 1

Invite a human ... communication i ... organizational c ... diversity in the v ... related to the top

...discuss ...nobiles, ...ps, and ...nallenges with employers ...roblem(s).

ENDNOTES

1-8 From *Interpersonal Communication: Building Rewarding Relationships*, by Kristen Campbell Eichhorn, Candice Thomas-Maddox, and Melissa Bekelja Wanzer. Copyright © 2008 by Kendall Hunt Publishing Company. Reprinted by permission.